Practical Spirituality

Steve Hounsome

Practical Spirituality

©1997 Steve Hounsome

ISBN 186163 015 8

Cover design by Paul Mason

Published by:

Capall Bann Publishing
Freshfields
Chieveley
Berks
RG20 8TF

Acknowledgements

Grateful acknowledgment is made to Builders of the Adytum, Incorporated, 5105 North Figueroa Street, Los Angeles, California, 90042, for permission to use their Tarot Keys on page13. The permission granted for the use of materials by Builders of the Adytum, Incorporated, in no way endorses anyone's interpretation thereof.

I am indebted to the following for their willing assistance in creating the artwork you see in this book:

Carrie Hounsome for the Chakras, Sundance, Sacred Circle, Human Energy System, Mountain of Universal Love
Neil Moore for the Spiral of the Sun and Moon
Antoinette Everts for the World Tree, The Sacred Spirit in Physical Form, The Sacred Birth Ceremony

You have each expressed something of the sacred within yourself and for that, be blessed.

I would like to give thanks to all those who have inspired me by their creativity and continue to do so and so for making me the person I am. Each has therefore contributed to this book, most without ever knowing. Mention must be made of Julian Cope, Robert Godfrey, Neil Young and The Levellers.

Respect, thanks and all love to: Faith, Anna, Abby, Neil and Hazel.

This book is dedicated to all those on the sacred road. May you walk with deliberate intent, beauty and joy.

As ever, my heart belongs to my beloved Carrie.

About the Author

Steve Hounsome works as a Spiritual Therapist based in Winchester, Hampshire. He uses a combination of Tarot, meditation, direct guidance, healing, ceremony, remedies and counselling to help people on their sacred road. He has qualifications in Healing, Psychic Studies and Tarot. He has also studied Meditation, Natural Magic, the Qaballah and the Western Mystery Tradition extensively and continues to do so. Steve was a founder member and former secretary of the Professional Tarot Society. He has written two other books for Capall Bann: *Taming the Wolf: Full Moon Meditations*' and '*Practical Meditation*'. His fourth book, '*Tarot Therapy*' is currently in preparation. Steve has also recorded a collection of highly acclaimed meditation and development tapes. He is a member of the Pagan Federation and the Order of Bards, Ovates and Druids.

These organisations can be contacted at:

The Secretary, The Pagan Federation, BM Box 7097, London, WC1N 3XX

The Secretary, Order of Bards, Ovates and Druids, PO Box 1333, Lewes, East Sussex, BN7 3ZG

Contents

Introduction

This book has been inspired by two things. First, a deep and powerful conviction and belief that for the world to improve its current condition it must rediscover a sense of the sacred as its prime focus. Second, that to do this we must first learn to blend the spiritual with the practical. It is my hope that through this book you will be encouraged to find a practical, spiritual path of your own.

In keeping with our modern 'global village' understanding of the world, we are able to blend wisdom, knowledge and practices from many and varied cultures and traditions in the search for this approach. Such an eclectic mix heralds the dawn of a spirituality for the Aquarian Age, a vision of a world where a majority of individuals have a higher goal than their bank balance or type of car. The soul, the spirit and the sacred become honoured first and foremost and life is cherished and sanctified before all else.

This vision is one which will take many, many years to become a reality, for it encompasses not only a change of humanity's heart, but a basic shift in society. This shift is away from the material towards the spiritual. Such a shift strikes at the roots of both our society and the individuals that comprise it. As such it is to those individuals that we must turn for what could be our last, best hope for the future and even survival.

This turnaround must take place in the heart of each one who is willing, for it can be forced in no-one; each must come of their own free will to drink of the healing waters on offer. To do so takes courage and faith aplenty, but it is precisely these qualities that we look for in the heroes that urge our race forwards, just as the myths of old show us. Just as the whole is greater than the sum of its parts, so we must strive to reach a point of critical mass whereby the number of souls alive focussing primarily on the spiritual is enough to bring about the shift for humanity as a race. This books hopes to show you ways in which you might make this a reality for yourself.

1

Yet it is naive to expect this shift to bring about a sudden transformation, individually or globally. Grandiose visions of a new world are positive in that they give us optimism and hope, but of themselves these qualities are pointless. The vision must be backed by action.

From the myriad forces of destruction that threaten us, survival, both individual and global, is a real concern for many. With an understanding of the sacred spirit as the basis for your life, a peace is instilled within that transcends these concerns. We can perhaps best define this sense of the sacred by realising that everything we do, say, think and feel is a manifestation, in some degree, of the Divine, whatever you conceive this to be. This will be looked at in greater detail, as we progress.

Again we come back to the individual. Since we have no right to evangelise or push our particular beliefs on any other, we are left with the self. If we feel we have to encourage others to change and 'progress' then we must do so only by example, without conscious awareness of this. Those open to receiving our 'message' can then change from their own freewill as surely they must if the change is to be total and permanent. Such a commitment being the minimum required to truly live the way of the spirit, especially in todays materialistic 'developed' world. A process of self exploration and development must take place, with the sacred spirit at the centre, coupled with the eternal, if apparently pointless, optimistic vision that by doing so we are creating a world more akin to its intended purpose, however this should manifest itself.

There are many people who are already striving after this and are reawakening their own sacredness. To this disparate, brave bunch we turn for guidance and inspiration, taking what supports and nourishes us. We are also able to draw on past cultures such as the Native Americans, where the way of life itself was sacred, applying the perennial wisdom demonstrated there to shape our own future. This book is simply an exploration, at the individual level, of the Aquarian Age vision, from the past and for the future.

In the book we will see how the basic structure of our modern, technological society can still contain a sense of the sacred. We cannot advocate a 'back to nature' or Luddite approach of dismantling and undoing the scientific knowledge we have gained and developed, since this is just not in our nature and is contrary to the progress we must make. Rather we must embrace the

2

discoveries made and realise that we have to adapt their use to work with the forces and powers of the Earth and nature, using the wisdom of discernment where necessary in their application and use. We cannot hope to master or control this planet which is bigger, stronger and older than us. Instead by rediscovering a sacred respect for the land and the Earth as a whole, we must look to ways to enhance and work alongside natural forces. In this too, can our lives become centered around a sense of the sacred once more.

In this book we will look at ways in which we can blend the business of living with the spiritual life. Time and again on my own spiritual path and life, I have struggled with trying to balance these two seemingly opposed facets. With the inner realisation and embrace of the sanctity of life as the central focus, the tide turns and we come to view all our actions as the outworking of the Divine within us. It matters not what tasks you are involved in; life is magical. When the focus and reason for living becomes sacred, all else follows.

By the application of this principle in the most practical of ways, we arrive at the best method for each of us to walk tall and proud, with our feet on the Earth and our head in the clouds, fuelled by and focussed on, full and vibrant awareness of our own sacredness. I hope that this book enables you to discover fully your own sacred spirit and in so doing realise that you hold the key to bringing the world closer to fulfilling its intended purpose.

N.B. None of the exercises or practices in this book should be viewed or treated as a substitute for orthodox or complementary medicine prescribed or given by a qualified doctor or therapist. They are however, useful additions to have!

Chapter 1

The Sacred Spirit

Humanity has acknowledged the existence of a spirit, in various forms and in as many ways, since the very earliest times. This spirit may be seen as the Sun, the Moon, the Earth itself, a race of gods and goddesses with different characters and attributes, one ruling god - or all of these. Cultures across the globe and throughout history have venerated their own particular deities in their own particular way, demonstrating in this an instinctive need in the human condition or psyche to acknowledge the presence of a force or being that gives a reason and purpose for the life led on Earth.

A study of these multitudinous ways of worship will reveal a great many things, not least of which is that the practice of a particular culture's spirituality adapts itself to the needs of those people, their living circumstances, bodies and time in which they live. Or it may be that the people adapt their spirituality to suit the limitations their lives and cultures place upon them. Whatever way round it is, it is certainly true that individuals, either alone or in groups, will go to extraordinary lengths to practice their own expression of the sacredness within them. Throughout history people have striven against enormous odds simply to show their love of their particular deity: the Jews, Aborigines, Native Americans, Baptist blacks in America and witches are just a few random examples, though many more exist. Why would any individual insist on the practice of their spirituality, with the guarantee that by doing so they risk beatings, imprisonment, torture and death, as has invariably been the case?

I believe it is safe to assume that it is something more than just 'blind faith', an empty belief that the head and heart need constantly convincing are true, to withstand such treatment. The numbers of such people who have only faith in this singular sense, to base their beliefs on, must have been comparatively low through history. Faith must be very strong indeed to remain true despite months or years spent alone in a dark, damp cell, receiving daily mocking, beatings and even torture, existing only on the barest, poor essentials to keep you alive. This has doubtless been the case, not just through history but even in our modern, 'developed' world today. If we are honest, there are few of us who would say that we would still insist on our beliefs given the above, if we had nothing but faith; no outer signs, inner responses or tangible results of our beliefs. In short, if we had no proof, as is the requisite definition of faith.

In the present time there are a great many people in my own country who have no 'religion', no faith, no belief in an afterlife of any kind and no sense of the sacred in their lives at all. Equally there are a great many people who say that they believe there is 'something', but as they do not know what, they do nothing about it. They prescribe to no fixed doctrine of belief, perhaps visiting church at the required occasions of birth, marriage and death. Such has become the norm for arguably the majority of people in the developed, industrial world.

There is certainly more than a little truth in the maxim that the god of these people is Mammon, their lives being one big shopping expedition, 'shop till you drop' taking on a rather different emphasis in this analogy, culminating on going to the great shopping trip in the sky! As more and more of us succumb to the short lived but very real 'high' we obtain from the acquisition of goods, so ever more do the wheels churn and clank that provide us with these goods. This provides us with jobs, which gives us money and security and we are happy in this knowledge and prospering economic climate - or so the politicians tell us. But what if we're not?

We have seen that religion, as 'faith without proof' is the answer only for a very special, perhaps 'chosen' few and that the modern approach to life creates only a need and greed for more and more of those consumable goods, presumably to make us happier and happier. This brings us back to those cultures who suffered for the practice not of their religion, but of their spirituality, their sacred life.

It is folly however to suggest that we must revert to their so called 'primitive' approach to life, modern investigation and understanding of course revealing that this primitivism was in many ways much in advance of our developed world. We must of course look to their wisdom, often from simplicity, and adapt this to our brave new world. We must go beyond

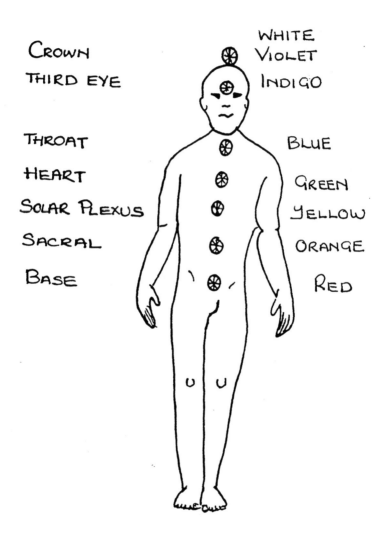

CROWN — WHITE VIOLET

THIRD EYE — INDIGO

THROAT — BLUE

HEART — GREEN

SOLAR PLEXUS — YELLOW

SACRAL — ORANGE

BASE — RED

The Chakras - the Personal Tapestry

religion and empty faith and (re)discover a practical spirituality for ourselves. Other approaches to life such as habitual use of drugs, sex, abuse etc. we can justifiably look on as escape routes from the acceptance of reality, tough though this is. We are left with the principle that life is sacred, in all senses of the expression and that we must spend our time on Earth accordingly. Also, we must find ways of adapting this spirituality to our current needs and times, as shown above. We each must find our own sacred heart and start living in accordance with this.

So what is it that allows for the strength, not just of belief but of sacred understanding, to practice ones spirituality despite the harshest of adversity, as many have done? What is it that beats in the hearts of those people the world over that grants then such magnificent dignity and stature? From whence comes their humility and acceptance of what the Earth gives them, regardless of how hard they must work to obtain it? What is it that takes us beyond the religion of faith to the sacred focus and way of life? This is the sacred spirituality we must find and live by.

We must examine and discover for ourselves what this 'sacred spirituality' is, for its nature can be different for each person. This is because it is alive, it beats within the heart of all that lives, whether mineral, vegetable, plant or animal. It lies at the very centre of the being, wherever that might be. In the case of the human being it is usually viewed as being the Solar Plexus, the name of which tells us much. The Solar Plexus is located at the soft hollow that exists just below the rib cage, in the middle of the body. This is the energy centre or 'chakra' (a Sanskrit word meaning 'wheel') through which you receive and formulate within you that life force energy that gave you life and keeps you living. We will discover more of the chakras later, there being many in the human system, and their importance in practical spirituality.

This Solar Plexus centre can be viewed as the physical centre of the sacredness that you are, but equally there can be other centres. Since the total being must have a recognition of its sacred nature to be complete and whole, it is necessary to find what is the sacred nature of your emotional self, your mental self and your higher, spiritual self. Each of these must be located, accepted, then blended with each other to form the complete, sacred awareness of the human nature. Everything we do, say, think and feel has a higher equivalent and we must recognise the nature of this and learn to blend it with our everyday acts, words, thoughts and emotions.

To help in this, we might look more closely at the nature of this word 'sacred' and discover what it really means. There are several definitions given in my Collins English Dictionary, the most relevant to our purposes being 'to set apart as holy' On checking the definition of 'holy' I find that the word 'sacred ' is given! So sacred then comes to mean to set apart.

This implies that the sacred is separate and distinct from the ordinary. As such this means that at certain times and in certain places we turn to our sacredness, acknowledge its presence and perform certain acts, say certain words, think particular thoughts and have particular feelings to demonstrate this sacredness to ourselves. All these things are vital and laudable, but we can do so much more than this, if we but strive towards a higher goal than donning our Sunday best and getting on bended knee for a time.

Whilst it may be necessary to first identity those parts of ourselves and our lives that we consider sacred, we must progress from this identification to integrating this sense of separation to our basic awareness and complete selves - our bodies, minds and hearts become united as one and so we arrive at a greater, holistic personality, more akin to the true human state.

To achieve this takes many years and can rightly be seen as one of the purposes of our lives. More practically, we can achieve this sense of unity and completion by turning to another of the given dictionary definitions of 'sacred' - 'dedicated to'. This dedication must be complete and total, to reflect the end product of the total human being. It must include all your actions, thoughts, feelings and aspirations from birth and before, to death and after. There can be no secrets, parts thought unworthy, shame, guilt or limits. All must be faced and embraced and brought into the loving light of sacred spirituality. By this we become 'enlightened', a being operating from a basis of higher dedication and sacredness. The method by which we achieve this is the nature of the text of this book.

Thus we come to see the sacred not as a separation but as an inclusion. We embrace and include all of ourselves and our lives as sacred, not setting apart particular places, within or without ourselves, for worship, ceremony and the like. This certainly has its function however, more details of which are given in Chapter Seven. Instead we simply live in a sacred manner and we know with our total being that all we are and all we do is sacred. In this sense we become 'enlightened' - full of the living light of the Spirit, in whatever form you conceive it to be, that is its Creator.

To achieve this inclusive and inherent, natural sanctity we must first dissect the self into its various parts, rather like the process of learning the rules before you can know how not to break, but transcend them. This, I am told, is the same with many things in life and is why 'rules are there to be broken'. To break a rule you must first know it exists and what it is. Apparently great blues and jazz players stick to no formula or methods in their playing, responding intuitively to each other and to the feel of the moment, thereby expressing perhaps an inner, more sacred part of themselves.

However, to reach the heights of this fantastic achievement, one must first learn and obey the basic laws of playing that type of music and understand its methods and structure. Once this method of playing has become instinctive and natural, the musician is then able to extend beyond those boundaries, becoming individual and innovative in their interpretation of musical scores. They are able to give of themselves as a whole in their music and thereby transcend, rise above, the usual everyday nature of their playing. To do this takes years of practice and requires dedication, but the end result is genius and ecstasy - both for the self and others, since the sacred and the spiritual seems to have a natural tendency to radiate out.

Once dissected these various parts can be known for what they truly are, then reassembled to a more unified, united and closer knit whole than ever before. This is really a process of death and rebirth, symbolised in many different cultures and ways across the world for thousands of years. This is why a total spirituality demands all. The rational, secure humanistic approach must be discarded and the self placed in the hands of a higher, often unknown and feared force or power. This force is in essence and nature unconditional in its giving of love and support to all who come to it, but we must first show some sign of trust and faith for it to respond.

Perhaps the most dramatic example of the death and rebirth process comes from the ancient and eminently practical spiritual nature of the many Native American ways. The ceremony known as the Sun Dance, held each year by the tribe, can rightly be viewed in this context. After a month of preparation which includes fasting, prayer and purification rituals, the chosen warrior still needs great faith and courage to undergo the physically arduous test over the coming four days of the Ceremony, held at the hottest part of the year. Through piercing his flesh the warriors blood is allowed to mingle with the Earth, as the feminine source and aspect of himself. His heart is given to the power of the Sun, as the masculine source within and without.

The Sundance

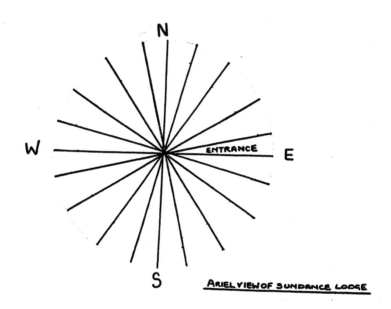

N

W   ENTRANCE   E

S

ARIEL VIEW OF SUNDANCE LODGE

SIDE VIEW OF SUNDANCE LODGE

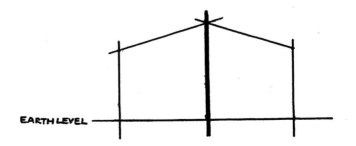

EARTH LEVEL

11

During the ceremony, the warrior has no food or drink and so must give of himself totally, as he hangs suspended from the branches of the specially chosen tree. Visions, dreams and symbols are often received by the warrior as portents of things to come, messages regarding the power and abilities he has received, not for himself, but for the good of the tribe as a whole.

It should be understood that whilst only males partake in the Sundance ceremony, females are viewed as having their own, perhaps more natural equivalent, that of childbirth. Here blood is shared and the mother gives of herself, beyond physical pain like the warrior, so that she may achieve the respected status of child bearer and nurturer. These aspects are given by Mother Earth and Father Sun, in this manner the same as through the Sun dance ceremony.

This ancient practice was much misunderstood, as is often the case with spirituality. Such was the mistrust of the United States Government that they banned the Sundance in 1941. Only recently have the indigenous inhabitants of 'Turtle Island' begun to receive this vital connection with their spirit back. Unless of Native American lineage, it is not necessary to submit oneself to such practices, though they are to be viewed with utmost respect.

Through more traditional ritual and symbolic acts we can achieve the inner shift that tells us we have allowed the old self to die and the new to be reborn. To further illustrate the necessity of this we turn to that consistent source of wisdom, the Tarot. The essential card of the Tarot and its central pivot is that of the Fool. Here we have a young person, living an instinctive life, following their path this way and that, seemingly without direction or focus. They are full of the joy of living, following their natural human desires and motivations.

We see them at the edge of a cliff, showing us that their natural instincts have taken them to the edge of the precipice, over which they must go, to experience the world, with all its trials and tribulations. The Fool must submit to this procedure, trusting that he will survive the plunge over the cliff and come to a safe rest below. This he or she does and continues on his way.

His journey takes him to encounters with symbolic characters which are aspects of himself, each of which he must face and embrace, thereby transcending that part of himself. Eventually he meets the figure of Justice,

The Fool, Hanged Man, Death, Temperance, by kind permission of Builders of the Adytum, Incorporated, 5105 North Figueroa Street, Los Angeles, California, 90042. The permission granted for the use of materials by Builders of the Adytum, Incorporated, in no way endorses anyone's interpretation thereof.

13

the mirror image of himself at the centre of his journey. Justice speaks only the truth, of the bare bones of oneself, 'warts and all'. This self must also be accepted and so transcended.

To do this requires a total giving of oneself to a higher purpose, just as with the Sundance ceremony. Indeed the Native American Tarot deck assigns the card of the Hanged Man, which follows that of Justice in the order of cards, to the Sundance. The Hanged Man is that which the Fool becomes when he accepts himself as he truly is, with Justice. Now he finds himself hung upside down, tied to a tree. This image reflects that of the Norse mythological figure of Odin, who hung for nine days and nights on the World Tree. Here he suffered great physical discomfort, having an eye pecked out by a raven and more besides. At the end of this time, he received the knowledge of the runes, spiritual knowledge and power for his journey forward, now that he has been through the symbolic death and rebirth.

That the death is symbolic is something that is the subject of the trust that needs to be shown. Being attached to a tree in such a manner as with the Sundance ceremony, or like the Hanged Man, in the power and ability of the Spirit, there can be no room for doubt, fear or shame in the self. This is why the total self must be encountered, 'faced and embraced' and then put aside, for the ways of the spirit and things of a higher nature. The Hanged Man image often shows coins falling from his pockets to symbolise the rejection of materiality and the ways of accepted society. The Cheyenne name for what we call the Sundance is 'The Offering'. It is the death and offering of the old self and the birth of the new. All that we truly possess is ourselves and this too must be relinquished to Spirit. This is why Death is the following card in the sequence of the Tarot.

Trust in the higher force and spirit to prevent us falling into oblivion, the vacuum of non-existence, when we are faced with our own symbolic Sundance, is essential. It is my belief that there can be no spiritual awakening without there first being an act of freewill on each individual's part that shows an openness of heart and willingness to accept what life gives them.

Faith and trust in this way is demonstrated in John Boorman's breathtaking film 'Excalibur', the modern retelling of the story of King Arthur. Here we see Perceval seeking the Holy Grail, the symbol for all that is pure and able to provide for all and that which will save his King and his country, the quest for which he devotes himself to. After many years in which he sees "nothing but sorrow and death" his efforts result in his being hung on a tree by his neck, beside other Knights who have failed previously. As he feels his life force begin to ebb away he has a vision of the Grail and with it something of the knowledge of spirit. He is unaware that the spurs from another Knight are slowly cutting at the rope around his neck, ensuring his survival. At the last moment his faith fails and he is cut free, to endure more suffering and torment before finally undergoing a purification by water, to clean him of his self doubt and inner torture. He goes on to achieve the Grail and save the day. That he would have survived anyway is the salient point here, but he lost faith and trust in this.

This Death experience and Tarot card, is followed by Temperance, the Angel of Peace with one foot in water, one on the land, a foot in both worlds, as we must be. We cannot ignore or neglect either the ways of the Earth or the ways of the Spirit. We must look after ourselves and the Earth, as well as honour the higher sacred spirit and learn to live in accordance with this. Does it not seem that the best way to do this is to blend the two together, living a life that is grounded in the physical, yet rises to the tallest clouds, the formless spirit from which all matter comes? By this blending our whole lives and all our actions can come to be seen as sacred, as a manifestation of the spiritual, which is our everlasting reality. The Temperance card is a picture of this state.

This gives us a good principle on which to base our lives. We cannot avoid that which is real and which is tangible. We must realise that the ways of humanity must be accepted both as a whole and individually. The best way for us to do this is to be fully present and awake in our everyday actions. By focussing fully on the present moment and applying ourselves completely to each task we undertake, so we learn to see beyond it and gain a sense of control over it. It is of course necessary to see the higher reflection in all we do and so we must learn to reach up to the clouds and breathe in that formless substance from which comes our material structure.

Such is the nature of our separation from Spirit, as we have come to term God/Goddess/Great Spirit etc. here, that we must daily, without exception, seek a meeting and uniting with its power and presence. There are many methods to do this, from as many different traditions. Included at the end of this Chapter is the simple yet effective method I have found works for me. This higher awareness eventually becomes a more tangible part of the self, one's basic identity. Consequently, as Spirit is contacted in this manner, we come to the point in our lives and selves where everything we do is motivated by Spirit and thus we come to have the same intention from within.

It is useless however to think that we can live our lives in a state of detached bliss with this connection, where we no longer must face problems and suffering. Rather we gain strength and understanding from our connection and learn to face and embrace what life throws at us. We have a sense of knowing that we can handle anything, even our worst fears, for we are truly never given anything more than we can cope with. Help is always given, when it is asked for. As such we can willingly look in the face of suffering, act as we believe best and move on. This requires that we be grounded, fully rooted and attached to the Earth, able to see things clearly and sharply, to recognise any messages applicable, learn from them and keep going. This is not to say we become cold or unfeeling, indeed quite the opposite, but that at the very root of our being we know that we cannot perish in the midst of our trials. This grounding is again required on a daily basis, both to help us remain strong and in control and also so that we are able to draw the higher connection with Spirit we have achieved, down to Earth. In this way are we each the Angel of Temperance.

That we have no or very little conscious memory or awareness of the Spirit world and of who we were in our previous lifetimes is a good indication that there is a chasm between our Earthly realm of existence and that of Spirit. This is why each must seek and undertake their own symbolic death and rebirth process. We emerge from this with our essence changed, an awareness of who we are in its most basic form. This is not to say that you undergo this process and change character that same day. It is usually a gradual process that we come to learn more about as we continue on our Quest.

It is necessary, if only to show we are willing, to perform such acts as we deem appropriate by way of Sundance, ritual, meditation, baptism, or prayer, to take ourselves through a specific time of death and rebirth. These outer acts are an indication and assistance to the inner shift that takes place as we continue. We may of course feel the need at appropriate intervals to renew the vows we have taken and give ourselves up to Spirit more than once, but these acts must be recognised as specific and special and honoured as such. When we perform this major ritual with our full intent and give of

16

ourselves completely, we are taken at our word. The daily act of grounding and connecting ourselves can be seen as a lesser reflection of the specific rebirth process, but is no less important.

There are many other methods of achieving our rebirth and as we cast our eye across the world we see its equivalent in many cultures and spiritual traditions. Traditional witches have degrees of initiation that require a giving of the Self to the God and Goddess and is a dedication for themselves of what is to come. This is also 'celebrated' each year with the celebration of the sacrifice of the Horned God as the personification of the male aspect of nature, who is cut down and harvested, only to be reborn anew, deep in a cave in the womb of Mother Earth. Perhaps it is that we too need to undergo an annual letting go and renewal process. Such is the pace and pressure of modern life that an annual retreat of a very different kind to the 'two weeks in the sun' approach is needed - a Sundance of a different kind!

The Buddha showed a more passive approach, sitting at the foot of the same, 'World' tree, the bodhi, until he had achieved enlightenment. This showed us that by looking within and seeking purity and highest intent of thought, word and deed, can we achieve the purging of the old self and so allow the light to shine from within that demonstrates to all, at the instinctive level, that we are reborn.

Modern, so-called charismatic Christians have an outer demonstration of 'giving your life to Jesus' that is their own interpretation of a rebirth, hence the name 'Born-Again' Christian. These people are also inclined to practice adult baptism, the total immersion in water for a moment that allows for the submission of the self to the cleansing and purifying properties of water to achieve the inner side to the rebirth. Such things are often loudly mocked, but can carry spiritual power and effect.

Jews have the Bar Mitzvah ceremony, the time when a boy is viewed as having left behind the ways of childhood and is now responsible enough to undertake full religious obligation. It is again, a death to the old way of life and a beginning of the new adult one. The ancient Egyptians also had complex rituals that had a great deal to do with the dead. It has been suggested recently, with some impressive evidence, that one of the functions of the pyramids was in order to bring about the actual physical rebirth of a dead pharaoh, as their representative of God on Earth.

This also brings to mind the Biblical account of the raising of Lazarus by Jesus, another symbolic death and rebirth ceremony. There are a great many other historical and current examples given to illustrate the importance of the rebirth process, along with a myriad of stories from mythology the world over. What is important and relevant from all such illustrations is that the process of giving up the self to Spirit is thousands of years old and is central to every spiritual path.

The spiritual process that includes psychology known as Psychosynthesis also shows us this framework. This postulates that there is a basic, core Self which must be identified and then separated into its constituent parts, called sub-personalities. Once each sub-personalitie's role is recognised so it can be given back to the Self and a new, more complete and rarefied whole is constructed. There is a great deal more to this process than outlined here, which we will return to later.

Rebirth is a natural process to which all must succumb or turn at some stage in their evolution. It is the in-built instinct within each and every human being, however far off some may seem to be by their attitude and actions. It is hard when we see the murderer, rapist and road builder (allowing a little personal jibe here!) but we really cannot judge others by their actions for we know not what stage they may be at. This is hard teaching, but truth.

Whichever way you turn, you will eventually fall over the cliff and experience the quickening that is the rush of energy and life force flooding through your veins when such a breakthrough is achieved. It is true that this may herald a time of difficulty and setback, but these are precisely the times when we can learn and make progress.

It is said that we learn by our mistakes and by difficulty and blockage. It can be difficult to see the sacredness in the inability to pay the mortgage or rent that results in our becoming homeless, or the spiritual nature when we are robbed, beaten or ridiculed by others. There are countless other " what about all the suffering" arguments, to none of which there is an adequate logical answer. So we will not be logical!

Instead we will turn to that which cannot be explained by logic, only known within by experience, the way of the sacred spirit. Here there is no judgment, no figure that says 'you must suffer this or that experience because you have been bad before'. Instead there is a principle which states that all things must balance and all things have their opposite, equal and complementary reflection and action. Thus, as you sow so shall you reap. Hard teaching again, but still truth.

We must remain open and soft enough to allow ourselves to recognise the opportunities for learning and progress in our suffering. It is said that misfortune, illness and hatred are the three greatest teachers we have. This can only be the case when we allow ourselves to look for, recognise and then act on what we see as the lesson learnt. This may not be while we are in the throes of illness, grappling with misfortune or displaying hatred, but when the dust has settled and we can again centre ourselves to truth and balance, we can look within for why these circumstances came about and so learn from them. truly then, rejoice in your sufferings, for they are a sure sign you are making progress. Remember that humour is a great help in lightening the load!

In order to see the sacred within the most abject of suffering our heart's reaction is all important. If we seek to apportion blame, where there is truly no-one to blame, if we look for earthly justice in revenge, we find only pain and torment. Instead we must realise that we cannot have dominion and control over all things. Whatever we experience, or see our loved ones go through, we must again 'face and embrace' these as being correct. Above all, we must not turn away, close our hearts and become bitter.

Bitterness creates a hardness within that it takes great suffering and torment to break through to the soft centre. Life and the human being alike, is indeed a box of chocolates. Soft centres have always been my favourites! But how do we accept that it is part of life's process to witness and experience physical, mental, emotional and spiritual pain and suffering?

This brings us to perhaps the hardest teaching of all, that of personal responsibility. In order to fully accept responsibility for all our actions, thoughts and feelings and the consequences of these, we must consistently seek guidance from Spirit and in so doing, learn to follow 'its' ways as closely as we are able. This gives the very highest standards and requires the utmost commitment and dedication. Such dedication cannot be based on faith and trust alone, though this always plays its part. This is why there must be each individual's Sundance, symbolically or otherwise and in whatever form, so that we have an inner knowledge and presence that takes away uncertainty and doubt. This makes the heavy weight of responsibility easier to bear. There is always guidance given when asked, if we can but recognise it, and there is always love, which is all we need.

There are a great many people in these times who are, consciously or otherwise, seeking a greater comfort and meaning than the modern industrial and technological approach to life is able to offer. These souls must be allowed complete freedom to make the choice as to which spiritual path they follow. It is vital however that some choice is made, if the individual expresses a desire to learn more of the ways of spirit. With the pressures put upon us to pay bills, wash cars, shop, mow the lawn etc., we are allowed little time for inner focus and examination. It becomes all too easy to think that we will consider the spiritual when we have caught up with the day's activities and got the kids to bed. Instead we must change this focus and put the spiritual first, for all things truly come from spirit. This is perhaps the greatest challenge the modern world faces, to learn to re-evaluate its focus away from the material to the spiritual.

As each individual finds the inner strength and intent to do this, so does the collective whole of humanity turn its face a little further away from the cash register and towards the centre of itself and all things. The death and rebirth process is a time of outer recognition and demonstration, to the self and others, that the spiritual has become the centre of your life. This does not turn you into a 'religious nut' or a campaigning madman, since what must follow is an embrace of the material. This seeming contradiction is needed since, as explained before, we cannot avoid the necessity of living in the real world. Having gone through the inner awakening that the death and rebirth process brings, we are freed from the constraints of trying to increase the bank balance and acquire more goods and are instead able to realise that everything we do, say, think and feel reflects our spiritual nature and condition. It is in this way that we are able to see how all things are sacred.

These things cannot really be explained, only experienced. For now, you will therefore have to take my word for it! The death and rebirth process, whatever way you perform it, causes a deep inner shift that brings a gradual, gentle and comfortable change in consciousness and everyday awareness. This allows for the most basic level of the human instinct to be contacted, that of the will. When the will is focussed we are able to utilise our intent, from within our beings, rather than trying to manipulate an outside motivation that is not truly under our control.

We are now able to demonstrate a greater control over our lives with the knowledge that what we focus our will on comes into being in tangible form. If we recognise a need for a partner in our lives, for a teacher of a specific subject, even for money or a house, we are able to concentrate our will on this goal, knowing that all things come from Spirit. We must ask for what we need, have patience and wait for it to occur. When it does, remember that we do not truly possess anything other than ourselves and even this only temporarily, for as all things come from Spirit, so must all things return.

As more and more individuals open to the spiritual, having found the inherent emptiness that lies at the heart of the material and technological approach, so does humanity move ever closer to its natural state. This 'natural state' we can identify, if arrogantly, as personal responsibility for each individual, the care of the Earth and pro-creation as the basis for life, all centered and based around the Spirit that gives us these things. It matters little as to how you go about this, so long as you create no suffering to others in the process, so there must be room for a multitude of beliefs and practises.

This is not to suggest that the technological and the material must be abandoned. Rather they must be embraced and accepted, not as a means of salvation or as the focus of the meaning of life, but as a means by which we are able to live a spiritual life in an easier and more fulfilling way. We cannot bury our heads in the sand and expect the nuclear threat, chemical warfare or pollution to go away. We must again, face and embrace what we have done and find ways to balance our demands on the Earth and our use of what She freely gives us, with Her needs. It is in truth such a basic and obvious thing to realise that if we use more than we replace, we will run out! Truly it is by our own created misfortune that we are given the opportunity to learn.

When we do learn, the rewards are great. The achievements of technology have been fantastic and in general have made life, at least for those in the 'Western' world, easier. Whilst this is not always a good thing, for laziness and complacency set in swiftly, few would forego the warmth of their electric or gas fire and the ease of the cooker. Yet we have reached the point where if we do not agree to balance what we take with what we give, we will have to, for there will come the day when there will simply be no more gas or electricity to give. So we recognise that gas, electric, coal, solar power or any other form of fuel is sacred, is a gift from our Mother Earth and we must honour and use it as such. In this way we embrace the material and the technological as sacred and spiritual.

In this we are able to see the direct reflection of the spiritual in the material more clearly. Life is holy and sacred and this includes all things. Even when we return our waste products they have use for the Earth in order to make things grow. Whilst we must have times of specific and exclusive focus on Spirit, perhaps through meditation, we must also realise that this same Spirit is present and alive in all our actions, thoughts and feelings and intentions. The needs of each of these are addressed in the coming Chapters.

As we progress from the moment of dedication in our rebirth process we find that we can identify the outworking of the Native American maxim 'As Within, So Without', or put Hermetically, 'As Above, So Below'. This tells us that there is always an equal and opposite reflection in our everyday lives of the spiritual realms and vice versa. Equally that what happens to us is reflected and a result of what happens within us and vice versa. The more we can see and realise that all things are sacred and a manifestation of Spirit, the more we are able to draw to us that which is uplifting and helpful, rather than energising and manifesting suffering, in whatever form. This is again why we must accept our sufferings and look for the lessons.

We must apply discrimination however, for not every tiny circumstance contains a message of great significance. In my work as a professional Tarot consultant I have come across many clients who have described occurrences along the lines of 'I bumped my car/lost the keys/spilt the milk the other day, what do you think that is telling me'? My response is to repair your car/cut new keys/mop up the milk! There is usually a lesson in becoming more grounded applicable to these noble folk, (as there is to all of us at some time) but beyond this, there is little.

Should circumstances begin to repeat themselves however it is usually safe to assume that there is some underlying pattern trying to tell you something. Look at things symbolically, not literally and allow yourself to relax and let the answer come to you. Inner realisation will occur if you take a little time to let the whirl of your mind stop and let the deeper, more knowing part of your brain help you.

With a close connection to your true Self and Spirit within, brought about by daily contact and dedication, you will also find that you have an inner sense of instinct and intuition that alerts you to when a lesson is applicable. You simply sense and know that what you have just experienced is demonstrating something to you that you need to know. Give thanks for this, take time to stop and realise the answer, accept it and move on.

With the recognition of all your actions, thoughts, feelings and intentions as sacred and from Spirit, comes a difference, not in what you do but in how you do it. This is perhaps chiefly expressed through attitude and a sense of directed purpose that comes from within. You are no longer motivated by outside forces, manipulated by whims and pressures from peers and authority. Instead you become self governing and responsible, able to harness your will and focus your intent.

You are then able to experience the quickening through your veins and in your life. This quickening is the bringing to the conscious level of your awareness, that which has been released and realised deep within your being with your rebirth procedure. As you continue to dedicate your self and your life daily to the sacred spirit, so you slowly and gradually draw up through your being, past blockages, doubts and fears, the basic truth that you are sacred and that you are loved as you are. When the security and feeling of love strikes you at the everyday level of your brain and functioning self, you feel a flow of life force energy and power that can catapult you forward, out of an ordinary life and into a supernatural extra-ordinary one. You may not change what you do, but the way in which you do it does, as does the reason for doing so. You have a passion, insight and ability that you 'never knew you had'.

This quickening can then be used throughout your life, not just for your own needs and self, but for the good of the whole. In this way we are able to fulfil not only our individual but also our collective destiny. Humanity has a role to play in the unfolding of the Universe, which will take place at it has always been intended. Should we threaten the unfolding of that process however, it is likely that we will be removed, for this is the nature of the Universe. There is no judgment, only love and truth. The Universe, God, Spirit etc. has love as a basic state of being, which flows out continually to all living things, but It/He/She cannot or will not force us to respond in the proper manner. This is matter for us, for each individual and as a whole.

That we are each connected to this whole has long been an accepted fact in the more aware of our historical cultures. I am again forced to turn to the Native Americans to illustrate this, though the example I give here also occurs in other traditions and mythologies. This is to see the world and on a wider scale, the Universe, as a spider's web.

Native American legend tells us how the creator placed Grandmother Spider in the sky to keep the web which connected the stars together in good repair. These stars were formed by the creator, being the crystallised form of the water he sprayed from his mouth. Grandmother Spider's first task was to make a huge circle and throw this into the air, thus making the Sun to guide people and warm them. However this left half the world with darkness, so the stars were brought into being to guide people through the dark times. The stars were then viewed as witnesses to all actions, another represent-ation of all things being sacred and connected. So we have the constellations to guide and inform us, linked by the image of the spider's web.

That all things are connected is a fact that is becoming increasingly accepted by scientific understanding too, specifically from quantum physics. This tells us that the basic constituents of matter are interconnected. Atomic reality has shown that particles of atoms - electrons and neutrons - continually vibrate and collide with each other, thus showing that they are related in some way. Since these atoms are the basic stuff of material form, it follows that all things are connected. It seems that the ancient cultures were aware of this process and their deities and beliefs reflected this.

This also means that what we do individually, makes a difference to the whole, collectively. Every one of your thoughts, feelings, actions and impulses has energy, has particles that flow out, collide with other particles and create a new unified form from which our reality is formed. This is why working at this basic, atomic and energetic level for the healing of the Earth and people is so effective and powerful. In such work, we really do make a difference to the reality that we experience. Not just for those who are performing the work, but for every living thing on earth, for they too are connected to this web and form part of its whole identity and reality.

This is also why we must come to see all things as sacred and why personal responsibility for the impression we make on the web and the effect we have, is so important and why this is arguably our biggest challenge. As more and more people seem drawn to the way of the sacred spirit so are they

The Maze

able to accept their responsibility, from the increased awareness that their rebirth and spiritual awakening brings. It is a typical irony that it is perhaps precisely the overwhelming materiality many people are faced with that causes them to turn to the ways of the sacred and the spiritual.

Since there is no sacred or spiritual base to the path of materialism, as a living energy or entity, it is no surprise that once the emptiness of this approach to life has been felt that people turn to that which has life and gives love. This is an instinctive response, which ever increasing numbers of people are responding to. For this, we can give thanks to Mammon and all he has brought to the world. If we can but acknowledge that he has a place and role to play, by blending his technological expertise, power and money away from self gain and towards the good of the whole, then we have hope.

It is this sense of hope that may carry us forward into the much talked about and envisioned Aquarian Age. This is the coming new age of humanity, renewed each 2000 years and is explained much more effectively than I am capable of by many others, so I simply direct those readers who wish to know more of what this means to the book *'Phoenix from the Flame'* by Vivianne Crowley (Aquarian 1994) amongst many others.

It is perhaps relevant that so as each individual must undergo the inner rebirth process, so is this happening on a global scale, showing how all things are inter-connected and part of an intrinsic whole. It is easy to view the current large scale of natural phenomena, such as floods, earthquakes and the like that we are experiencing as Mother Earth initiating her own necessary purification process. There is much of significance here that we can learn from.

We are reminded here of the flowing of the Warrior's blood and his suffering in the Sundance ceremony, which is endured for the good of the tribe to seek guidance and visions to help that tribe survive. It is the basic, unconditional nature of the sacred spirit to love.

So as It, He or She loves us, so must we learn to love ourselves, which is the most direct and effective method of coping with the weight of personal responsibility. Of course there can be many blocks to loving oneself that we must again face and embrace, but this is the process of the sacred life. When we have the inner intention of loving without condition or judgment we are

26

supported at every turn by the infinite and abundant love of the sacred spirit. As we turn to the needs of the body, heart, mind and will in turn so we learn to accept ourselves as we are, recognise our sanctity, feel the spirit within and so love ourselves, others and the Universe of which we form a small, yet significant part.

First must come the inner acceptance of the sacred spirit and the rebirth process. To assist you in this we can also look at the needs of the body, heart, mind and will, to examine the constituent parts of ourselves, accept what we find there and work on it. So we are led to the centre of the maze which the ancient Celts of the British isles chose to symbolise both this process and the workings of the Universe.

In many Celtic sites around our islands we find this image, such as Newgrange and Tintagel. The symbol of the maze shows that each warrior and Seeker must find their way to the centre of themselves, accept what they find and in so doing transform or rebirth themselves and journey back out again, reconstructing their life and reality as they go. As they do this, so the whole tribe, race and world is transformed about them. As more and more Seekers fulfil their destiny in this way, so is the nature of the world rebirthed and transformed.

This is a continual everlasting process that is akin to a purification, of ourselves and the Universe. This is why we need to come to the basic identity of ourselves on a daily basis, to reconnect and bring to the conscious level that which we know to be true but is so hard to remember and carry with the present structure and focus of our society. As we journey out, purified and transformed we reach the edge of the maze and the spider's web and find ourselves again at the precipice of The Fool. Will you now jump?

COME TO THE CLIFF, HE SAID
THEY SAID, WE ARE AFRAID
COME TO THE CLIFF, HE SAID.
THEY CAME.
HE PUSHED THEM
AND THEY FLEW.

Exercise 1 - Grounding and Connecting

This exercise can be used on a daily basis, to establish and maintain the necessary grounding and to allow you to soar to spiritual highs safely and realistically. Once grounded you are able to journey where you will in your spirit, knowing that what you experienced is real and that you are able to collect experiences and realisations and bring then back to apply in your everyday life. Being grounded is also a state of being, that with repetition of this exercise, will find its way into your self and life. This enables you to accept whatever you experience in your life, face and embrace it and provide for a real understanding, stopping you becoming one who drifts about a few inches off the ground, seeing a false, rosy reality that just does not exist.

Connecting does the same thing, but from above. This provides you with the necessary connection to spirit, like tuning in a radio station. It needs to be maintained and renewed on a daily basis, as does grounding. Being connected also ensures that you are able to be guided by spirit, whether unconsciously or intuitively, in your everyday approach to life. Once this state of being has become the norm for you, you will find that you have an increased awareness and understanding of the spirit worlds, seeing how they operate alongside and closely linked to, our material dimension and existence.

This exercise will take a little while to begin with, but you will find with regular practice that you perform the whole thing effectively in only a few minutes. It is always a good idea to make a few brief notes to record and be aware of your progress. This may not seem important now, but it can be so useful in the future. This applies to all the exercises in this book.

For a complete explanation of Grounding and Connecting, please see my book '*Practical Meditation*' (Capall Bann 1996). For those that find it helpful, I have produced a tape of this technique, details of which are at the end of the book.

To begin, sit comfortably, whether in an upright chair or on the floor. Try to avoid slouching and keep your back reasonably straight, but do not tense your body in the attempt. Close your eyes and just relax for a few moments. Let the outside world drift away, forget all your responsibilities for a time and just relax and be still and calm. Let your thoughts come and go as they please, moving through your mind naturally and without holding onto them at all. Now do the same with your emotions. Relax your body, letting go of any last areas of tension or ache as you become more and more calm. Your concentration will keep you awake, but if you find yourself nodding off, do not worry. You are in need of rest before you are able to delve into these deeper levels of yourself, so take time for extra sleep and rest and begin when you are ready.

Now let your breathing relax fully and let your breath happen by itself, without strain or effort from you in any way. Let a natural rhythm emerge and take you deeper within. As you do so, imagine and try to sense the flow and movement of the life force and energy that flows throughout your body and being. This flow responds to the force or energy of your mind and thoughts, so focus these on your feet and on the earth beneath you. This energy moves through solidity easily, including you, so imagine and sense it flowing down into the earth, then taking root just like a tree or plant.

Remain with this for a short time, however long feels appropriate to you. Then draw the energy and life force of the earth up into your body and being. Perhaps use your in-breath to help, but do not change your breathing in any way. Imagine and sense it flooding your entire self, inside and out, filling you with its presence, power and strength. Let this continue to rise, grounding you more clearly with each moment, until you feel that the force has reached the top of your head. Keep it inside here, it is meant for you.

Now focus your concentration on the higher flow of life force that comes from above and all around. These flows are infinite and abundant. Open yourself to this energy and imagine that you receive its gentle, beautiful power flowing into you through the crown of your head. Let yourself drift up to receive it and connect with your higher senses and self in this way. Perhaps draw this down with your breath too. Feel this flowing through your body and being and mingling with the grounding energy of the Earth.

Soon these energies settle and you will feel them balance within you. In this you reach a point of perfect balance and peace that is the centre of your being. You are now grounded and connected, centred within yourself and able to extend your awareness out and journey where you will. In the early stages, just remain with the wonderful feeling you achieve by finding the centre of your self. Remain there for as long as you wish.

When you are ready to return, focus gently on your breath once more and gradually and slowly increase this back to its usual, everyday level. Slowly adjust your senses back to their usual state and let your feet rest firmly on the floor to establish contact with the material world once more. Take your time returning as it is vital to do so fully. When you feel ready open your eyes and adjust before you move.

Exercise 2 - Dedication Ceremony

This exercise is intended to be an outer demonstration, to yourself and spirit, that you recognise the reality and necessity of following the ways of spirit. It may be performed once, as a special ceremony, after careful thought, planning and meditation, and never used again. You may find it necessary however, to use this ceremony once a year or at suitable intervals when you feel you need to regain your focus and intention onto spirit and away from the material. It is a serious exercise that should not be treated lightly, or its effects underestimated. They may appear to be subtle and intangible, but over a period of time they will have repercussions that can have some major implications for your path through life.

Begin by choosing an area to perform your ceremony. This may be in or out doors, whatever feels appropriate for you. If outdoors, choose a secluded place where you feel safe and know that you will not be disturbed while you perform this ceremony. If indoors, clear the room to give yourself the maximum area possible to work in.

Light some incense if you like it and place some special objects at the centre of your space, that represent your sacred spirit and life. As we progress through this book, we will work with each of four Elements in turn, being Earth, Air, Fire and Water. Gather together something to represent each of these Elements. These might be a bowl of salt or soil, a stone or sand for Earth, some incense or feathers for air, a candle for Fire and bowl of water, sea shell or beach pebble for water. When you have found these objects, place them neatly in the centre of your working space.

Now take a seat beside them, and sit for a short moment, recognising and considering what you are about to do. See the place you are in as a place that will become a gateway between this world and the world of Spirit. Feel it as a sacred area and feel yourself as part of this. Now close your eyes and perform the grounding and connecting. Take as long as you need over this, for this is vital to achieve clearly to give you the necessary awareness of what you are doing.

When you feel ready, pick up your Earth Element, face the North of your working area and say:

"The Element of Earth is placed in the North as witness to this ceremony. I bring the qualities of Earth within me".

Pause for a moment to reflect on what these qualities are within you and be open to receive any impressions, thoughts or feelings as they arrive. Then place your Earth Element down at the North edge of the area. Now return to the centre and pick up the candle. Walk to the South, and say:

"The Element of Fire is placed in the South as witness to this ceremony. I bring the qualities of Fire within me".

Light the candle and pause as before to receive the Fire qualities and become aware of them and their effect. Place the candle down and return to the centre once more. Pick up the Water Element and walk to the West. Hold this Element up and say:

"The Element of Water is placed in the West as witness to this ceremony. I bring the qualities of Water within me".

Remain open to receive these qualities, perhaps sprinkle yourself with the water, feel what these are, then place the Water Element down in the West and return to the centre when you are ready. Pick up the Air Element, walk to the East and say:

"The Element of Air is placed in the East as witness to this ceremony. I bring the qualities of Air within me".

Stand and receive these as before, then place the Air Element down in the East. Now return to the centre and pause, sitting or standing as you wish. It is also a good idea to involve yourself with the Element in some way. This may be by sprinkling or drinking the water, gazing at a candle flame, letting sand or Earth fall between your fingers, wafting incense smoke over you and so on. Obviously what you use for the Elements will dictate this.

You are now in the centre of you own sacred space and circle. Recognise this as such and close your eyes to reflect on this and how it feels. When you are ready, read aloud a prepared statement that describes the dedication you wish to make to Spirit. This can be as far reaching, as general or precise as you wish. For guidance only, as it needs to be personal to you, it may be something like:

"I pledge my actions, intentions, feelings and thoughts to all that is Sacred. I declare I am a Sacred Being and offer myself in recognition of this sanctity. I ask for guidance and help in this service. May my life demonstrate the love that exists at the heart of the Universe".

Be careful about what you say, as it will be heard, noticed and acted upon. There is much truth in the old saying 'Be careful what you ask for as you might get it'! Think seriously and meditate before deciding what to say and be absolutely sure before you do so. If you have any doubt, wait. You are responsible for what you declare and demonstrate here and it represents an important transition in your life that will have an effect in your everyday life. It is also a very beautiful, private and powerful moment than can be fulfilling and inspiring to an amazing degree.

Having said your piece, pause and wait for any response that seems to occur. This may be emotionally, mentally or physically, but if nothing seems to happen, do not despair! It may be sometime before you sense or recognise a tangible effect from this ceremony, if ever. If you are sincere, it will have been heard and responded to. You are taken at your word.

To conclude the ceremony, give thanks, aloud, in your own words for the guidance, inspiration, help and so on that you have received and declare that the ceremony is at an end and closed.

This ceremony is written here in a deliberate manner so as to make it necessary for you to study it and adapt it for your own circumstances and preferences. Read it thoroughly and decide beforehand on your own words to use, make any additions or alterations you wish to make and plan clearly what you are going to do. Choose a specific time, do not tell all and sundry about it and above all, treat it as a serious and significant time in your spiritual life and it will succeed and have effect within you and your life.

Exercise 3 - Discrimination

This exercise is a method of defining what is imagination and what is real, in the guidance, intuition and messages you receive from spirit, as you go about your life. It is not failsafe, since we are all fallible in different ways, but once you have learnt it and it becomes habit, you will find that surety of what is real and what is not becomes a natural process.

This exercise requires that you take a few moments out of the speed and activity of what you are doing and find somewhere to sit quietly. Close your eyes and perform a quick grounding and connecting, which is always good to do at any time. Now recall the experience, circumstance or message you feel you have received from spirit. Bring it to mind fully and hold it in your focus.

Now ask clearly 'What is the meaning of this'? State this clearly in your mind once and once only. Pause and observe the answer you receive. This may be a sensation in your body, an emotional feeling that wells up within you, a sudden thought that occurs to you, an image you see clearly in your mind or something that happens as you sit. In the altered state of consciousness that the grounding and connecting puts you in, you will know then what the meaning is, if you allow yourself to sense it. Do not analyse, but let yourself take part in the experience fully. Analysis can come later. If nothing happens at all, you will usually sense that this means that you have an active imagination. If so, perhaps look at why you conjured this 'message' up and what you are trying to tell yourself. If you cannot seem to stop these messages occurring, learn to channel your over-active imagination into some creative endeavour. You have this ability, so use it!

Take time to return from the grounding and connecting fully back to the everyday world, bringing with you what you have learnt as you come. This exercise may not seem very reliable or significant to do, but you will find that once you have learnt the grounding and connecting process fully, you perception will be quite different.

Chapter 2

The Sacred World

It used to be the case that wherever one lived on the Earth, there lay one's spirituality. Indeed, this was frequently in the Earth itself, many native cultures taking their teaching directly from the Earth, as well as the unseen realms and worlds that exist about it and about us all. This native spirituality was not 'set apart', as with our modern interpretation of the sacred, but was simply life. Spirituality was fully integrated into the practical necessities of life.

Food was doubtless blessed before being eaten, as well as the spirit of the land on which it grew being venerated by the worship and acknowledgement of the deities seen as residing in and overlooking it. The greater spirits of the seasons and the years were also given recognition, the agricultural relevance and necessity of the 'powers that be' to be placated so that they bestowed a bountiful crop was essential, not for luxury and making life easier, but for survival. The winter brought with it a dearth of food supplies, for humans and the animals they were dependent on. Life was not an idyllic splendour lived close to the Earth. it was a harsh, often cold existence, with a constant hard working regime, needful for life continuing.

Now it is a very different picture. Our food supplies never seem to dwindle, and in the so-called developed world we are given access to the Earth's bounty from all far flung corners. Life is, in many ways, easy. We do not, in the main, worry over where the next meal is coming from or if we have enough stocks to last through the winter when the Earth gives us little. Hardship comes to us in different ways, brought about by the world we have created and in which we must live.

Now the 'powers that be' are Governments and mutli-national corporations that control our lives by directing what laws we must obey and what food we eat. We have work, for which we are paid money to buy those things we choose. This chase occupies the majority of our time, leaving little, once children have been cared for and our houses cleaned, for recreation and simple pleasure. Next, all too often, comes spirituality, if we are of a mind to pursue such things. Most have sparse energy for this, or, perhaps understandably if there is no direct cause or need, cannot be bothered.

Consequently, our roots become forgotten, our past left to rot and decay. Yet the Earth annually shows us, that which is left in this manner feeds the new and stimulates new seeds, life and potential. So it is in the Earth and in our past we can find that which has been forgotten and that which can produce new growth within us. It becomes our task then, to seek out that which has been lost.

If we have little or no time for spiritual pursuits, sitting to meditate or perform sacred ceremonies or rituals, then we must integrate the sacred with our daily lives and activities. To do this takes resilience, discipline and tenacity. We must be firm in our commitment and have clearly defined ways in which we reflect the spiritual in our actions. It is simply not enough to have vague beliefs and ideas about which we do little, except plan to begin a practical search and 'live a better life', when we have brought the children up, paid the mortgage off or retired. Other obstacles or perhaps excuses, are sure to present us with another distraction or seemingly so-important task that shields us form turning to the spiritual.

First we must place the sacred at the heart of ourselves and our lives. This, as explained in the last Chapter, having been done, we can direct our energy and motivation to adapting ourselves and way of life towards becoming a reflection of this sacred influence, within and without us. One of the most vital decisions we must take is that of choosing which path and manner we will pursue the sacred in.

It should be made clear that this choice is often not a matter of simply sitting and thinking to ourselves, 'I like the way the Egyptians do this or that, I'll follow their ways'. Nor am I speaking of a conversion in the sense of a sudden acceptance of one god or another or a philosophy of life.

It may well be that a conscious choice is in fact, never made as to which spiritual discipline you make your own. It is more common that the spiritual chooses us and we find ourselves one day having become a Buddhist,

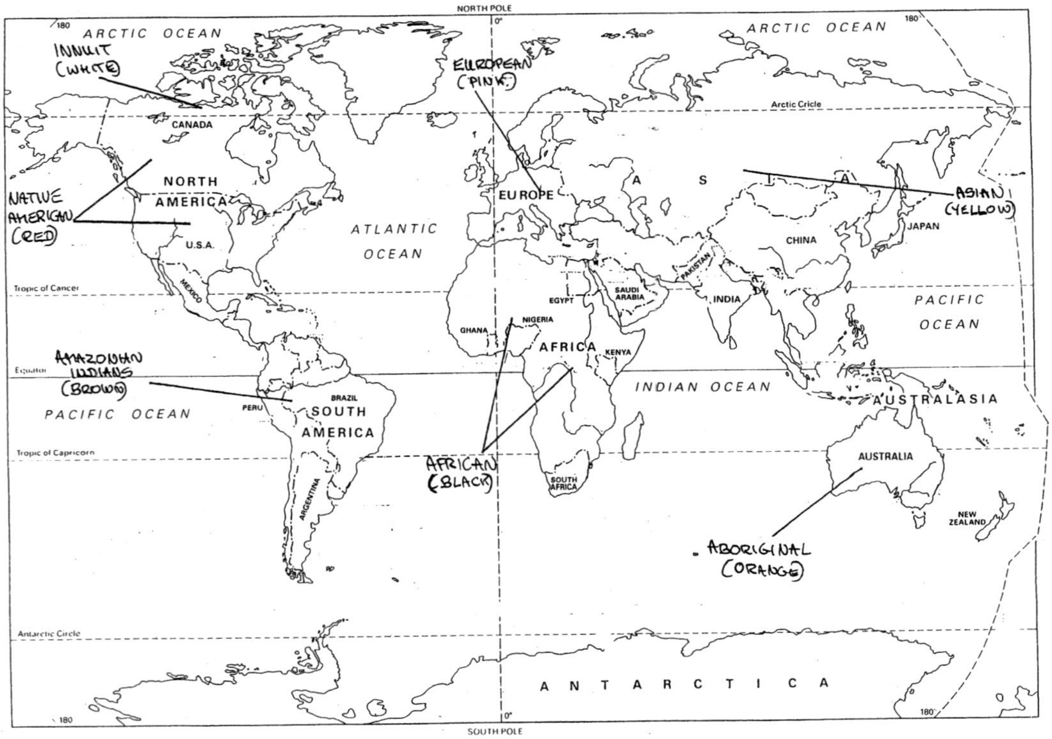
NORTH POLE
ARCTIC OCEAN
INNUIT
(WHITE)
EUROPEAN
(PINK)
ARCTIC OCEAN
Arctic Cricle
CANADA
NORTH
AMERICA
NATIVE
AMERICAN
(RED)
U.S.A.
EUROPE
ASIAN
(YELLOW)
JAPAN
CHINA
ATLANTIC
OCEAN
Tropic of Cancer
MEXICO
EGYPT
SAUDI
ARABIA
PAKISTAN
INDIA
PACIFIC
OCEAN
GHANA
NIGERIA
AFRICA
KENYA
AMAZONIAN
INDIANS
(BROWN)
Equator
INDIAN OCEAN
AUSTRALASIA
BRAZIL
PERU
SOUTH
AMERICA
PACIFIC OCEAN
Tropic of Capricorn
AFRICAN
(BLACK)
AUSTRALIA
SOUTH
AFRICA
ARGENTINA
NEW
ZEALAND
ABORIGINAL
(ORANGE)
Antarctic Circle
ANTARCTICA
180
0°
SOUTH POLE

The Global Tapestry'

Wiccan or whatever. It is simply that 'things' have evolved in such a manner as to make this or that way the most fulfilling, pleasing or meaningful for us.

Another major bearing on our present day spirituality comes in the shrinking of the world. As technology, in its various forms has enabled us to travel, publish globally and interact across the world, even instantly now, with the advent of the 'Internet', so are we able to read, learn and even meet those from drastically different histories and cultures than our own, learn their ways and even adopt them as our own. Spirituality is no longer a local matter. Though applied in a directly ecological sense, the phrase 'Think globally, act locally', comes to mind here. It is vital, however physically distant our chosen methods may be, that we have a defined and structured manner in which to practice them. We may not be able to express this definition in logical terminology to another, but it is enough to know it for ourselves.

Global culture and interaction brings with it many benefits, as well as drawbacks, for ourselves and those we contact. This is also true spiritually. Now, as never before, we have access to a myriad of sacred paths, the result often being an eclectic mix understandable and practical for us, but a blur and impractical to any other. Perhaps it is that there is now a call for a world-wide spirituality, a global method of honouring, worshipping and depending on the Earth and the Divine. If we look closely however, we may find that this has in fact existed for thousands of years.

In the rich tapestry that is human nature and the Earth, we see many different colours and shades within those colours, each practising the sacred in a different manner. As we step back and enlarge our image and vision, we see that each of the different practises is linked to the other in some way and that placed alongside each other in this way, they form part of that global spirit. To complete this image we see that the tapestry is woven onto the Earth, forming the foundation and structure on which all those paths are built and out of which all grow. So we come to see that a spirituality for the coming Aquarian Age has been with us, in red, white, yellow and other skin colours, for much of our history.

The nature of colour is such that when it blends, all colours eventually become white. So we are linked by the colour of our skin, not separated. Yet we must glory in that link by embracing that which we are, both outwardly

The Universal Tapestry

SUN
ORANGE
MERCURY/VIOLET
VENUS/GREEN
EARTH/YELLOW
MARS/RED
JUPITER/BLUE
SATURN/INDIGO
URANUS/MIXED COLOURS
NEPTUNE/PASTEL SHADES
PLUTO/BLACK

and inwardly. The many practises of the sacred that the different colours offer us all have something to offer. It is vital that we recognise that no matter in what form, or what colour you paint yourself, all the colours merge to the same source, the Divine white light, if you will. It should be said here quite categorically that this does not mean in any way that the 'white man' is better because he is white - he is not white, he is a murky kind of pale brown!

So how you follow your spirituality is in the higher sense, not important. That you follow the path is. What we must turn to now is the choice of that path, not in the sense of which path, but choosing a path. This can best be done by looking at what the sacred is to us and how we would wish to demonstrate and reflect this in the way we are and the manner in which we live.

In this we must look within ourselves, to who and what we are and what has gone before us, in all senses. We must turn inward, seek the sacredness within and then turn outwards, taking deliberate and conscious steps, armed with knowledge and certainty of what we are about. Then we can widen our minds and hearts and turn to the Universe to discover our place in it and come to understand a Universal tapestry too. As such we come again to the understanding that all is sacred and that all paths converge to reflect and be part of this same divine spirit.

In turning within we encounter ourselves, including all our faults, hang-ups, fears, motivations, inspirations and cares. This we must do if we are to accept perhaps the biggest of all individual challenges, personal responsibility. Consequently the manner in which we turn within must be open and honest, fuelled by the sense of inner knowing that tells us that all is well. We must recognise the limits of our conscious outlook and view of things and so learn ways in which we can transcend or bypass the logical view.

The exercises in this book, together with its text, will help you to achieve this. as well as the necessity of looking within, identifying your needs and then working with them, to produce the optimum person possible. This is done by taking as our basis the Four Elements of Earth, Air, Fire and Water that form the quintessence of Spirit, or the Sacred, that constitutes our being, at all levels. We explore the needs of each, both personally and Universally, to bring about this effect.

In our Quest to identify and integrate our own particular view and relationship with the sacred we must learn and accept what is right for us, discarding (but not belittling) that which is unsuitable for us. This is a basic part of our personal responsibility, which to a large degree means understanding our part in the wider Universe.

That we are a part of this 'grand scheme of things' must first be recognised and accepted, with the realisation that our planet and all individual life upon it is necessary for the Universe to unwind, expand and evolve as it should. There is perhaps a level of which we have no knowledge, where things may indeed be planned and so we must accept by faith that everything is working out as it should. The first exercise at the end of this Chapter should help you come to an awareness of your place in the Universe and so help you to value yourself and your life. This forms the first step on the path of personal responsibility.

History and experience has taught us that there are certain principles which we must learn to live by, if we are to play an active part in both our own evolution and that of the Universe. We will examine some of those principles now, by way of helping you to choose a path and manner in which you can live with the Sacred at the centre.

If indeed there is a level beyond our comprehension, we must reconcile ourselves to this and so question our own sense of freewill. The concept of fate and destiny is a much vexed one that causes a great deal of debate and disagreement. What is important to realise here is that, in principle, what you believe does not matter as much as having a belief that you are comfortable with and that allows you to live in a manner that allows you freedom to be you and maintains the Sacred at the focus.

Do not allow yourself to be trapped into having to justify your views and beliefs to any other (except, to yourself) or even at being able to explain them in a logical fashion at all. The spiritual world is not limited or trapped by human logic, operating at a level beyond that of mere rational thought. The proof by logic approach used to decry much of what the esotericist believes stems from the humanistic approach, upon which the Sacred cannot, because of the blockages we present, encroach. That is some people's prerogative of course, as it may be that they need to experience this kind of life and approach in their evolution, but it does not mean that the whole world must conform to their views. If you cannot explain your beliefs in a rational way, it may mean that though you know what you believe and feel to be right within, it is not applicable to any other, or simply does not have a means by which it can be explained, such is its nature. So abandon logic all ye who enter here!

Consequently I do not propose to debate the issue of freewill, fate and destiny, save to say to be sure you are not limited in your zest for life, conscious evolvement and above all, sense of personal power, by letting fate or destiny claim such a hold over you as to demean or belittle the strength of your motivations and actions. We are beings of incredible power, achievement and strength, it is sad to see it when it is disempowered and made disfunctional by our own self-imposed perceptions. Expand your mind and the Universe expands with you! Or put another way, and to quote a recent song, 'Free your mind and your arse will follow'!

Having stepped into a Universal perception, consciousness and understanding of the nature of things, we must of course look at what we find there, learning to obey the rules that do exist spiritually. Not to limit or contain us, but indeed, to free us so that we can fulfil the amazing potential we all have. When we learn to step outside of and beyond the limits of our conscious mind, we encounter, almost as a regard, a feeling of peace that truly does surpass all understanding. This sense of peace, for me a daily requirement in these troubled times to maintain balance and hope, can be achieved by the effective use of the Grounding and Centering technique. The peace is experienced within, yet stems from without, for it is felt inside your body and your mind, yet is able to be there because this is the nature of things at the higher or Universal level that you have accessed by use of this technique.

This takes us to one of the most used, but often misplaced spiritual principles, that states 'As Above, So Below', or alternately 'As Within, So Without'. The inner peace and calm is within, and has its reflection without, in the individual and then the Universe, and of course, vice-versa. This principle also enables us to go a long way in accepting personal responsibility for all that we are and do, since every thought, action, word and emotion that we have is reflected in some way in the wider world and Universe.

A simple illustration of this reflection can be made using colour. In cultures the world over, the chakras or energy centres of the body are each given a colour, that describes its nature for us. Based on the frequency and effect of the colour, formed by the speed of vibration of the energy or force that forms colour, each chakra is perceived to vibrate at a different rate, having corresponding functions in the human system.

Firstly these chakras are both within and without the body, being located at different points up the spine, yet extending out into the aura, the body of energy that surrounds all living things. Secondly, the colours of these seven main chakras are also the colours of the rainbow, these being formed by water but appearing as colour, so energy again. The inner showed in a bigger and wider format on the outer.

Be aware of the principles, but not wary, that everything you do is projected to the Universe and so quite literally and in a physical, tangible way, builds the world we live in and are part of. This is another reason why we must take responsibility for ourselves. We must come to an acceptance that we play a vital part in the Universe and use this awareness to empower ourselves, not frighten us. We are loved and accepted just as we are, for we have chosen to have the kind of life we have, though of course we may not logically agree with this. But we have left logic behind, transgressed and moved beyond the need for it. Instead we follow a higher mind and a wider perception of things.

With the recognition of our part in the Universe and humanities collective identity and experience, comes the realisation that if our actions are self centred, brought to give us more money or possessions, so we are depriving the world, not just of the material goods we stockpile, but of growth, expansion and ultimately, love, this being at the height of all things. If we choose to believe we cannot do a certain thing or we carry with us unconscious beliefs from pre-conditioning, whatever its origin, we are limiting not just ourselves but the rest of the Universe too. We are quite literally, in this together, to quote another recent song.

This is shown in St Paul's maxim that we are *'Members One of Another'*. Esoterically, this means that we are all linked to and part of a force or energy from which all things take their body and which binds all things together. This is precisely why personal responsibility is so important. the more we accept that we are masters of the Universe, in a non-egotistical sense, the more we help everything, including ourselves, to evolve. The nature of this energy is that of unconditional love and this is the reason why

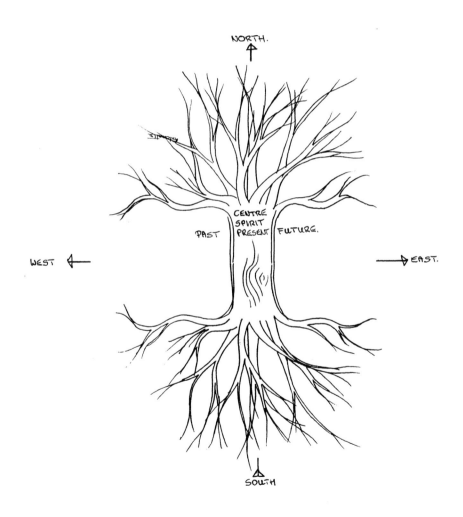

The World Tree

we experience the reflection of 'as above, so below' and why 'everything that goes around, comes around'.

This in turn brings us to the law of karma, which we will deal with fully later, but suffice to say for now that it is a law that says that all things must balance, no more and no less. Our personal responsibility must extend for the whole of our evolvement, not just the current, worldly life. Our British ancestors the Celts knew this and this is why they were able to arrange loans in this life, repayable in the next. Somehow however, it is difficult to see even the 'bank that likes to say Yes' responding positively to a request for this!

Having entered into the realm of Universal awareness and consciousness, and found the peace that presides there, we must begin to explore the world that we find, shaped by that higher level of perception and again with the Sacred as its focus. We must find a way of learning about this new world and applying the lessons we discover to ourselves and our lives. The myths and legends that litter the world contain such stories and revelations that give us these lessons, so it is to our own ancestry and pre-history that we must turn for education about the make-up and construction, not just of our world, but of our Universe.

In historical shamanic tradition the links between the world and indeed worlds, was shown by the image of the World Tree. This occurs in more than one tradition and myth, each having a slight variation of the tree that stands at the centre of all things, giving us the means by which we can, not only discover our links to all things, but to actually journey between these worlds.

This tree, known as the 'Axis Mundi', occurs in Norse mythology, with the well known story of Odin who hung upside down suspended from it, suffering greatly, to obtain the knowledge of the runes. We have already encountered some mention of this tree in the previous Chapter and you may like to look again at the Tarot card of the Hanged Man. The Buddha sat under the same tree to gain enlightenment and the Native Americans strapped themselves to it for symbolic rebirth. Its trunk is of mighty girth, its roots strong and deep and its branches wide, plentiful and beautiful. These qualities are reflected in its power and ability to stand at the centre of the world, reaching down and up to the different worlds.

These are the worlds of the shaman, in Celtic tradition called the Under, Middle and Other worlds. These three worlds are open to our visitation, journeying being achieved by the many different methods that result in an altered state of consciousness. Some such methods include trance, meditation, dance and ritual or ceremony. For a detailed explanation of those three worlds I would refer readers to Caitlin Matthews' excellent book. 'Singing the Soul Back Home' (Element 1995). Suffice to say here that we will encounter these worlds again when we look at the Needs of the Mind, their relevance being explored in a psychological context there.

In Celtic and specifically Druid tradition the World Tree was an Ash. The Ash is seen as linking the three circles of existence which we perceive as past, present and future. So journeying beside the Tree, as in Exercise 1 of this Chapter, we are not only able to travel 'up' and 'down' between the worlds, but backwards and forwards too, since the tree stands at the apex or axis of all things.

These myths and legends can teach us much about choosing and following a spiritual path, for entwined in their fabric are the very principles, ways and means that we need to live by. Many cultures, not least the Celts and the Norse were and are great storytellers, this being their prime method of teaching, especially in the spiritual arts. These stories still survive in some corners of the world, known more often than not now as fairy tales and folk stories. Often we see in them the archetypes of our modern world, the symbols that the figures in the stories represent teaching us much about ourselves and the nature of the world we inhabit.

Before we begin to look forward at our development, personally and spiritually, it can be helpful and clarifying to look back, both at our own past and that of our ancestors. To do this we can read the stories and tales of old, examine the lives of the heroes we find there and apply those same principles to our current selves and lives. In our own Celtic tradition there is an extremely rich wealth of legends and figures that we can call on to help and guide us in this manner, not least the likes of Cuchulainn and Llew. Search the stories and consider what they are saying, beyond the content of what is written. Apply instinct over logic and you will discover a teaching that is timeless and can apply directly to you in the 20th Century world as much as when they were originally told and subsequently written down.

This is perhaps because that it is said that all myths are based on fact. This may well be the case when we consider that our own current perceptions and principles are based on logic and science, that inevitably walk hand in hand. These stories and teachings come from a time when the scientific approach was at worst blended with intuition and the inner human instinct looked upon as the best of guides as to future action and current thought and opinion. By looking at our history in this manner we can learn and adopt the ways of the heroes of old, by applying those same instincts, which are as strong in us as they were within Odin, Bran, Taliesin and the like.

By examining these stories we can establish a deep and inner link with the tradition from which they come. Look at the myriad of titles on offer concerning myth, legend and folk tales. Do not discount children's tales too, for in these is much wisdom, helpfully put in a style that is understandable for even the small and growing brain. The Brothers Grimm stories are the obvious example here.

Be instinctive in you choice and read what appeals to you for whatever reason. Allow yourself to be open in your approach and learn from all traditions. In time you will find that the stories from a particular tradition and culture will seem to make more sense and speak to you more clearly and meaningfully than others.

This may in fact be because you have been there before. We shall examine the subject of past lives in more detail when we look at the Needs of the Body, but suffice to say for now that we are often able to connect more readily with one period in history, place in the world and therefore the teachings it gives us through its stories, simply by virtue of having lived there before. We now carry an unconscious memory of that time in our bodies. The stories we read and hear can be a powerful way of unlocking this rich store of inner wisdom and knowledge that we all carry with us. We will see how we can unlock that store in due course.

The thought of sitting and reading all these books may fill you with dread and seem like a long winded way of discovering where you came from and who you are and to which tradition you should apply yourself. If this is the case, you may well find that there are alternatives. Many books are now available as spoken word cassettes and it is worth searching for these. This allows for a different atmosphere to be created, where the story is read by what could be viewed as the modern version of the ancient bard or storyteller, the character actor. You can then sit back, close you eyes and let yourself be transported to a world of wonder that is as real now as it has always been.

There is a frustrated storyteller buried within many of us and most never get the chance to let it out. Telling stories to our children is an excellent way of developing the intuition and imagination, for them as well as you. Let yourself visualise the stories you tell, for you can be sure the child is doing the same. It is then a short step to reading your own stories on to tape, or getting someone you know who loves to do so (or perhaps loves the sound of their own voice!) to do it for you.

If you felt truly adventurous you may like to form a small group to tell stories, traditionally done inside at night and only in the dark half of the year as the Celts viewed it, between our November and May. This winter time was seen as the time when we are more still and receptive and therefore able to take more into our minds. To sit in a candle filled room, if you are lucky these days with a real fire, is an excellent means of providing a suitable and relaxing atmosphere, the participants perhaps loosened by a glass or two of mulled wine to warm the bones. As the stories are told, you can feel yourself slipping back in time and living alongside the heroes and villains of old. In this you can effectively meet yourself and discover the direction your spiritual path has taken and so where it is heading now.

There are a great many ways in which storytelling can be utilised, not just reciting old verses and scripts. You may like to begin with an agreed first line (for those that have seen it, recall this scene in the film '*Out Of Africa*', with Meryll Streep providing the story in exchange for dinner), or perhaps choose a theme. You can have one long story told by each person, or have more, shorter stories.

You could use the Tarot as a basis for each person's portion of the story (may I recommend here the *Arthurian Tarot* by Caitlin & John Matthews for those of a Celtic leaning).

We can also look to modern drama, in all its forms, for our modern storytellers, who do exist between the dross that is also churned out on a daily basis! In many films and even television drama we can find nuggets of truth and tales of old recreated in a modern form. The recent animated versions of some of Shakespeare's works serve as a good example, making these sometimes complex works available even to a young mind. (Another way of understanding Shakespeare is to examine the *Shakespearian Tarot* by Dolores Ashcroft Nowicki).

The heroes Hollywood and the television companies give us are in many ways not so different to the likes of the Arthurian Knights and so on. Now we have James Bond and Indiana Jones, Superman and Batman, Luke Skywalker and Captain Kirk (or Captain Piccard, depending on which Generation you come from!). The settings may be different but the heroes and the archetypes they bring with them come from the same mould. With the advent of the publishing industry, many such heroes first came alive in book form and were then presented to us on the screen. First however, they existed in the heart and mind of their creator and it is there that we need to find them, alive and teaching and inspiring us still, exemplifying at best what we aspire to and can achieve if we look deep enough. This is not just within the creator, but within you. When we look beyond the mega-bucks and the gloss, we can still see a spirituality and a sense of what could be. This can be of great help in identifying where we come from and where we belong.

Having connected us to our ancestry in this manner we can follow this through logically and look to our personal history to see in more and closer detail who we are. Many who now claim to be Celt are in fact of Saxon, Norse or other blood. Learn what you can of who you are, who your grandparents were and theirs in turn where possible. This can be of enormous influence, not just mentally, but physically and emotionally, on who we are now. Esoteric teaching tells us that many things stay with us across the generations and science has now discovered the truth of this in DNA and its workings.

Our native and family roots influence us subconsciously, shaping much of the person we become. With a little effort we can get a feel for this person and absorb the influences from our family past in a more defined and holistic way. As such we become a little more aware of our identity and a little more complete.

The family is currently much maligned, taking a different form for the 21st Century. This can be a great shame since it can cut us off from our past in this sense and so a great store house of wisdom and help for each individual. Should we find ourselves in a position that is essentially family-less, we can still tap into the roots of who we are and where we come from, by tapping into the land we live on.

Again with the advent of modern technology, we can choose anywhere on our planet to live on. However, we each have a land of our birth and so we are truly a part of that land. The land, its buildings and structures, as well as its people, serve as a conductor for its tradition and its spiritual ways and principles. As such they all soak up the influences and energy that we give out, so there is an intrinsic link between ourselves and the land we live on.

In choosing a spiritual path to follow, we are able now to pick any culture that appeals to us, even to the extent of, literally 'uprooting' and living there. Be careful however, not to disregard the land of your birth, for 'you and the land are one'. As such you can tap into the memories the land contains, learn about your ancestors, and examine your roots. You may of course still feel that your chosen path needs to be that which is a continent away, but by discovering your roots first, you will take with you a connection that is a foundation upon which your chosen direction will be much the stronger and more focussed. You may well find that the two seemingly separate or even opposed traditions may blend at a certain level, for the Earth is still the Earth, wherever you are upon her body.

Looked at from the opposite point of view, the Earth and its peoples are a fantastic and wonderful mix, full of the most amazing practices and beliefs and since we have nearly all of these at our disposal now, it is a shame and an ignorance to dismiss any of them as cranky or weird. Each has something to offer, whether we can see this or not, so be open and eclectic in your influences, but look at yourself first, where you came from and so who you are. The past is only the past on the Earth plane and level of existence. Elsewhere it is an ever present living thing, still alive and working and it is easy to open to its influence and learn.

Much of our spiritual development and focus is to do with our search for wholeness and the instinctive and basic need we all feel to be complete, free of pain and a sense of being alone. All these things can be adequately filled and more besides, by a life led that has as its central axis a sense of the sacred, backed up by whatever practices we deem fit.

Indeed we may find that with the advent of the truly global culture that is upon us now, that we need to look at those seemingly opposing cultures and

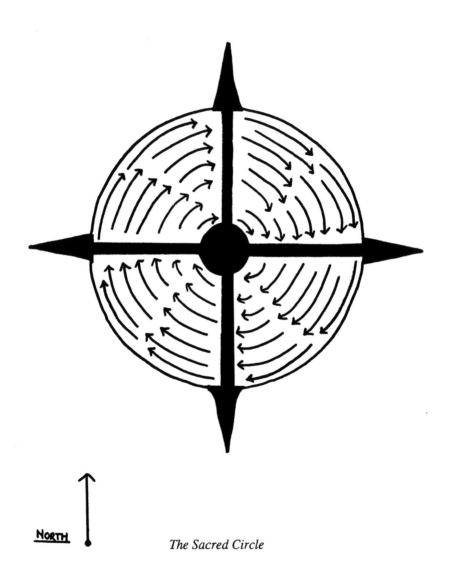

NORTH

The Sacred Circle

ways in order to feel complete. We are no longer limited to our own area or even our own country, such as has been the case. We may find that in time a new global spirituality emerges that includes elements of practices as different as Witchcraft and Christianity (chosen specifically to create a good debate!). In our differences and oppositions may lie the key to our wholeness and healing.

Like the Holy Grail, that is able to heal and provide for all that come to it, we must not discriminate, judge or otherwise have an opinion of others and their particular spirituality and method of manifesting the Sacred. The Sacred is the Sacred by whatever name we call it and whatever face we give it. We must realise this and move beyond our own limited, flawed, thinking selves. With the peace that passes all understanding that comes from our own contact with the Sacred, so we can discover an instinct that tells us we are indeed all linked together, part of the same land and so part of the same body. We are therefore all of 'like mind', it is just that its images may appear different to the conscious level, depending on where we are born and what we look like.

This basic link means that we can learn from both our own ancestry and that of others that may seem at first glance we have little to do with. In fact, we have everything to do with them and it may well be that this 'global identity' is vital to our need for future understanding and co-operation, if we are to live peacefully as a race on what is now a small and overcrowded planet.

In order to become whole, we must look backwards, forwards, up and down and see how things from all these directions visit us. Put another way, we must travel round the Sacred Circle or Medicine Wheel of the Native Americans, looking at what we find each way, learning what we are able to and moving on. The following Chapters constitute a journey round the wheel, exploring the influence and attributes of each Direction. By the end of your journey, it is my hope that you will have found, not necessarily your wholeness, but at least the identity of the parts that make up the whole and realised your own individual key that enables you to put those parts together.

The spiritual instinct is one which is natural to every person. It is part of our fabric, constitution and body. We each have an in built desire to re-unite with the source from which we came. We have created a great many things that distract us from that search and can provide us with an alternative.

However these false representations of the Sacred, be they drink, drugs, music, sex, money or whatever all take their toll when granted the excess that is required to make them a sufficient substitute for the Sacred. Eventually all must capitulate, or simply, die. History is littered with the remains of those who have not heeded this lesson.

When we begin on a spiritual quest and path and try to live a life that is focussed on this, we are not so sensitive as we may become to the inner promptings, messages and influences that come from a close connection that truly takes years to build for most of us. So we must have something else that will keep us going. That something else is the much maligned and ridiculed faith.

If we can have no immediate 'signs and wonders' as is usually the case and we have not advanced enough as yet to have the feeling of knowing within to guide and direct us on our path, we have to again step beyond logic and embrace a belief in the unseen, unknown and unheard. This means that we must hold to an unproven faith in our particular god or goddess (or both). Of course, many would argue that all gods or goddesses are unseen, but for those who have seen them in their visualisations, felt them in their rituals and experience their workings in their lives, they know that they are real. However, this experience is subjective and cannot be proved by or for any other.

The same is true with your faith. It cannot be proved, so do not try, to yourself or others. When you begin your quest and search for the Sacred, it is tough but gets easier. You must effectively prove your worth. You may wonder why you should do so, but remember that it is you who are searching, not the Divine. We have free will and so must make our own choices and take responsibility for them.

It may help to consider that this is much like the way of the world. When we look at the world today, we see violence and war, conflict and greed, selfishness and poverty, hate and gloom. There appears no reason to have faith and those who seek to despise religion in whatever form (or themselves really!) will use the argument that if 'God' loves us, why is suffering allowed and why is the world in such a mess. The answer of course is that we have made it this way, not 'him'. From here we can go round in theoretical circles, the only escape route being that of faith.

When we bring faith into this equation, we find that we have a reason to have hope and belief, though there is no logical proof for us to do so. In effect we become a 'pointless optimist', a way that I have described myself for years since seeing an unknown author of advanced years describe himself as such with a smile. Whoever he is (or was) I am indebted to him, for he is quite correct. In the beginnings of our Sacred journey, as well as in our worldly lives (the two of course needing eventually to become one) we must be a pointless optimist, to rise above the fears and traps that logic, greed, doubt, other people, money and so on lay for us. By embracing the foolishness of our faith, we are able to laugh in the cold, expressionless face of logic.

What we must be careful to ensure as we progress on our path is that we turn this faith into practice. Sooner or later we must come to the realisation that if we are living a sacred or spiritual life, it is primarily one of service. As such we must act accordingly. This is not in some holy life style that does not allow us ever to have a drink again or go into a pub for fear of contamination by the lower vibration that tends to exist in some. Rather that we almost unconsciously teach by example. We are not called on to separate out the sacred and save it for the times we are meditating or feeling good.

If we are sacred, we are sacred to the same degree when we are eating dinner, sleeping, doing the weekly shopping or making love. Our awareness and perception of this may change depending on what we are doing and you may certainly find that some activities take you away from this essence of the sacred within you, but in essence, our sacredness remains whatever.

Some people fear they are going mad or will be perceived as such by others when they give their lives over to the spiritual way in their heart. This rational fear is largely the product of the general mistrust of things of the spirit that results from our reliance on logic and humanity for so long. Now we must learn a different way once more, a way that puts the sacred first and a way that is not limited by other's opinion of us. Quite simply, if you are holding back from living a life that your family and friends will not approve of for that reason, then you need to realise that this is their problem, not yours, for you are just living your life the way that you need to. If you still cannot bring yourself to go vegetarian, study healing, learn the Tarot or whatever, then you may need to question just what your motives are.

Eventually, with patience and perseverance, you will come to the realisation that it is more that the everyday world around us is the one that is strange and unreal and that the 'Otherworld' with all its fantastic images and ways of working is the one that lasts and has existed far longer than the Earth. This is akin to the view of many mystics across the world, not least the Native American Crazy Horse, who maintained that this life was but a dream and the Spirit World was reality. Do not lose your grip on reality, above all stay grounded, realise that you are in control and all will be well. You can then take the plunge, give yourself over to spirit, put the sacred first and experience a world and life that takes you far beyond what you thought you were capable of and gives you more fulfilment than you really expected. All the things of the Earth must eventually wither and die, that is their nature. The things of the spirit, that which is sacred, endures forever. Let yourself realise then that you are sacred, live in accordance with your perception of this sacredness and remain true to it.

We can then realise that the subject of which way to express this spirituality and which tradition to follow does not matter, in a higher sense. There are many cultures, traditions and paths to follow and as stated before, it is my personal feeling that we need at this stage to be looking for a new 'global spirituality' that embraces the principles and ways of the sacred that have existed for thousands of years. It may well be that such a spirituality glorifies and revels in its diversity, which is firmly established in our Western society now and that we each need to accept and celebrate.

This is best done by tapping first into your own roots and ancestry and that of the land of your birth. If you then wish to explore another way that is good, for your foundation is of yourself and who you are, you are not then searching another tradition for a meaning and basis for yourself, but to enhance and develop what already exists. There is therefore no wrong choice you can make, for all roads do indeed lead to Rome. In a spiritual sense this means that at a certain level all the paths converge to the one and same route, that ultimately leads straight to the Divine.

At this convergence lies we know not what, but we must continually strive for it. This is the continuing work of faith, the belief that despite what heartache we have and what evils we see loose in the world, everything is working just as it should. We have a choice either to play an active part in the workings of the Universe or to opt out and therefore to work against them. Rest easy then and follow your own sense of the sacred. Look to yourself and work out from there. You cannot go wrong or lose your way, for all ways lead you back to the same source. In truth, the only wrong choice is that of no choice.

Exercise 1 - The World Tree

This exercise uses as its basis the mythical World Tree, spoken of in this Chapter as standing at the centre of all things and providing a link between this and the Otherworlds, of Celtic view. The exercise allows you to become balanced and centered against the Tree, providing you with a strong force of power and a means of central focus around which to orientate yourself and your life.

The exercise begins in a similar way to the Grounding and Connecting technique, here directly utilising the image and substance of the Tree. It is better to sit than to lie for this exercise, to assist the feeling that comes with the imagery and to allow for the maximum flow of energy through and around you.

When you have become comfortable, close your eyes and allow yourself to relax. Take a few deep breaths and let yourself and your body settle where you are, taking your awareness inside. Just relax in your own way for a few minutes. Often people who are experienced at meditation or esoteric work do not bother to include this relaxation, thinking that they have progressed beyond this. This invariably leads to a lesser degree of depth to the experience achieved and a less focussed contact, in this instance, with the Tree. Take a deliberate few minutes to relax then and let go of your outer perception and awareness completely.

When you are ready, begin to imagine that you are sitting with your back against a huge Tree. Let yourself feel its trunk against you. It is a huge Tree, old and massive of girth. You can smell its essence all about you and see the thick branches hanging over your head. As you sit and look up at the Tree, it is as if you can see a soft yellow hue or glow about it that makes you gaze in wonder. You find that you are completely comfortable in your position and relax again. You can see little detail about you, but are aware only of the Tree.

What strikes you most about this Tree is its sheer presence and power, that you are aware of as soon as you see the Tree. As you sit there, gazing up at it, you become more and more aware that this power or force is moving through you, as well as the Tree. This is a subtle sense within your bones and your veins, but it is there and you can feel it, all the same. As you consider this power moving through you, look down at your feet and at the ground about you. Study what you find there, notice the textures and colours, perhaps pick up a few stones or leaves.

As you do this you find that the power seems to have moved down with your thoughts and that your feet and legs have become very heavy, yet not unpleasantly so. Close your eyes to sense more of this power and you become aware within of that power. It is almost as if you can see it now and feel it ever more strongly. It seems to be pulling you down with it and you know that it flows beneath the Earth. This feels comforting and warm to you, so you go with it.

Your perception and awareness changes as you go and you see the power moving and spreading out in different tendrils and strands. You realise then that it is moving down through the roots of the Tree, taking you with it. You let yourself go, for it feels pleasant and strengthening, even though you may not understand what is happening. It becomes darker, warmer and very humid. Still there is movement down, but now the restriction of being in the separate roots goes and you find yourself in a quiet dark place, much like a cave.

Exactly where you are depends entirely on you. You are in the Celtic Underworld, a realm with many strange, wonderful and empowering experiences and teachings. Each person's perception of it seems to differ. However, for the purposes of this exercise it is not necessary or indeed advisable to wander out into the Underworld. You may look and see at this stage, but that is all. So just spend a few moments considering what you see and perhaps asking yourself if this has any relevance to you at this time.

Next, take your awareness back up through the roots of the Tree, by simply focussing on that same power and this time drawing it up through your body. Feel it move, almost solid, slow and sticky through you, touching all parts. Soon you arrive at an awareness of the great trunk of the Tree stretching up above you and of the branches moving out beyond that. As you do so you find that the power follows you again and seems to lift you, taller and stronger than ever before. Again there is the awareness of the power in separate strands, this time moving up through the branches.

Let yourself be taken by the power and drift up. Soon you come out above the branches and arrive at a different place. Here is the Celtic Otherworld. Again look around you and see what is there, but do not go wandering, lest you disappear with the fairies and are not seen again! See what you may and when you are ready come back down in your awareness to the mighty trunk once more.

When you arrive back here, just sit for a few minutes feeling the strength, power and presence of the Tree, Here at its centre you are at the Centre of all things and of yourself. See what this feels like, feel the great peace and let this soak into you. This is the peace that passes all understanding. Absorb it into your being and become part of it, deeply and fully.

Remain with this peace for as long as you wish and when you are ready, bring your awareness back to your body, sitting against the Tree. Become aware of your breath again and deepen this, returning refreshed and strengthened. Take your time in returning after this powerful experience and make notes on what you saw and felt.

Exercise 2 - The Story of Your Life

This exercise utilises the teachings of ancestry and the art of storytelling. It attempts to drag, willingly or kicking and screaming, the storyteller out of you. Set aside an hour or two when you will not be disturbed and you do not have tasks on your mind to do. Create an atmosphere, perhaps put on a relaxation music tape, some incense or oil, some candles. There are now two options of how to create your story - you can either write it down or record it. If you truly do not like the sound of your voice (remembering that you do get used to this) then write, if you cannot write very well, then speak.

All that is now required is for you to tell your own story, from beginning to present. Put it in story form, give yourself another name if you wish, but tell your story. If you are clever you can put yourself in another time or place, but stick in some way, to telling the story of your life. Let yourself go and be creative. It does not matter how 'good' the story is, for that is not the point of this exercise. It is simply to connect you with your past, encourage creativity and allow you to realise what you have achieved so far and where to go next.

If you wish you can continue your story into the future, making the story an exercise in affirmation and goal setting. Do not try to write a book, just a few pages or one tape, telling what you make of your life and self so far. Do not write in the first person ('I') but in the third (He, She, they etc.), as this will help you to be objective and more aware. It is often surprising what this exercise can reveal.

Exercise 3 - Choosing a Path

This is a guided journey that will enable you inwardly to make a choice as to how to express your spirituality and search for the sacred and allow you to know which way to go in that search. It is a simple journey where the use of symbolism is paramount. You will therefore need to decide how to apply what you see, sense and feel in your journey, seeing for yourself what it means and represents to you. As you do this, let your inner feelings and intuition guide you and you will not go wrong. Do not attempt to be clever and mentally analyse what you received, but just let the message come to you.

Begin the exercise by sitting and becoming comfortable. You will need to perform the grounding and connecting, as it is given in Chapter 1 Exercises. If you have skipped this or not learnt it yet, then go back and do so, for there are no short, easy cuts here.

Once you have duly arrived at the centre of yourself, as the Grounding and Connecting allows you to do, imagine yourself then walking along a road. This can be any type of road, but one that takes you forward. Walk along the road and have a sense of forward movement. Realise that this road reflects and is connected in some way to the path of your life. Look around you and see what is there. Be aware of how this place feels, for this is the landscape of your present life and current self.

Look at the contents of what you see and reflect for a short time on what is there. Continue to walk as you do so and soon you come to a roundabout. In the centre of the roundabout is a tree that looks somehow familiar to you. You walk around the roundabout, looking at the tree, finding yourself curiously attracted to it. As you walk around it, you see that strange yellow glow about it and you realise that this is the same World Tree you have been with before.

Then you arrive back at the beginning point of the roundabout. This time you take another walk around it, looking away from the Tree and at the roads, paths, tracks, rivers, canals or whatever you see leading away from it. Pause as you walk around and see what is down each one as far as you can. Do not go down any of the roads as yet, for again, that is not the point of this exercise. Just look and see and let yourself respond as you wish.

Take your time to complete your trip round. If you feel it necessary go round again. The object now is to choose one path down which to go. You may do this in this journey, or leave now and return when you are ready. If you are absolutely sure which path is for you, then go down it. You may have seen something or had a feeling which leaves you in no doubt. Unless you have this feeling, come out of this journey, look at what you have seen and return when you are ready and feel that the choice will be easier.

Otherwise walk down the path or road and see where it leads. What you see, think, feel and experience will be symbolic of your spiritual and sacred path and will give you some clues as to what to do. The symbolism can be direct or abstract. It is only you that can know how it applies. With a little sensitivity and feeling you will know what it means.

Take as long as you need down your path and then come back to the roundabout. If you are leaving without going down a path, turn and look at the Tree. You may like to sit against the Tree and use this to ground yourself before you leave. Otherwise just stand and lean against it and feel its power. Let this root you to the Earth as you return. Separate the awareness of your body from the Tree and focus on your breathing. Take your time and ensure you return fully then just sit and let the symbolism speak to you, draw conclusions that you wish and determine where the Sacred Spirit lies for you.

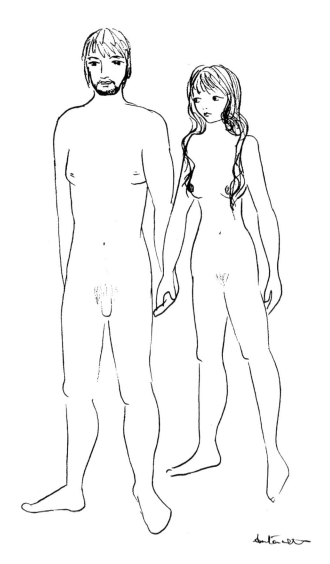

The Sacred Spirit in Physical Form

Chapter 3

The Needs of the Body

We come now to our exploration of how we can apply the nature and methods of the Sacred in our everyday lives. For this we turn to the four Elements of ancient philosophy that have long been viewed as being the constituent parts of all existence on the Earth.

These four Elements, Earth, Water, Air and Fire are seen as comprising the human being and we are indeed dependent on each in some way for our daily survival. Each Element represents different qualities, principles, areas and methods and a great deal else besides. By examining each in turn, as they relate both to our individual selves and to the planet and the Universe as a whole, we can see how we can form a structure for ourselves whereby the Elements themselves come to be our guide, expressed as they are through the annual cycle of Nature. This and the subsequent four Chapters will explore the nature and methods of each Element in turn, together with a look at the quintessence and higher nature of the result of combining those Elements into one workable whole, known as Spirit or Ether. Lastly we place all this into the context of the movement of nature through the year, thereby giving ourselves a sacred calender, ready made for us to follow.

Before we undertake this weird and wonderful journey, and by way of introducing us to the Elements themselves, we will pause to see the body in a different context, whereby human physicality is by itself linked to the four Elements. In this system, the front of the body can be seen as the east, the direction of the rising Sun and the pointer to where we are headed in life. This is the softer part of the body, open (if we allow it to be) and yielding to the influx of light and energy, chiefly from the Sun. If we are free and flexible across the chest and breathe easily and freely, we are showing we are open to accept life and with a willingness to move forward, progress and evolve.

The back of the Body, is seen as the West, being firm and strong and the place of the setting sun, shows us how we relate to the physical world and bringing things into matter from energy. If the spine is straight and free, loose and flexible, we can easily pull toward us that which we need. If the back of our body is strong, the front can open easily to receive what we need.

The top or upper half of the body can become the South, from where we receive warmth, love and inspiration. This reflects in our face, the outer appearance always showing the condition of the inner state. Equally, the bottom, lower half is the North, the place of stability, earth and grounding, where we root and establish ourselves in what we are doing. From this we can easily see how a good and clear influx of energy and life force, reflected by a free and healthy body, is necessary for our whole well being and evolution. So let us examine the needs of each in turn.

We shall take as our starting point the Element of Earth, as the foundation, cornerstone and building blocks upon which the others rely for security, safety and strength. Thus, the Element of Earth is related to the Body in the personal scheme of things. Here we explore the needs of the Body and of the Earth as we relate to it (the needs of the Earth as a planet are explored in Chapter 7).

The Earth provides us with all we need, however many there are of us, if we but give it a chance. In the industrialised world, we have machines that provide our food for us and the extent of our 'hunter, gatherer' activity now is to take the food from the supermarket shelf and put it into our trolley. Very few of us actually have contact with the soil, tree or plant that presented us with our food. We need give little thought or concern to the origins or supply of the food we eat. We now simply take it for granted that, even if the shop has run out one day, there will be plentiful supplies the next and such is the case. Rarely do we consider that whilst our shelves groan under the weight of all that we have and our cupboards are weekly stocked full to bursting, there are millions across the world who are dying of starvation.

It is however, futile of me to expect any change by preaching to you through this book. Rather, the best that I can hope for is to make a few more people aware of the food they eat and where it comes from and ask you to consider the nature of what you put into your body.

First in this comes your view of your body. An excellent, though surprisingly difficult exercise to do to give you an idea of how you really feel about your body is to stand naked in front of a full length mirror and examine your body (See Exercise One at the end of this Chapter).

Having performed this exercise we can come to be aware that our body is a receptacle for the sacred spirit inside us. The body expresses the nature and condition of that spirit or soul and shows it, literally, as clear as day. The trained and experienced eye can see at a glance the nature of another's soul, whether it be in agony, defeat, joy or exuberance. It should follow that the nature of what we put into the covering for our soul should be as pure and unpolluted as possible and be only that which contributes to the health and development of that body.

I am not however advocating that you never eat a cream cake or chocolate bar, as the temptations put our way by the merciless marketing people of the global companies is very strong, often without our realising. The power and effectiveness of subliminal messages and graphics is far from lost to these people, who see profit resulting from increased production, rather than poverty, debt, obesity, disease and addiction that more often occur on an individual level. What is required here in the first instance is to see food as part of the sacred spirit to which all things exist and therefore that the kind of food that you consume reflects that spirit.

This basic premise becomes a yardstick to measure all that goes into your body by. When we hold clearly in our minds that all things are sacred and a part of the same spirit, then food comes to be seen as one of the most primal forms of that spirit, giving an immediate and accurate reflection in the state of our bodies, the result of the goodness and properties our bodies derive from our food.

When we begin to appreciate that the Earth is a living being and symbolic or literal Mother, we realise too that the food that grows from her body, is just like the milk that flows from our own human mother's breast. If that milk is full of pollutants and chemicals, then so is the baby who drinks it. This will soon come to have an effect on the baby's health and overall being. Nowadays we hear of babies being born addicted to caffeine from the effects of coffee and other foodstuffs to which it has been added and worse to various narcotic drugs. In such cases, the addictive substance has become part of the baby's system, requiring injections of it to stop them suffering from withdrawal. We are all babies of our Mother Earth and can too become addicted to the many and varied chemical cocktails that are added to the majority of our foods these days.

With the sacred spirit at the heart of our priorities and motives, we can appreciate that we need to have pure, unadulterated and natural food to reflect and maintain the sanctity of our body. This requires that we inspect the ingredients of what we eat as much as the finished product itself. Given that we also are each quite literally part of one another, linked by the vital energy and life force of sacred life, we may also feel the need to consider the circumstances of those who may have worked elsewhere on our Mother Earth to produce the product we buy. The power of the Ethical Consumer is one that should never be underestimated, by the recognition of those multi-nationals whose methods and practices are most often questioned. This is not just a case of easing our conscience, but of recognising that the right and correct treatment of all individuals upon our planet is the responsibility of all of us, for we are all a part of that spirit that links us together. This fact cannot be over described or stated too often.

The ethics and activities of the companies from which we choose to buy our goods are of course not just limited to food, but include everything that is manufactured, grown, developed etc. In short anything that we buy must have some effect on the Earth and on some people. Recognise all these things as part of the inter-linked fabric of all people, wherever they may be on Earth and let this guide your choices, rather than the comfort, short term pleasure or little saving it may make you. With a concentration to your buying and perhaps a little more effort and investment of time, you can know that your possessions are free from the burden of guilt, contamination and destruction. All this is a major step forward at this stage of our evolution to accepting responsibility for our actions and ourselves, individually and globally. As mentioned before, this is one of the most difficult areas of living a practical and sacred life, but it must be achieved if we are to continue and improve.

With this awareness, even the weekly drudge of the supermarket trip can become an exercise in sacred living, as it can become an almost furtive celebration of not giving your money to those that seek to decry the existence of the spirit and energy in all things, turning this instead into profit and gain for themselves in the short term. Of course, it may be that your new found ethical awareness does not allow you even to shop at a supermarket, but seek out organic grocery delivery services, the health food shop and the corner store (if you can still find one). Better still, you could try growing your own, providing the optimum of contact with the sacredness of what goes into your body and this brings us to our next consideration for the needs of the body.

If we accept that the Earth has a life force, energy or power of its own, then it follows that so do all things upon it and in it. This of course, includes that which you decide is food, whether this be vegetable, fruit, animal or mineral. It is not the subject of this book to determine the rights and wrongs of eating animals, or their products, for that is a matter for each person's conscience. What I ask you to consider here, as the view of food as part of the sacred spirit, is the nature and condition of the life and force and energy that you ingest as you eat each article of food.

That we consume the energy, power or force of the food we eat is a logical conclusion if we accept the reality that energy exists in all things, which is now scientifically proven. The type and nature of that energy is affected by everything it comes into contact with and so this is passed on into our bodies, becoming a part of our very existence as it is absorbed into our body through our eating.

We must also give mention here to the kind of food that we eat. Different types of food are known to have a different rate of vibration of the life force within them that they contain and that we absorb when we put the food into our bodies and absorb it. The lighter and more liquid the food, in general, the higher the rate of vibration it contains. This means that it is absorbed into the body quicker and gives us energy only at the higher end of the spectrum. To bring about a balanced flow of life force within us, from the food we eat, we need to ensure that we consume a balanced variety of food stuffs. Of course to provide an exhaustive list of the rate of vibration of all the foods in existence is not possible here, but we may take one example, that of fruit and vegetables, to illustrate our principle.

Those vegetables or fruits that grow on trees have a higher rate of vibration than root crops such as potatoes and turnips, growing beneath the Earth and therefore absorbing the denser, more solid Earth vibratory force. Meat is often thought to have a similar earthy, grounding quality. What you do to the food as you cook it, can also have an effect on its life force. sadly in most cases destroying it. The longer a food is boiled, the less life force is left within it. Steaming is more efficient way to cook your vegetables and retain the life force. Fast food has very little life left in it and microwaved food is generally thought, in terms of its life force, to be dead and is best avoided.

In this you may also consider the colour of the food you eat, as this can be a useful indication of the level of vibration it may have. A meal of carrot, swede, turnip and beetroot will have a much more dense and grounding energy that one of white fish, yogurt and eggs (though I do not recommend these combinations!).

Another point to make here is to try and avoid eating while you are angry, depressed or upset in any way, as this also affects the goodness you are able to absorb from your food. At the very least take a few deep breaths before you eat and try to calm yourself inwardly. This allows the life force in the food you eat to flow into your body unblocked or tainted by negativity and its effects within you.

The main and most helpful principle to remember and view what you eat by, is 'you are what you eat'. As the food breaks down eventually into life force and as that force is absorbed into your being, you literally become what you eat. As your body is, if you will forgive this pompous sounding maxim, the temple of the Divine, you should always remember that what you are is a reflection of the Divine and as such requires your absolute highest regard and consideration. The more healthy your body, the better will you be as a person, able to develop yourself to the best possible degree and level.

So the condition of our food begins with the Earth itself, absorbing nutrients, goodness and life force from the Earth, rain, sun and air. Immediately we can identify areas of trouble as we know of the poor condition of much of our soil, the acidity of our rain, the lack of protection from the power of the sun and the contamination of our air. When we consider that all that exists, exists first and has its counterpart as an energy or (life) force then we can see the gravity of our situation.

Of course the best answer we are able to give to this is to grow our own food on soil that is as organic as possible and the food be eaten as fresh as possible. However this is often not practical or possible for many of us and we should therefore explore the next best possibilities. If we are left with no alternative but to buy from a shop or supermarket, then we need to consider the ethical questions involved in its manufacture and delivery. Again, it is the awareness with which we do things that can make an enormous difference.

The manner and style in which we cook and prepare our food is also important, from a practical, spiritual point of view. This is because there is a constant flow of energy in and around ourselves that in turn affects everything we do, say, think, feel and touch. Should you be angry when you are cooking, then part of that anger flows into the food and thence into the person who eats it. This may be fine if you are the only person to do so, for this is an excellent way of helping you learn from your anger, but not so if you are cooking for another, especially an innocent child. Eating is a sacred act, for we directly add to who we are by the food we eat. It is not an act of a responsible individual to allow anger or any detractive quality to become part of another by literally feeding it to them.

It is common to hear is said that food always tastes better when it is cooked by someone else. This is usually the case because it is prepared with love and a desire to please its recipient. The food not only tastes better, but in all truth helps the diner's evolution along in its own small way, for from this food they are empowered to grow and develop, aided and abetted by the positive power and energy of the food they are served. So it is we come to see cooking and eating as sacred acts, with sacred materials.

Whilst it may be true that boiling and generally cooking our food may purify it to some degree, we can never be sure that what we eat is pure in terms of energy and power. We have already illustrated the damaging effects of consuming food that may not be pure in the life force it emits to your body and being but we can consider this subject from a more esoteric viewpoint too.

It is often only with Christianity that we associate praying before eating, but the act of blessing one's food prior to eating it can be a powerful act of consecration, sanctity and recognition. This can be done to suit the individual preference as to terminology. Please see Exercise 2 for this Chapter to assist in constructing your own.

The reason for saying a simple, focussed blessing prior to eating our food becomes clear when we turn to the maxim of 'Energy Follows Thought'. There is little better way of our focussing our thoughts than by the use of speech. When we speak aloud, or silently with concentration on what we are 'saying', the mind is more completely engaged in this activity than is usual. Consequently the energy that follows these thoughts, has power. This power, prayer or blessing then becomes an active substance in the field of energy and therefore the food before us. Since the nature of this thought form is to bless our food, as this is the way it was programmed or created, then this is what happens.

The saying of such a blessing before one eats any food is perhaps the most powerful way that we can ensure its purity, as its basic energy level. This precedes the physical, so whatever is done to our food, the Earth it comes from, the air it breathes and the rain it absorbs, is underlined by the energy of our blessing. This need not be complicated and takes only a moment. The result is that the energy you absorb from your food, not to mention the goodness, is increased and so you become a more whole, more complete being.

Abstinence from food can also be a part of the acknowledgement of our sacredness, through the practise of fasting. Abstaining from food can be an effective means of eliminating toxins that have accrued in the body and also of helping the body and the psyche access the 'Otherworld' or a vision for healing or any particular project. Before one embarks on any fast, preparation needs to be made and advice sought as to exactly how to gradually cut down one's intake of food, how long to abstain completely for and how to build up again after the fast. This is the general method for fasting, which eases the hunger cravings that are inevitable after regular eating habits, but each individual's requirements are different, according to metabolism, preference and simple will. Indeed it may be such that your metabolism does not permit or tolerate complete fasting but this can still be effectively achieved by undertaking a fruit only fast. Consider your own requirement and what you know you can realistically tolerate and respect these and your fast will be all the more effective.

As part of the sacred attitude toward food, attention must also be paid to nutrition and here again the principle of purity and wholeness seems paramount. I am not qualified to give advice as to nutrition, but even the briefest attention to dietary recommendations shows that a majority of fruit and vegetables, fresh and organic if possible, is the best way of ensuring the maximum of goodness and use to the body. Following our esoteric line of thinking, this means that the more whole, pure and complete our food, the more whole, pure and complete the energy that we derive from it and so we become. When we view ourselves as beings of force and energy we begin to see the true reality of all things and so we must appreciate this esoteric truth in all things we do.

Not least in this is the attention we give to our body's needs, apart from the fuel we give it in food. The body must be maintained at the optimum level possible, so as to generate, maintain and develop the maximum energy levels and condition we can. The body must be given sufficient supplies of as fresh an air as possible to oxygenate its cells, thereby creating the most efficient energy and life force we can.

High in our list of priorities in recognition of the sacredness of our bodies is its need to be exercised and maintained physically. Again, the better the performance of our body in daily life, the more energy we are able to generate and conserve, and so the more whole we feel and become. I am not suggesting that it is necessary for us all to adopt a strict exercise regime and become marathon runners, but that we should pay attention to what our body tells us.

If we ache or have pain, our body is attempting to communicate a message to us, that something is not as it should be. This causes a depletion in our energy and so this occurs physically too. If we ensure that our basic energy is free of blockage and interruption as it flows through our body and being, so we are able to prevent a physical replication of the malfunction of our energy that is the true cause of all disease. Exercise 3 gives some suggestions for this.

In practicality, we at present seem unable to prevent the onset of some physical malady occurring at some point in our lives. When this occurs, we must turn to healing ourselves, by the best means possible. It may be expected that a recommendation to utilise complementary therapies be given here and indeed I would advocate this. However, I am qualified in only one of these therapies, (healing) so can comment only from this limited view. This and my experience as a patient, is enough to convince me of their validity and effectiveness and I feel that knowledge and use of such therapies and happily their availability is accessible enough for me to resist further promotion here.

I would however, point out that these therapies are not alternative, not to be seem as a replacement for many of our scientific, more mainstream medicines. They are just what they say, complementary to what our traditional hospitals and surgeries can provide. In your enthusiasm for natural medicines, do not discount the need for much of what science gives us. What is perhaps needed, as in all things, is a balance and at best a blending of the abilities of science with nature. Many new and exciting innovations are constantly being put forward in the field of medicine and we need only to include the esoteric aspect and effect on the human being of our approaches and we are complete.

I would exhort you to examine the likely effect on your energy, at the physical, mental, emotional and spiritual levels, (as indicative of the needs of the body, mind, heart and spirit respectively) of any medicine you may choose to take, be it natural or artificial. All things have such an effect and it may only be by experimentation that you discover the exact effect for yourself. However, one thing is certain and is often neglected in the treatment of the ill and this is the damage done to the aura and energy body of the person affected, either by the dis-ease itself or the treatment given.

Whilst any therapy may treat the physical symptoms and cause of a dis-ease, the energy aspects and level are often sadly neglected. If we can combine treatment to the energy bodies of the human system our recovery will be more swift, effective and complete. For any who have experienced surgery and then recovery from it, they will be only too aware of how unpleasant this is. This is largely because, apart from the shock to the physical system, the energy flow that underpins and reflects the physical is greatly disrupted and disturbed too.

Were the energy in the auric field that surrounds and interpenetrates the physical to be realigned by a healer expert in such matters, working alongside the surgeon as they go, the better the patient will be and the swifter and more complete their recovery. If this is not possible, then seek out healing treatment of this kind as soon as is practical. This applies not just to surgery of course but to any disease, be it a 'simple' headache, common cold or a long term or even terminal condition.

It is the natural inclination of every human being to heal another, since any disease in another is in some small way, a disease in ourselves, since we are each and all a part of the same global, human energy field, body and life force. Therefore, to heal another is to heal yourself. This is indeed the most effective way of bringing about global healing, improvement and development of any kind and on any level.

This natural tendency to heal others and indeed ourselves is manifested daily in many ways, from the Mother's 'kiss to make it all better' to the placing of a hand on the forehead or neck. This instinctive touch allows for the transmission of energy to take place which stimulates the body to provide its own physical healing. The human body is a fantastic thing, reflecting many of the principles of the Universe. One such principle is to grow, expand and evolve to wholeness. This is again reflected in the human body by its natural ability to heal itself and its brothers and sisters. We have only to provide the direct conditions to facilitate this healing to occur. The nature of such healing depends largely on the nature of the dis-ease, but you will hopefully find sufficient material in the pages of this book to apply in this respect.

It is but a short step from this natural healing of the self to applying the same principles and in many cases, techniques, to others. Whilst there are many courses available these days to teach you the finer and more specific points of healing, it is perfectly possible and quite safe to have knowledge and use of some of the basics, for use in everyday life.

The intentional touch of a hand to a wound, of whatever kind, is sufficient to generate a healing force to the patient. This follows our previously met principle of 'energy follows thought', combined with the knowledge that all things that exist, exist first as energy. So if we focus the power of our thoughts on healing the person before us, place our hands in the appropriate position to give the means for the resultant energy to travel, we are manifesting a healing energy and power that gets in to the patient underneath the dis-ease. From this basic 'building block' level of physical life the energy works its way into the body and is transmuted into the physical means necessary to help heal the particular dis-ease.

It is not necessary to try and force this energy in and to be sweating with the effort whilst giving healing in this manner. Remember that its nature is to heal, for that is the intention you have in doing it. The more focussed your thoughts, the clearer and more focussed the healing energy. This may mean that it is necessary for you to clear yourself and your own needs out of the way for the duration of the healing. It is worth noting here that since you open yourself to the Universal and constant flow of life force energy to heal another, the flow moves through your own being and so you benefit from giving healing. The healing power moves through you, not from you. To provide the correct conditions for healing is just as important as the healing itself.

This is a matter for personal preference, but for some direction you may like to consider the following. Firstly, take the phone off the hook and be free of interruption. You may wish to perform a simple relaxation, perhaps with some deep breaths to start, to let go of tension and then just relaxing in whatever way is comfortable for you. The more natural, relaxed and easy you are, so will your patient be. This provides for optimum release and reception of the energy generated. Your patient may prefer to sit or lie so consider where they will be placed, giving some thought to allowing for your being able to move around them, in order to give healing where it is needed. You may like to play some suitable music, light a candle and so on. Do ensure that your room is comfortably warm too. Lastly, consider a prayer or words of affirmation, asking for guidance and protection in the healing work and asking for healing too, of course.

To begin a healing session, I recommend standing behind a sitting patient and placing the hands lightly on the shoulders, closing your eyes and just standing there for a minute or two (which will seem like longer). This allows for your two separate energies to blend to an extent and for each of you to become comfortable. This can be a good time for prayer too. You will soon notice, if you are a little sensitive, a flow of energy down your arms and through the palms of your hands.

You and/or your patient may notice an increase, or decrease, in temperature as you give healing and perhaps a tingling 'pins and needles' type sensation. This is normal and is an indication that energy is moving. This also may not be experienced, but this does not mean energy is not flowing. If you are following these steps, it will be working, but it seems to be the case that each individual's perception and experience of healing is different, for many reasons.

Take as much time as seems needed to give your healing, remembering to tell your patient where you are going to work and giving absolute consideration to the ethics of touch in certain areas. If you are going to touch your patient, tell them before you do so. Usually the patient will have

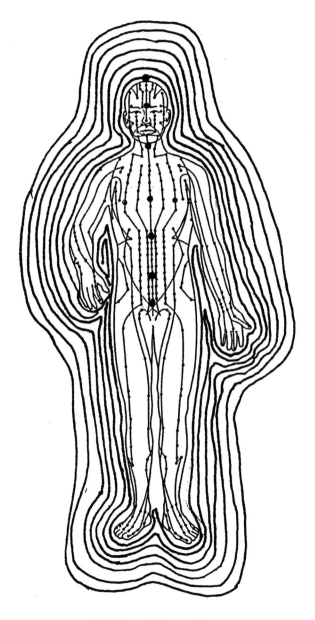

The Human Energy System

their eyes closed and will be relaxed. It is the worst thing to suddenly and unexpectedly feel a hand touch your leg, causing you to miss a breath, jump and jar the sprained ankle you are attempting to heal!

If the nature of the dis-ease prohibits touch, whether by ethical reasons or otherwise, healing can certainly still take place and be as effective. The human physical system has its counterpart or reflection in its energy system too and it is possible to work within this, without having any physical contact with the patient at all. Before we explain this, a last word concerning the healing session.

At the conclusion of your treatment, it is wise to place your hands on the patient's feet and direct a brief flow of energy there. This ensures that the patient is properly grounded when you finish and is safe to go out into the world again. This takes about 20 seconds but is vital also in sealing the patient's energy for themselves, rather than it being soaked up by the first person or situation they come across in need, whether conscious or not.

It is also good if not necessary to cleanse the room you have performed the healing in, so that any residual energy is dispersed. This can be done by prayer or perhaps by using incense. To do this, light the incense, enter the room and walk around it, wafting the smoke from the incense to the walls as you go, upwards. Walk round and out of the room, and preferably the house, focussing on clearing any negative or unwanted energy, emotions, thoughts and physical conditions as you go. This will purify the atmosphere in your room and ensure that it is clear for the next patient you treat there. These 'unseen' measures may seem very ceremonial and pedantic, but they improve the quality of what you do and yourself a great deal.

There is a Native American practice of smudging that equals this cleansing. This is used both in clearing sacred spaces and people. A stick of dried and bound sage is commonly used, but the herbs can be varied, for their particular properties. We use a mixture of Sage, Sweetgrass, Cedar and Lavender, for a potent, effective and beautiful smelling smudge mixture that seems to do the trick. To use this, you need to chop the herbs into small pieces (an arduous task!) and mix together. You can burn a pinch of the mix on a charcoal block or sprinkle some in a small earthenware dish (not a sea shell as is often used as the watery link is looked on as putting out the fiery power of the herbs when lit) and the herbs will smoulder.

Then as the smoke rises, fan it around the room, or person you are working on. If a room or space, follow the outline, fanning the smoke as you go. Walk in, around, then out again. Smudging is an effective means of clearing the aura, or energy field of a patient, prior to beginning healing on them and also as a maintenance and preventative measure to use every so often and prior to performing ceremony, ritual or any important act. To fan the smoke, a feather is best, which you will need to go out and find from nature by yourself, remembering to thank the bird that has donated it to you and acknowledging this exchange by putting some bird seed or crumbs down. Say a prayer of thanks before you take the feather and pause to ensure that it feels right for you to do this. If not, leave it as you find it, for there will be another for you. Cleanse the feather in the smoke before you use it each time, to ensure its purity.

Now, beginning behind the patient's feet, use the feather (or your hand is sufficient) and fan the smoke towards them and upwards. Work your way over their head and down their front. Then work from side to side, beginning at the floor and ending the other side. Finally, place the feather or your hand on the floor, to earth the energy and yourself and pass the feather through the smoke to cleanse it. It is good then to say a blessing of thanks.

This is an excellent healing technique that does not involve touching the patient at all. It effectiveness relies on the properties of the herbs used and their effect on the energy system of the human, if treating a patient or the residual energy existing in the area if purifying a sacred or other space (remembering that all 'space' is sacred!). This energy system is quite a complex thing but the basics are easy to grasp and can be of great use in maintaining health and providing for the needs of the body.

The human energy system exists both within and without the human body, the human being comprising if you will, both the physical and energy systems of the individual. This is illustrated here, in simple and nearly complete form. The existence of the seven main chakras is now well known, but rather less attention is paid to the lesser chakras, situated on various parts of the body. These all have a function and role to play in the health, growth and development of each of us, just as do the organs and systems of the body. Also, just as all these organs and systems are interlinked on the physical level, so they are on the energy level, each affecting the other and each being a part of a whole greater than the sum of its parts, just as is all humanity, our solar system and the entire Cosmos. The smaller 'subsidiary'

CHAKRA	BASE	SACRAL	SOLAR PLEXUS	HEART	THROAT	BROW	CROWN
LOCATION	Base of Spine	Between pubis and navel	Beneath rib cage	To right of heart	Base of neck	Between eyes	Top of head
GLAND	Adrenal	Gonads	Pancreas	Thymus	Thyroid	Pituitary	Pineal
COLOUR	Red	Orange	Yellow	Green	Blue	Indigo	Violet
BODY	Large Intestine, Rectum, Legs, Feet	Kidneys, Reproductive System	Stomach, Digestive system, Nervous system	Heart, Lungs Blood, Arms	Throat, Neck Shoulders	Ears, Nose, Left Brain	Right brain, Whole being
NEED	Physical health	Self acceptance	Understanding	Love	Truth	Divine love	Serenity
ABILITY	Movement, Presence	Feeling	Intuition	Love of others	Communication	Sight	Knowing
MALFUNCTION	Obesity, Sciatica Constipation	Impotence, Kidney & Bladder disease	Ulcers, Stress	Asthma, heart & lung disease	Colds, thyroid problems	Headaches, nightmares	Immune deficiency
AURA	Etheric	Emotional	Mental	Astral	Spiritual	Celestial	Ketheric
QUALITY	Grounding, Stability, Survival	Desire, Pleasure, Sexuality	Confidence, Control, Will, Feelings	Love, Harmony Compassion, Service	Creativity, Synthesis, Communication	Vision, Wisdom, Mastery, Ideas	Fulfilment, Completion Enlighten- ment

Table of Chakra Correspondences

chakras are therefore to be found at the main intersection points of the meridian lines through the body, thus providing for a maximum efficiency in the flow of energy distributed.

The existence and awareness of the chakras is also happily well documented now, as is the aura. What follows is a brief introduction to these, to assist you in the awareness of yourself and your sacredness. The location of the chakras can be seen in the 'Human Energy System' picture. Listed overleaf are some of the correspondences of these chakras.

As can be seen from the picture, the chakras are located at points up the spine and above. However, we need to be aware that these chakras exist at the front of the body too, being three dimensional. They are looked upon as spinning vortices or power centres of energy. One of their principle functions is to receive energy from the aura, which in turn receives its supply from the Universal flow of constant life force energy all around it and all living things. The chakras receive and then transmute this energy into forms that the body can absorb. This is done via the various glands that the chakras are aligned to, as listed above. From this we can see how vital the optimum performance of the chakras is to our overall well being and effective functioning.

It is necessary to maintain this performance to ensure maximum physical health and well being. This can be done for yourself by a variety of methods. The use of healing to treat the chakras is excellent, but should only be performed by those expert, experienced and preferably qualified in their field. Physically, exercise is one of the best ways to give the chakras a good clear out! The chakras are trumpet shaped and can become clogged with accumulated 'negative' or unwanted energy, produced by sluggish physical performance, worry, stress, dis-ease, fear etc. Remembering that the energy reflects the physical and vice-versa, if the body is stimulated to work harder, so are the chakras, since more energy is required to push the body's system to work more. The chakras therefore spin faster (they are constantly turning, to produce the energy flow) and so are able to clear out what has become static and neglected within. One comparison we can make is that if the body is sweating, so are the chakras!

At this juncture, the point should be made that one of the strong needs of the body is that of sex. We each have a sexual urge and this energy, like all others in our systems, must be allowed expression. The type and mode of expression is of course, entirely up to you, so long as it harms no-one. We have seen that if energy is suppressed it results in dis-ease and the same is true of the sexual energy. We need to view the sexual urge and energy as a part of our sacredness and allow its expression as such. Quite blatantly the sexual act is a sacred one (as well as being immensely pleasurable!) for what could be more sacred than that which can create life. This does not mean that we must be solemn and only use sex for the creation of life, but that we recognise its sacred nature as well as acknowledging our need for release of the sexual energy flowing through each of our beings.

Another physical method of clearing the chakras is by the use of Yoga. For particular positions you can use for each chakra, I would refer readers to Naomi Ozaniec's book 'The Elements of the Chakras' (Element, 1990), being more capable than I in this department. Other forms of physical/energy exercise, such as Tai Chi, Chi Kung and the like can doubtless be used too, but I have too little knowledge of these subjects to comment here. If you are a practitioner of these arts however, you will soon be able to deduce how this can be done.

Visualisation and meditation can also be utilised to maintain the chakras, since they directly employ energy for their working. Please see Exercise 4 for this Chapter for a full chakra and aura cleansing meditation/ visualisation.

In closing this section, let us give mention to various certain exciting developments in the field of healing that concern 'energy medicine'. This, we are told, is the medicine of the future, perhaps instigated by the albeit unconscious recognition of the truth of the existence of energy and its effect on all things physical. Even a cursory glance at the specialist magazines of this field very often carry articles or advertisements explaining and demonstrating new methods and machines that utilise energy in their treatment and address themselves to this aspect of the person. This is most encouraging and can lead us to believe that it may not be too long before we are able to see the healer alongside the surgeon in the doctors surgery and operating theatre.

In truth we have seen energy medicine at work for some time, through the use of some Herbal Remedies and now especially Flower and Gem Remedies. These utilise the properties of the herbs, plants, trees and flowers used, in the same way as our smudging, except in liquid form. Many such remedies, notably the Bach Flower Remedies but now many others too, pay specific attention to the cultivation of the materials used to ensure that the plant etc. contains the maximum energy with which to treat the patient. This is usually achieved by cutting or collecting at a specific phase of the Moon and time of day, so as to trap the maximum possible sunlight which gives rise to the energy flow of the plant. By this we can come to see the sacredness of not only the aforementioned plants, trees and flowers but also the sun and moonlight that animates them.

The place that we choose to live in has an enormous effect upon our well being. Of course the needs of the body are such that we need a roof over our head and a source of warmth and comfort, for rest and sleep. Nowadays many of us live in square boxes, or worse, high rise flats that are not even in touch with the Earth. It is strange that we now choose to live in unnatural square shapes, rather than the circular shapes of our ancestors. All of nature exists and lives in circles, from the planet itself, through bird's nests to the circling of dogs and cats before they lie down. The life force and energy of the circle allows a flowing of energy around it that is far more conducive to our well being than the harsh corners of the modern home.

As such, what we put into our homes is vital to improve our condition as far as possible. Consider the effect the decor and colour of your house has upon you and also the objects you surround yourself with. Walk around your home slowly and meditatively and see how you react in different rooms and areas. Resolve to remove anything you feel detracts from your well being. Be aware too of electrical appliances, as they radiate an energy that is not helpful. It is recommended that you have a minimum of one plant per electrical appliance in every room of your home. This is not so that the poor plant can absorb the rubbish, but that you can counter-balance the energy you receive as you live there. Your home should be a reflection of yourself and show the sacredness that you consider you have. It is your place upon the earth and as such is a sacred environment, that you can create and make as you wish. Here you create life, evolve and learn and may uncover the key meaning for life to you, so is it not worthwhile of your attention and highest regard? Let your home become sacred.

Through such sacredness, we can come to see that we are also linked to all things in Nature and indeed that we are a part of that Nature. What we see around us is a reflection of the state and condition of humanity, which at present paints a sorry picture. This however can change, the more so by the acceptance of ourselves as sacred beings, here to live a sacred life and to care for the planet that gives and maintains that life. This first requires that a psychological leap of understanding be taken, in our view of ourselves.

To begin this needs to be in our view of time. We know only the present moment exists, for we cannot prove what has gone before or is yet to come, except by memory or prediction. These however are subjective to the individual and cannot be seen to be fact by any other. We can exist only for the everlasting Now, the present moment that lasts forever. Yet many esoteric systems of thought and belief have shown us that we can access far memory of past times and lives we have led previously. The doctrine of reincarnation exists in belief systems worldwide and is now accepted by millions. In order to become fully aware of who we are, it is perhaps necessary to look at what and who we are now as the outcome and product of all and indeed who, we have been before. In this, it becomes necessary to open ourselves to the possibility of having lived before.

As such, we can gain a sense of being far more than just the limited view of who, where and what we are in this lifetime. This sense, once opened to and accepted, allows us to feel and therefore become, more complete and whole and so more sacred. In actuality, our past lives can go a long way to explaining our current one, assisting us to deal with the pre-conditioned fears, beliefs, loves and hates that we each seem born with, in our own individual way. The last Exercise for this Chapter gives you one easy way by which you can discover some of the influences of your past lives.

It should be stressed here that the object of casting ourselves back to gain information regarding our past lives should never be simply to satisfy curiosity. In examining your own past lives, by whatever method, do not fall into the trap of only discovering what your name was, what you looked like, who your family were and so on, for these things are but trivia in the grander view. We need to realise here that when we die, it is literally only the physical body that dies. In our deep and irrational fear of it, we place a great emphasis on death, yet at the same time shying away from this one true certainty of life. By fully integrating our past life influences to our present being, we are able to take a big individual step towards removing the fear of death as the end of all things. If you have some experience, however fleeting, of a past life of your own, it can be enough for the mind to know deep within, that death does not mean the end of its existence.

If we continue to exist, there must be something in some form, physical or otherwise, that carries on despite the physical body ceasing to function. Again, we come back to the energy system, which in one form, does continue. It is taught in healing and esoteric circles, that the chakras and the aura itself collapse immediately prior to death. What remains beyond this is the totality of that individual's experience in life, their thoughts, feelings, activities and beliefs, in energy form. It is this that is contained in the essence that inhabits a new body, when it is ready and decides to be reborn.

By 'going back' to become aware of our past, or more accurately, previous lives, we can learn how the beliefs, loves, hates and so on are affecting us in the present. Each and every pre-conditioned state we are born with must be faced and embraced if the individual is to become truly whole. If the energy dies with us, then so do the love we feel, pleasure and pain we have experienced, beliefs we hold and memories we cherish or have buried, die with us too. As such past life work assists us in discovering who we are now and more importantly, why we are the way we are in our current life and perhaps why we are doing the things we have chosen to do.

In this we can come to see that our previous lives are now a part of our accumulated individuality. This can only serve to increase our view of ourselves as sacred and helps us in our quest to live a practical, spiritual life. We can come to realise that contained within the human being, as body and energy systems, is all that we need to know. As such we gain a complete picture of the needs of the body in living a sacred life, honouring ourselves and the others of our race with whom we have chosen to share that sacredness. In this, life becomes not a drudge or a chore, but a hard work of progress and celebration, led with honour, intent and purpose and resulting in achievement, satisfaction and evolution. Life looks very different when the sacred is placed at the centre of its mysterious and wonderful circle!

Exercise 1 - The Sacred Body

For this exercise you will need to ensure that the room you are in is comfortably warm for you to stand naked in and also that you will not be disturbed. Remove your clothes and stand before a full length mirror so that you have a complete view of your body. The exercise will be even more effective if you can arrange a mirror behind you so that you can see yourself from behind too. Stand comfortably and perform a brief Grounding and

Connecting exercise with your eyes closed. This is done so that you are relaxed and to ensure that your perception is unbiased while performing the exercise. Grounding and Connecting ensures that you are operating from a place of balance and sacredness within yourself.

Now open your eyes and look at your body. Examine yourself from toe to head with a steady and relaxed gaze. Let your gaze run slowly over your body, working round its outline and simply absorbing what you see. Notice the colours you see, the shapes, marks, scars, hairs etc. In particular, pay attention to the feelings that come to you as do this. Let yourself react emotionally as you look at yourself, as you truly are physically, and be aware of these emotions. It is a good idea immediately afterwards to write down brief notes as to how you felt and what you experienced and what this may have told you about yourself and what you may have realised by doing so.

Be aware as your gaze moves up over your body that you are a sacred being. Ask yourself what is it that is sacred about your body. Consider that you have a 'Divine Spark' within that body and ask yourself where this is, seeing if you can pin it down to one spot. Just remain still and silent for a while and see what thoughts and feelings come to you. Then move about and watch your body and the way it works as you move. Allow yourself to realise and appreciate what a wondrous thing the human body is, considering the array of muscles, tendons and so on that move, just by your raising an arm above your head. Perhaps you may like to speak aloud your feelings about your body, allowing yourself to accept what you realise through this exercise, by doing so.

This exercise has no point other than self realisation and a greater awareness of who you are. Take as much time as you feel you need to achieve this. If you find that you are ashamed or have a dislike of what you see, ask yourself lovingly why this is so and try to determine to change what it is you do not like, if at all possible.

Exercise 2 - The Sacred Blessing

For this exercise you will need pen and paper, quiet and time. Make yourself comfortable in a favourite room or spot, perhaps the place you use for meditation, reflection, reading etc. Make this a special exercise, that you have prepared for, perhaps by buying (or making!) a candle specifically for the purpose, prepare or light some incense, put on suitable music etc.

Now perform a grounding and connecting exercise, to put yourself in the best possible condition to receive the words of the blessing you will use prior to eating your food. After your grounding and connecting, you may like to speak a few words of prayer or request, perhaps asking the Mother Earth and/or Father Sky to give you the words to use, as they can be viewed as the source of all food. Let your request be in simple, natural and sincere form, as it occurs to you then.

Now breathe naturally and let yourself relax deeply. Simply wait and see what words come to you. You may feel an immediate inspiration and direct flow of words that spring into your mind. You may decide to open your eyes and begin to scribble some random words or phrases down that you like. Follow whatever seems natural to you in this and continue until you have arrived at a blessing you like. There is nothing to stop you changing or adapting your blessing as you go and remember that there are no rights and wrongs here, only a request that you be true to yourself and honest and sincere in your words. To give you an idea, here is a blessing I have just written:

GREAT MOTHER EARTH AND FATHER SKY
I HONOUR YOUR POWER IN THE GROWTH OF THIS FOOD
AND ASK FOR YOUR BLESSING UPON IT
AS A SACRED ENERGY FOR MY BODY
SO LET IT BE

When you have arrived at the blessing you will use, close your eyes and take a deep breath or two to relax yourself again and become aware of the sacred within and without you. Speak a few words of thanks for the guidance and inspiration you have received, ground yourself by focussing the flow of energy to your feet and bring yourself gently back to normal waking consciousness. You now have a blessing, that you will soon memorise, to recite each time before you eat.

In the saying of your blessing, try to avoid repeating empty words, but pause, take a deep breath before you say them, feel your sacredness and that of the food and be aware of the meaning of what you are saying. If in time you feel that the words have become stale, change them, if just a little. If you are in company and feel embarrassed, it is easily possible to say the words silently, without anyone knowing.

Exercise 3 - Sacred Exercise

As part of our view and regard of our body as a sacred object, it is important that we do not subject it to practises and substances that poison it to a degree that it cannot cope with or that adversely affect its condition and performance. I am not suggesting here a puritanical approach to what goes into the body, for each must follow their own conscience in this regard, paying respect to their limits and bodily response. This exercise is designed to make you aware of your body's needs in order to achieve and maintain an optimum level of performance, so as to instil and improve a quality of life for you.

This exercise, you may be glad to know, does not contain any exercise itself! The point of doing this is to make yourself aware of what exercise your body gets and how your body is used in your life. The decision and subsequent action to perform exercise, of whatever form, must be left to you, for in order to continue to exercise your body, as part of your sacred spirituality, you must find and maintain your own motivation within. It is naively hopeful of me to expect you to begin a strict regime of exercise, just because you have read this book. You must want to maintain your body as part of your acceptance of yourself as sacred. This no other can do for you, it has to come from within.

This exercise can assist you in this endeavour however. To begin, take a piece of paper and again, perform a grounding and connecting, or at least become relaxed, letting yourself be objective, truthful and honest in your outlook now. Mentally go through what you do on each typical day of the week. Consider what your body has to do from the moment you rise until you go to bed. As you do this, write down the forms of exercise you give your body. Think about the different parts of the body. See if each part of your body is stretched in your activities or if it is generally left dormant, with little demands made on a certain group of muscles. Be aware as you do · this that for energy to flow freely through the body and maintain good health, the body itself must be moving freely and smoothly. At the very least, each set of muscles really needs to be exercised each day, just to remove the accumulations of tensions and relaxation that sets in with sleep.

Of course we need to be relaxed and to sleep adequately, but when we are awake, we need to be properly and fully awake.

When you have completed your review of your typical week, look at the notes you have made and consider the amount of exercise this reflects. You will need to be scrupulously honest with yourself in this and do bear in mind your feelings and reactions from the previous exercise as you looked at your body. As you look over your notes, any areas of neglect or need in your body should become clear.

From this, determine what needs your body has that are not currently being addressed. Then think about how you will be able to redress this imbalance. There are many non-intensive and gentle forms of exercise that can be learnt for only a small cost and that do not require lots of materials, special clothing etc. In particular, you may like to consider Yoga, Tai Chi, Chi Kung and the like as such. These forms of exercise do not require you to adhere to the misplaced Western maxim of 'no Pain, no gain' in your exercise, instead focussing on the movement of energy through the body and being, seeing this as central to the maintenance of health and performance. It is then just a matter of beginning to exercise your body. In all this, remember that the point of this exercise is to come to view and treat your body as sacred.

Exercise 4 - Energy Cleansing

This is a meditation/visualisation that provides a thorough cleansing and servicing for your body and being. This is achieved by focussing on the energy of these and makes use of the breath and colour as the means by which it is achieved. As before you will need to ensure that you are not disturbed and have created your own meditation area, using incense, music, candles etc as you wish.

Begin with the grounding and connecting, as outlined in Exercise 1, Chapter 1. Now, in your meditative state, focus on the life force and energy moving naturally in and around your body, as you sit or lie there. Let this awareness settle until you are familiar and comfortable with it. Be aware that you can direct and alter the flow and condition of this energy with your thoughts. Spend a few moments before you begin focussing on any specific needs you have at the time, letting them rise to the surface.

Next, imagine that you breathe in a red energy flow, each time you inhale. As with all the colours used here, this should be an even stream of red, untainted and not too dark or bright. Breathe this into your body and as you breathe out, breathe this out, around and over your body, out to just a few inches from your body. This refreshes and cleanses the first, Etheric layer of your aura and the Base chakra and the aspects this controls. Each subsequent breath and colour you ingest does the same for its corresponding chakra and layer of the aura. Breathe each such breathe in for as long as feels necessary to you, with a suggested minimum of three and maximum of nine. The breaths should be deep and regular, but not so as to cause you to strain. The breaths out should be equal.

Follow the structure of colour and breaths as listed below, in the manner described above, for each chakra and layer of the aura in turn. Let yourself pause between each colour and become aware of any changes in your feeling and perception as you go. Please refer to the picture of the energy system for clarification as to where each breath should be located. Each layer of the aura is a little further out than the previous, until you reach a distance of three feet from the body, though this does vary from person to person.

BREATH	COLOUR	CHAKRA	AURA LAYER
FIRST	RED	BASE	ETHERIC
SECOND	ORANGE	SACRAL	EMOTIONAL
THIRD	YELLOW	SOLAR PLEXUS	MENTAL
FOURTH	GREEN	HEART	ASTRAL
FIFTH	BLUE	THROAT	SPIRITUAL
SIXTH	PURPLE	THIRD EYE	CELESTIAL
SEVENTH	VIOLET	CROWN	KETHERIC

When these seven breaths have been completed, pause and let yourself settle, allowing a little time for the energy you have generated to settle too. While this is happening, let yourself become aware of how you feel now.

This exercise regenerates a positive flow of life force through your being and cleanses and flushes out accumulated 'muck' gathered by daily living. It is important not to destroy the force and boost you have just given yourself, by leaping up immediately and running a marathon or some such tomfoolery! Ground yourself as before, prior to finishing the exercise. It may be appropriate for you also to say a brief few words of blessing and thanks for the sacred energy you have as your being too. I would recommend you perform this exercise once in each Moon, perhaps around the time of the New Moon, to capitalise on the fresh energy coming our way then.

Exercise 5 - Previous Life Influences

This exercise is a simple and natural means whereby it is possible to discover some of the pre-conditioned influences you have with you in your current life, from various previous lives you have led. As with many such reflective exercises, it is helpful to perform a grounding and connecting first and to create a suitable atmosphere for yourself, utilising such materials as you see fit.

Now sit and write on a piece of paper your answers to the following questions, letting answers come intuitively to you:

What are the main cultures in the world you are drawn to and why?
What countries in the world do you especially like and why?
Do you prefer hot or cold weather and why?
Are there particular kinds of foreign food you like and why?
What kind of music or sounds do you particularly like and dislike and why?
What do you like to read and why?
What kind of landscape do you like and dislike and why?
If you could alter your appearance to be anything you want, how would you choose to look and dress and why?
Imagine you are a time traveller. When and where would you go and why?

When you have your answers, read over them and see if there are any common threads that make themselves clear, as to a particular country or area, which you seem naturally drawn to. These are only some of the factors that can indicate where we may have been before and what kind of experiences we may have had. Our natural tendencies, likes and dislikes, especially those we have as young children, can often give us strong clues as to previous life influences that we carry forward, for whatever reason. You are asked to examine your dislikes as well, since not all of your previous experiences will have been pleasant and positive! Look at your list objectively and simply see if you are able to pick up any threads that you feel are from your previous lives, helping you in this way to discover who you really are.

Chapter 4

The Needs of the Heart

We now move around the wheel of our beings and the world a little, to look at the watery, emotional aspects of ourselves. Here we need to identify what our particular needs are on this level of our beings and then ascertain what we can do to maintain balance emotionally. In this Chapter we will see how our emotions form a vital part of our sacredness and the role they play in the overall well being and growth of us as sacred beings.

The needs of the heart - healthy emotions - are expressed esoterically and symbolically through the Element of Water. The nature of Water is such that it is adaptable in that it forms a shape that adheres to the container it is in. Our emotions too, are shaped by the circumstances that induce them. We may feel excitement at listening to music or watching sport: the inner response to the outer action. This Element and therefore part of us, is therefore an inner one, regarded as being of the feminine rather than masculine.

Our emotions are fluid, like water in that they come and go, always changing as the situation demands. If left to stand, becoming in the person cold and unfeeling they become like the stagnant pool, poisoned and polluted. We must ever be on our guard to remain open and trusting of our emotions, unafraid to accept them as a part of the sacred being we are. We must face and embrace our emotions, both good and bad, pleasant and unpleasant, as a valid response applicable in that moment of time, Indeed, it is this very acceptance and openness that allows for much of our fulfilment, happiness often being regarded as a measure of how one feels.

Above all, our emotions cannot be ignored, To ignore them is only to suppress them, to place a lid on the container of water that prevents it from breathing and being alive. Such is the case with us. Our bodies are, according, in an episode of *Star Trek*, (to a life form that advised humanity to return to it three hundred years hence to see if its arrogance had calmed) 'bags of mostly water', confirmed later as over 90% water contained within a flexible structure!

That we are to such a degree water is also indicative of the degree of strength our emotions have upon our overall being. Emotions, as said previously, cannot be ignored or dismissed, or even prevented from occurring. This is helpfully illustrated for us again in that fertile ground for comparison, Star Trek, when Spock in attempting to re-learn all he had previously lost as a Vulcan, was unable to answer the question 'How do you feel'. By trying to ignore the human half of himself, emotions had become foreign and alien, yet he was incomplete until he had acknowledged that the 'needs of the one outweigh the needs of the many' This he was forced to do, foolishly only after every other avenue had been explored, by acknowledging the place of the emotions in his own self and in others. Please see Exercise One here for a method by which you can identify the true place of emotions in your being.

At a deeper level we can see emotions as a prime motivating force for our actions. What we do in life is rarely because it is the right and proper thing to do, but because underneath whatever mental excuses and logical reasoning we may convince ourselves of, we simply have a desire to. We must therefore seek to identify what our true and real feelings are at the deepest level, to ensure we remain true to ourselves, for only in truth will we find solace and peace, perhaps a truer meaning of happiness than a moments surface pleasure.

Yet everywhere we find in our modern society traps and tugs away from such a deep fulfilment with one self. With a sardonic smile we are advised to 'Choose life, choose a job, choose a career, choose a family, choose a f****** big television', the writer of such wisdom offering heroin as the alternative at the other extreme. Such is the claim on our lives by the forces of profit, promising happiness in the 'three piece suite in a range of f****** fabrics ... sitting on that couch watching mind-numbing, spirit crushing game shows'. How easy it is to bend to these mighty forces and accept the surface pleasure the above can only hope to offer us. It is this way that we become driftwood on the river, tossed helplessly this way and that as we deny ourselves for the temporary thrill of momentary pleasure, affected by all and sundry that may touch us - the starving children on the news, the lottery jackpot figure, the price of petrol per litre and the manufactured unfeeling muzak that daily stings our ears.

Beneath all this, despite its prevalence these days, there lies the still lake, the silent pool of untouched, unexplored emotions that promise so much and lies in wait to teach us until summoned, yet which we seem to shy away from, fearful of the murky depths we might plummet to. This is not to suggest that we must become people of such strong feelings that we are out of control. Instead the delicate balance must be struck that allows us to feel what we may, accept it and recognise what it is telling us and flow accordingly. Further guidance in this balance cannot be given, for each person and each circumstance is different and each must find the responsible and appropriate emotional response they believe fit, in every moment.

This in turn requires that we are alive and awake, watchful and open, eager to step beyond the robotic life that does not demand of our resources, inner powers and strengths. Here we must nurture ourselves, deep in the quiet lake of our beings and hearts, taking the time to be still ourselves and listen to what our heart is saying. At this deep level we find no betrayal or traps, but only truth, designed in its very nature to help and teach. Here we find the sacred nature of our emotions. To identify them we must become calm and placid, able then to be objective about the way we feel. To achieve this hallowed state I would recommend the Grounding and Connecting exercise, so valuable in so many ways. This lets you become an observer without denying the way that you think or feel. Rather, it highlights these aspects, thereby letting us face and embrace as we must.

It has been said that people who are unemotional are simply suppressing their emotions. This can never be a permanent state however, for emotions must be shown and be allowed out. As said, if we try to prevent their showing on the outside or even deny them to ourselves, we become the agent of our own pollution. The living nature of the human system is such that if the healthy and valid feeling cannot find its way out through the natural release of tears, love, anger, laughter, smile, or a million other expressions, then they are transformed to some other form by which they can find expression.

Here we discover something of the true nature of illness, for such is the most common result of ignored or suppressed feelings, that of disease. This is an apt description, for we are indeed in a state of dis-ease with ourselves, unable to acknowledge what we feel, frozen like ice, cold to the touch and unresponsive to others. Yet it is precisely in that disease that we find our message and healing. It is often that the nature of an illness or ailment tells us much about what we need to do at the emotional level. The links between arthritis and anger are commonly known now, yet there are many other conditions and dis-eases that tell us much in this way. Dying of a broken heart is not uncommon.

Literally, the most common of these, is the cold, which science for all its power and achievement cannot find an answer to. When we consider the nature of the cold, we realise that it blocks and prevents each of the five senses we daily have with us; sight from streaming eyes, smell from blocked passages, touch from aching bones, taste from bacterial activity and sound from a build up of wax in our ears. Clearly then, the message is to retreat within ourselves, be still and rest and allow what is within to bubble up to the surface to be dealt with accordingly.

When this is done, coupled of course with appropriate responses to the body's needs (in this case fluid and Vitamin C) we are able to recognise that we have brought about the right conditions for the cold to manifest by ignoring something of our own feelings and sacredness. Again, this is an individual matter for each to approach as they are able, for emotions can neither be forced, but as a guide and offer of help here, please see Exercise 2. The above is only one example but sadly, physical and sometimes life threatening dis-ease is all too often the result of buried, painful emotions escaping as they must.

The human potential movement, peopled by teachers far and wide offering many different methods for developing that potential, has grown to massive proportions, perhaps as an indication of the emotional need within so many people in these times. The choice of how one chooses to develop is again a personal matter, as is much of the subject of this Chapter. For the recommendation that comes from my own experiences, please see the Bibliography, where you will find several titles listed of such methods of development.

One common trait recognised throughout the human potential movement is the validity and sacredness of the human being and our condition. Too often we are given images from television and cinema that portray the human condition as one of squalor; pitiful and weak. Adversely the human potential movement sees the human glass as half full, not half empty, to return to our watery analogies! It is this view that we must realise is the truth and that such squalor and suffering as we may see around is of our own making and choosing, but not of a result of our natural condition.

Our natural condition, in terms of emotions, is one of peace and love. To deny these is to deny yourself, for these things are part of your natural state of being. You were created with love and with love you die, taking this with you, as you do many of your deeper emotions. Before we explore this point, we will pause to look a little closer at this natural state of being.

When a baby is born he or she begins to explore the world around them, through the natural and instinctive medium of their five senses. Things are identified and labelled by the experiences that touch, taste, smell, sound and sight. What comes next is a response to those senses and these are emotional. What baby does with the experiences whether they choose to explore further or keep away, is determined by how they feel about what their senses presented to them. This occurs without our considering anything further, it just happens and we react as we see fit, according to our individual psyche, memory and overall identity, shaped by so many things, as such emotions are an initial response to what we experience and are the yardstick by which we come to measure ourselves.

Because it is natural and instinctive and occurs each and every time without exception, we come to rely on and accept what our emotions tell us as truth. As we live and grow however, we experience unpleasant as well as exciting discoveries. Our mind files all this in its deeper and dormant layers and these are used for future reference. When we next experience something that recalls a previous unpleasant experience, the same negative emotions of fear, anger or whatever are stirred and pushed up to the surface to remind you: 'once bitten, twice shy' Hence the need again for feeling that emotion and response, but then detaching ourselves and being objective and balanced in our view. Here again, we can turn to the Grounding and Connecting exercise. If this exercise is performed regularly and preferably daily, we find that the centre of our being, where we are calm and still stays closer to us and objectivity and truth are easier to grasp and keep in our conscious field of vision.

We can now see more of the sacred and intrinsically helpful nature of our emotions, if only we will be open to them and let ourselves feel. It is this openness and trust that is the key to healthy emotions and their interplay with our whole and complete beings and as a result our ability to develop, learn and grow from what we feel.

The opposite to this is as illustrated previously in the 'cold as ice' persona of the killer that shows nothing when sentenced to their own death, perhaps this coming as a merciful release of their inner torment (not that this is in anyway an advocation of capital punishment). Pain, suffering and torment are the result of emotional denial. It is this that we must use to measure against the pain that powerful emotions might give us, from the severed love relationship or grief at the loss of a loved one. The pain of such experiences is undeniable but they are not in their nature harmful to us. In fact, the opposite is true. It is from the pain and associated feelings that we can actually grow in compassion, empathy and awareness of our fellow human's plight in their own times of pain. Emotions are seen now as a sacred part of the human condition.

What prevents us from feeling these emotions is often fear, based on the pain we felt at a young age when we first came across such a feeling. That fear is instilled as a defence mechanism and we must face that fear and accept that we must also feel the pain if we are to conquer this blockage and grow. The end result of blocking such uncomfortable and painful emotions is hardness and bitterness. It is true to say that the bitter person is one that another cannot help for they have imprisoned themselves behind a wall that is effective in preventing another to come close. They may fall in love still and be able to cry in times of grief and despair, but the real heart of true pain within them is blocked out.

There is a paradox here that must be realised, which is that we find our strength emotionally by accepting that we are fragile and vulnerable. By doing this, it is that very fragility and vulnerability that becomes our strength, Like the strongest tree, strength is to be found in the flexibility we are able to show, the openness to feel what we may and flowing with what circumstances bring us.

What prevents us from this openness is often fear. It is not that we can remove the fear, but that we can 'feel the fear and do it anyway' to quote a very useful book in this instance (*Love is Letting Go of Fear* - see Bibliography). Beware then of bitterness and the icy cold walls of fear that surround it. For an antidote to these traps. please see Exercise 3.

Perhaps the strongest and most powerful force that we can use to combat fear and bitterness is love. Love, we are told, is many things, not the least of which is God. Allowing for this to mean that we can apply our own interpretation of what or who God is, if 'God' or the Divine is love, then love is within all of us, since as we have seen we possess a spark of the Divine or God in us, that is ever present and constant. We therefore possess just what we need to combat fear and its workings, for to quote the Bible again, 'perfect love drives out fear' and 'there is no fear in love' (John 4:18.)

But it is easy simply to say that we must love or to naively assume that 'all you need is love'. Interestingly, when questioned 20 years after this view was first postulated by the Beatles, many prominent figures of the time, Abbie Hoffman et al, said that whilst this may be true, you must also know where the next meal is coming from, but that love got you most of the way there. This to me, is a good example of grounding and connecting in action! To return to love, my Dictionary gives, amongst many others, the definition of love as 'wholehearted liking for or pleasure in something'. The key here is in the word wholehearted. We cannot truly love with only a part of our hearts, only a part affection for someone or something. If we truly love, then we must give completely of ourselves, unreservedly and bravely, in the sure and safe knowledge that love conquers all fear and drives it out.

In this we have a freedom of choice. To choose love we must be open and soft, knowing that to do so we may experience pain and suffering, as many of the heroes and gods of old have done before, but that from this experience we might grow and learn. As such we are able to tap into a higher spiritual element to our emotions, as distinct from their sacredness, that lets us bring about the energy and power that love is. This fills us with security and confidence that we revel in and that gives us quite extraordinary abilities. History is littered with examples of those who in the face of great adversity and suffering triumphed against all the odds, as many cliched Hollywood films remind us, the key being that the whole heart remained opened, whether through faith, trust, belief, (blind or otherwise) or through sheer guts and determination. This openness allowed for the individual to win through so that all live happily ever after.

This brings us to our next point, that being the ever after. We have seen the importance and degree of influence our previous lives have over our present one, in the preceding Chapter. Now we must examine the principle that when we die, we die as we are, taking what we have become through the actions of our lives with us. This of course, includes our emotional state. As mentioned before, we take with us our love, joy, hate, anger, resentment, fear, and bitterness.

This requires that we must constantly be aware of not only who we are but what we are. When we realise that our emotions are energies, we can realise too that as we are a being of energies in a physical body, it is the force of our thoughts and feelings that make up those energies. Emotions then, outlast death and are not changed by it. We are then in turn our emotions and we cannot hide or run from them. We may construct all manner of barriers and walls but they will find us in the end, not matter how we convince ourselves we are something else. Should we be so clever as to ignore or hide from our feelings all through our lives, it may be that we meet them on our death bed. There are many stories we hear of the dying finally giving up and admitting they were wrong, or that they should not have acted, felt or believed what they did. Death indeed, is the great Leveller.

I would therefore exhort you to consider the effect your in-built emotions and conditioning has upon you. We have a need to seek the truth of our emotions and avoid building any kind of a defence to hide from our true, deepest feelings, for they will surely crumble at the last, where they will give us only fear and regret. Perhaps the strongest of all defences we must be wary of is that of bitterness. Bitterness is a hardness that prevents us from feelings and herein lies its power. Sometimes the hurts we are caused are such that we decide deep within our beings that we cannot risk feeling that pain again and our mind tells us that we must do something to prevent this threat to our survival again.

Thus, we harden our heart and swallow our tears. It may be the death of the one we love most dearly or of those who gave us our very lives that causes this, or it may be that we are rejected by the one we have given our heart to. Each of the above, and a good deal many other things beside can cause us to become bitter, sometimes even without our knowing.

Bitterness can creep up on us over the years, where we close a piece of our hearts off little by little as we are caused more and more pain through the seemingly random events of our lives. Finally, we can suffer no more and our hearts become cold, unable any more to feel the true thrill of joy, the peace and serenity of bliss, the rush of real anger or the tenderness of love.

In time we forget and become 'comfortably numb', until at length in death our bodies become numb too and our bitterness then dies with us.

Consider now, how you might be if you are born bitter and with your heart as described above, frozen over like the lake in Central Park each year. Others can skate over us, scratch the surface and perform all manner of movements and laughter, but never can anything really touch us. Imagine that you are a small child who can never really feel the love of its parents, experience the true joy of discovering who you are and what love is like. It is not a welcoming menu for life.

The prevention of bitterness is truly a matter of personal resolution and choice and requires of course much thought and contemplation, possibly and often, backed up by therapeutic work of one kind or another. Perhaps the strongest and most helpful guide I can offer here is to say that esoteric teaching and the ancient wisdom tells us that we are never given more pain and suffering than we can truly cope with. Remember that always we have a choice. We can choose to end our lives, or become bitter to stop us feeling the pain our lives will inevitably give us, or we can choose to become humble and open ourselves to what we are feeling. We can let ourselves cry and cry and keep on crying until we are dry. Then we can acknowledge our strength, for we are strong enough to wrench the very separation from the Divine in our hearts if we may and in this find our healing. If we are empty of emotion by our crying and softness, then we can become filled with the complementary and opposite to the pain that caused the tears - peace, calm and joy and above all, love.

We must be careful and sensible here to realise that there are those sufficiently distant from the Universal source of love, though it be open to all who come to it, that they rely on those who are open for their supply of energy. Such vampiristic tendencies are sadly all too common in our society for it is all too easy to take what is freely on offer from another who openly gives, without thought or consideration for the effects of your actions. Such people should not however be punished or particularly blamed for drawing on others for support, but neither should they be encouraged or helped in this.

The answer to this problem, which I have found in my experience as a therapist is quite common, is to utilise the practice known, tongue in cheek, as psychic self defence. There are many methods of protecting oneself from the unwanted attentions of another, on whatever level, so I give here one that embraces the spirit of love which we are focussing upon in our study of emotions.

Many techniques of psychic self defence take defence as their marker point for action and aim at shutting out what is confronting the person. This is valid and effective, but our aim here is love and love cannot be achieved by preventative methods such as these. Instead, by embracing and tapping into the great power that love is, we are able simply to rise above what may seek to threaten and make use of us without our permission or even knowledge.

So this technique is really a strengthening one, from which the practitioner benefits as does, it is helpful to know, the 'attacker'. If the attacker is seeking to obtain from another human what they need to make them feel comfortable or to help them progress or even just survive, as they see it, then they need to come to the stage where they realise that they cannot continue to rely on others continually. By refusing to give them support in the way they wish to take it from you, you are encouraging them in their quest for self love, acceptance and personal responsibility. They may be caused a little pain or suffering as a result, but this is really the only way in which they will come to find the truth for themselves. Put another way, 'if you want to defeat your enemy, sing his song'!

This technique does require a good awareness and basis of both self and Universal love, as the structure for its practice requires just that. If you feel that someone is 'getting at you' for their own needs or is taking from you by psychic or energy means, then choose a specific time for this technique, settle down and become comfortable. Close your eyes and let yourself imagine the constant and never ending flow of Universal love, flowing specifically to you. You can picture this as you wish, though giving it colour is very helpful. You may like to picture it as white or perhaps gold light and energy. See and feel this surrounding you and flowing right through your aura and your body. Feel it strengthening you, through every vein, bone and fibre of your being. Let this then radiate out to the edge of your aura, filling you with the very essence and power of the Universe.

Now focus on the person who is 'attacking' you See them as separate from you, and picture them as being filled with their own flow of Universal love, but with a different colour to yours. You could use violet or perhaps pink here, whatever you wish and feels right for you. Let this energy fill their aura and then picture the both of you as separate entities, each filled with their plentiful supply of Universal love, easily filling the needs of each.

Now imagine a cool, blue circle of light, energy and power that flows around each of you in a figure of eight formation. This separates each of you from the other, but does not detract from either's flow of Universal love, to which they are entitled. This helps your assailant and also helps you. Continue this image for as long as feels necessary and let the picture dissolve. You may like to add a few words, silent or otherwise, requesting guidance and assistance for the other person and lastly giving thanks for the help you have been given in this.

The effect of this exercise will then filter through to the person in need. They will recognise and sense this, unconsciously or otherwise and you may find that they withdraw from you for a time. This is because they will sense and feel that they cannot get what they were from you anymore, but you have done what you can for them and helped them in truly the most effective way possible. Allow them to do this to fully separate the unwanted links between you. If there is need for a true friendship between you, they will soon make contact when they have discovered an alternative source of energy. You can then go on your way, safe to be open and loving to those genuinely in need and requesting help which you may choose to give or not, as is your choice.

It may be that you require the services of another to assist you to remain able to fully feel and relate to all your emotions. If this is the case there are many therapies able to achieve this. Perhaps the most obvious here may be counselling, where the job of the trained counsellor is to actively listen to you, not to offer solutions. A trusted friend can be a big help too, but be sure that they do not offer advice, unless they have been through deep and effective counselling themselves. The point here is that the listener should only seek to validate and affirm your experiences and feelings for you. They need to be able to confirm for you that what you are feeling is real and is valid thereby helping you to accept the way you feel. As we know, this is the key to transcending that emotion that seeks to belittle or disempower you and you can move on once more, ever nearer to the sacred love that awaits you at the centre of the Universe and all things.

Another therapy I would recommend to help you deal with your emotional life, perhaps surprisingly, is aromatherapy. Firstly the essential oils used in aromatherapy massage can be of enormous help in lifting the spirits of the downcast and for helping to draw out suppressed or locked up feelings. Secondly, we need to remember that emotions are an energy and as such those energies exist and move within our bodies and our auras. Massage, when combined in aromatherapy with essential oils, is an excellent and largely pleasurable method of bringing to the surface deeply buried emotions. Often the release felt during and after a massage can bring about sighing and tears that bring a return of security and softness to the patient. We have also already mentioned the power and effectiveness of flower remedies and other essences, that taken over a period of time are a subtle yet powerful way of dealing with emotions we can no longer feel, for whatever reason.

Rejoice then in your emotions and your weakness, for in truth your emotions make you stronger. It takes far more courage and strength to be open, soft and emotional than it does to become cold, hard and bitter. The needs of your heart are such that they need to flow, like a clear and bubbling stream, turning this way and that with no seeming purpose or pattern, but flow they must, for that is their nature and instinct. If you waver and wobble a little too much, ask for help. Help is always at hand and is always given, but we must ask for it.

Who you make your request to and in what way is entirely up to you. Only be sincere, polite and honest and such will be your reply. You are unlikely to experience visions of angels or feel loving hands around you as you meditate immediately after asking, but you will get an answer. You may well forget you ever asked, when you wake refreshed after a night's sleep or you may find from somewhere a tiny portion of determination or motivation that allows you to sniff, smile a little and just keep on keeping on.

Be always aware of what emotions you have and what and who you are becoming as a result of them. You may like to use a quiet time each day, for just a few moments, to ask yourself what emotions you have felt that day and why and decide on any course of action that you feel needs taking. In this way you will negate the need for the forces of karma to affect your subsequent lifetime and bring about such circumstances that will bring things to balance, as all things must. So little effort for so much reward.

Another strong reason for avoiding the full force of our emotions lies with the fear we can feel about confronting and dealing with what our hearts' give us in response to what we experience. Fear is a force that hides us from truth. As a force, it is also an energy. As such, we can see that we can control it and have mastery over it. Fear is also a thing that has no object, no foundation and no physical presence. Again, we see that it is an energy. The nature of fear is such that it has no nature.

The result of fear however, is a different matter and that result is a similar one to that outlined above through bitterness. If we are scared and fearful of our emotions, we cannot feel truly what is in our hearts. To become open and able to love, hate and feel again, we must first accept that we have this fear. There is no shame or blame in this, it is just a recognition, nothing more. Once this has been achieved, we need then to consider why we felt fear and so address the object of our fear. The object once identified, can then be dealt with in whatever way we personally feel is acceptable to us, perhaps with the help of a therapist of group. We are then restored to our open, soft selves, able to 'face and embrace' the fear that has stolen our emotions from us. It is now that we are able to realise the truth behind the old maxim that we have 'nothing to fear but fear itself'. We must make a friend of our fear or it remains our enemy. It is really but a simple thing when we see that fear has no physical substance and that with a focussed and concentrated effort, it can be defeated by the vast and all conquering power of love.

Love of the self is perhaps the most powerful method of maintaining a healthy emotional state for ourselves. This requires that we are able to accept ourselves just as we are, with all our limitations, failings, faults as well as talents, abilities and achievements, emotionally and on all levels of our beings. This state of healthy emotions needs however, to be clarified - what are healthy emotions and how can we get them?

The answer here must be that healthy emotions are all of them, for they are each a vital part of our overall and complete beings. It is clear from our studies of the needs of the heart that we must be open to feel all of our emotions in a complete and thorough sense. Whilst it may be true that some emotions may seem to threaten us and cause us pain, it is also true that from a higher, sacred perspective, which we are concerned with here, our emotions are an excellent means of teaching and guiding us, when approached in such a spirit. This is because they are a flow of the energy that we are and as such we must find why we feel the way we do, accept this as valid and move on from there. Let us then examine the main types of emotion that we feel and in so doing discover their sacred nature as a part of our own sacred being.

Much has been said and written about love, throughout humanities history and so it is to love that we shall first address ourselves. The last 2000 years of our history has, from an esoteric view, been founded, at least in theory, on Christianity. This branch of religion and approach to the sacred has for its basis and foundation, love. Specifically, the unconditional love of both ourselves and our fellow beings. This, we are told, is exemplified for us in the life and ultimate death of Christ, there being no greater love than the laying down of one's life for another.

That the highest strain of love is unconditional is a fact we again, need to accept and embrace. Whilst it is very rare that we are called upon to lay our lives down to prove this, it is equally rare that we see a display of unconditional love in our society today. The forces of commercialism have instead placed at the centre of our hearts a dependency on the material and money such that we are in many cases only motivated to show love when it suits us and when we are able to obtain something in return.

When we look at unconditional love, we must realise that this is the only motivation we need as the reason for carrying out some act. It is rather like the mountain that needs to be climbed because it is there. Because love exists and is the force by which humanity evolves, we need to embrace its power and energy for others and so ourselves. Ancient wisdom tells us that what we give out to others is returned to us, three fold. Therefore if we demonstrate love and have love in our hearts, this is what we shall experience in return. With this in mind, we need have no thought for ourselves, only for others. This sounds very difficult to put into practice especially when motivated by profit or personal gain, but we must overcome this hurdle and realise that love is eminently practical and remember again, that love may indeed be all we need. If we have such a love, we are open then to the forces of the Universe that in turn love us.

Many of the sacred texts of the world, covering thousands of years of our history tell us that love is the strongest force and that is it out of love that humanity was first created. Love is sacred and so as we come to realise that we are sacred, so we know that we are love. If we move, live and have our beings surrounded by love, nothing can harm, threaten or destroy us. The 'hippy' ideals of the sixties may sound as if they are embedded in these words, but that love must include perhaps what those days lacked, a grounded, practicality that knew where its next meal was coming from! We must be connected to the higher power and force of the Universe, love, and be grounded in the real world about us and thereby able to exude or emit that real power and force through us. As such we are free from harm and know instinctively that whatever pain we feel has beneath it an everlasting and ultimately conquering power of love. With this in mind, any other emotions are secondary and sacred love wins out.

Chief in our quest for this Universal love must come self love. This is not a selfish, excluding love, but one that accepts us for what and who we are. True love of another is unconditional, it does not depend on physical appearance, the money one makes, music one likes and so on, but simply is. Such is the love we must have for our selves. We must come to love our failings and mistakes in life, for they are surely bound to occur, as the means by which we can learn.

Some may say that this is optimistic twaddle and indeed I would agree. But I would also add that to go through life in a pessimistic manner is not to truly live, but to deny oneself experience and evolvement. There may be no point, on the surface to our optimism, but that does not stop us from being optimistic anyway. Again, we climb the mountain because it is there!

Ancient wisdom teaches us, as does more modern science, that for every force and action in the Universe, there is an equal and opposite reaction, a complementary and opposite reaction. As such when we feel love we must look at hate. Our study of bitterness and fear has shown us the end result of hate, whether of ourselves or of others. We could perhaps see ourselves as standing somewhere on the line, with love at one end and hate at the other. (See Figure 1)

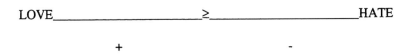

Figure 1

We can see from this that the forces and energies of love and hate are like the twin polarities that exist in all things. As the only thing that can destroy

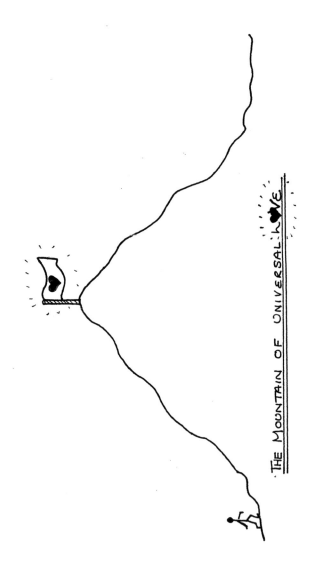

THE MOUNTAIN OF UNIVERSAL LOVE

energy is a vacuum, so nature exists at all times somewhere between the twin polarities that have an equal and opposite positive and negative charge. As such, the more you love, the more of a positive charge you receive from the Universe and the more you hate the more of a negative charge is felt. This is another reason why we must in the fullness of time come to accept responsibility for ourselves and our actions. It is a perhaps hard truth that we have only ourselves to blame for what we experience in our lives, for following this principle we attract to ourselves what comes our way, good and bad and so we must accept it. Only by this acceptance can we seek to resolve the difference in the polarities and find the point of balance that lies at the middle, of ourselves, the World and all in it and the whole Universe.

We can utilise this diagram above and ask ourselves in any one situation or circumstance where on the line we lie and what we might do to bring ourselves to balance. As an introduction to this system of self management and acceptance, you might like to consider how you are now, overall and in general in your being and in your life, taking into account everything that is happening to you now. Do not measure this in terms of satisfaction and certainly not in terms of how comfortable you are (financially or otherwise), but in terms of how much you love, yourself and others; not just those you know but the rest of humanity. Be truthful and honest for this is not a test, merely a simple means of becoming objective.

You can then list under Love all those things that take you this way and all the things under Hate that take you that way. By doing this, you can get a good idea of all the things that take you off balance and sway you away from the feeling of contentment that we all strive after. With a little thought and effort and perhaps some inner contemplation and meditation, some surprising and valuable revelations can be gained.

Many other emotions can also be measured this way, particularly those that are considered to be some of the strongest: Desire and Regret, Happiness and Sadness, Peace and Panic, Passion and Apathy, Pleasure and Pain, Truth and Confusion (seen in an emotional sense), Love and Anger, Passion and Passivity.

Of course there are many more that can be added to this list and you may well like to add your own, which I recommend. By placing each of the complementary opposite emotions at either end of the polarity line and following the method described above, you can learn much about yourself,

105

either in a general sense or for specific situations. Such exercises also help us to realise that we cannot avoid emotions, only move from one end of the line to the other.

One way in which we can come to view ourselves and all our fellow humans is that of being either a head or a heart person, responding first with either thought or feeling. These too can be placed at opposite ends of our line of polarities and by listing your tendencies under each you can come to realise which you are. If you find that you are a heart person, I suggest that you re-read this Chapter, taking it is as applying in particular to you. Then read the next Chapter, as subject matter for learning. If you find that you are a head person, read Chapter 5 as applying particularly to you, then re-read this Chapter for learning material. By this, you may each arrive at the perfect and serene balance that lies between the head and heart, the indwelling and constant sacredness within each and every living thing.

When we come to view the sacred human being as consisting of the four sacred elements we must accept that as such, emotions, forming at the very least one quarter of our complete being, are sacred. This view of emotions as a sacred part of the human being is backed up when we recall the link between ourselves and the earth that we have, reminding ourselves here that a majority of the Earth's surface is of water.

We must not run from our emotions, but openly accept them and ensure, by flowing with them just as the river runs its course, that we are neither flotsam, helplessly floating in the wake, or a stagnant pollution whose purpose is only to prevent the natural order and inevitable flow. Then can we come to the higher level of the collective, shared and related emotions that identify one with another, resulting in the highest power and emotion of all, love. Here we find our home in the open sea, blending with others, shaping ourselves around them and finally, merging with them to express something of the sacred and divine nature of the human being and system. Glory then in your emotions, revel in their passion and force and direct them to the highest good of your individual evolvement and that of the human race as a collective and lastly, embrace love always.

Exercise 1 - Sacred Self Identification

This exercise is based on an ancient and powerful Zen Buddhist technique for self identification. For our purposes, is also follows on nicely from Exercise 1 of Chapter 3, The Sacred Body where you identified the sacred centre and Divine presence within yourself. This exercise allows you to enlarge upon this and effectively sense and become aware that your whole body and being is in fact, sacred.

To perform this Exercise, you will need to enter into a state of relaxation and if you are able, meditation, thereby achieving an altered state of consciousness. This will be achieved if you are able to perform the Grounding and Connecting exercise, the first of the book, to a reasonable degree. If you wish you can ignite incense and play some suitable music in a still and warm, comforting environment of your choice. Make yourself comfortable, close your eyes and begin.

When you have brought your focus to the centre of yourself following your Grounding and Connecting you need to bring your mind into focus on yourself. First, let your awareness drift gently but firmly over your body, recognising its shape and outline. Now expand this awareness a little to gain a sense of the size and proportion of your aura. Become aware as you do this that you are both body and aura, and that together these things make your complete being. Allow yourself to sense too, the energies and forces flowing within your body.

Now inwardly speak the following to yourself, allowing yourself time as you go to absorb their meaning:

I have a body, but I am not my body, I am more than my body.

I have emotions, but I am not my emotions, I am more than my emotions.

I have a mind, but I am not my mind, I am more than my mind.

I am a being of pure energy, consciousness and will.

I am eternal, immortal and infinite.

As you work through these words, be aware of how you feel as you go and any reactions you seem to notice. Especially be aware of your feeling within when you have finished the words. Let this awareness sink into the very depths of yourself. Focus on this feeling as the sacredness of your whole and complete self.

Take a little time to absorb and enjoy this experience, for it is an uplifting and pleasurable one to have and return when you wish, by grounding yourself firmly and clearly, as in the grounding and connecting exercise. It is important to try and memorise the words so that you can maintain your altered state of consciousness as you go. Opening your eyes will bring you out of this and the focus will be lost. This may seem like a lot of effort to begin with, but after a few tries you will be able to do this easily. It is also important to ensure that you do allow time to consider what you are saying. Dryly repeating the words will do nothing at all.

Exercise 2 - The Healing of Dis-ease

This exercise is one of analysis and self awareness, to assist you to be aware of the causes of your illnesses and times of dis-ease. Through it you may be able to identify any underlying causes or patterns for such difficulties, whether of small inconvenience or life changing significance

For this exercise, you will need some uninterrupted time and a pen and paper. It is a good idea and helpful to enter a relaxation and to make your environment a warm, pleasing and comforting, safe one for you to be in whilst you do the exercise. Now make a list of all the illnesses, since birth, you have had that you can remember. This can be both small and seemingly unimportant things, as well as any major troubles you may have had. Work your way through your life until the present time.

Now go back through your illnesses and next to each one, try to recall what you were doing in life at that time. Write down any details you can remember or that seem to spring into your mind. Write down whatever you think of, as it may seem unrelated or even stupid but could be of surprising significance. Consider where you lived, how you spent your time, the people in your life and see if you are able to identify any other things that may be contributory factors to your illness. Pay special attention to your emotional condition at the time of the illness and how you think this may have affected you.

Now, work your way through your list of illnesses and see if there are any patterns that emerge, recurrent types of illness and more importantly, causes of them. Be open and honest in this and do not put yourself down or feel bad if it shows something you feel bad about or ashamed of. This is a good chance to put that right if this is the case. Let your intuition and instinct be open and guide you as you perform this analysis. If you feel tired by this stage of the exercise, it is better to leave it alone and return at a later date.

The conclusions you come to through this analysis are entirely a matter for yourself. The exercise simply provides the forum for realisation and illumination to occur. You may find that it is necessary to embark on a course of treatment or you may need to determine to yourself to avoid an allergic reaction to a type of food or some such material. You may find that you need to work on yourself emotionally, as you may discover that you become ill after feeling a certain way and allowing your emotions to control you in some way.

Exercise 3 - Dissolving the Walls Meditation

This exercise is based closely on a meditation given in the useful book 'Pathworkings' by Pete Jennings and Pete Sawyer (Capall Bann, 1993), to whom I am indebted. I have made some alterations to allow for adjustment to our specific purpose through this exercise, of achieving and maintaining an open, fluid and harmonious emotional state or condition within ourselves. I have chosen this exercise for this having used it many times in groups with an excellent response.

Prepare yourself in the usual manner for meditation, utilising incense and music if you wish. Begin with the grounding and connecting exercise to take you into the appropriate state for meditation. Now imagine that you are looking out from an inner, third eye inside your forehead. This eye allows you to see energies and forces that your outer, physical eyes cannot. In effect, it gives you a kind of X-ray vision!

As you look, you see that you are standing before a large, brick wall. It is quite dim, but you can just make this out before you. The wall is too large to climb over, but you spot an iron ring in the very centre of the wall. The wall seems to have an enormous pressure and heaviness about it. These are the pressures you face within you and your life, that have here formed themselves into bricks of hardness and even bitterness. Walk up to the wall and grasp the ring firmly. With some effort you are able to pull this ring out and in so doing release the keystone from the wall. This collapses around you and you can now walk forward, through the rubble about you, feeling the sense of release this gives you.

It is a little lighter now and you can see a wall before you, covered in a sticky, treacly substance. When you reach out and touch it, it stretches and clings to your fingers. This is made of the lack of motivation you can sometimes have and the lack of self love you may feel for yourself at times. You notice as you touch it that it has no solid form at all. Now summon all your inner power and let yourself feel a self love for yourself as you are. Focus this into your hands and push and lean against the wall with all your might. After a short time, the wall will collapse into a mess at your feet, through which you can carefully step forward, letting a little more light around you.

Now you are faced with the next wall, this time of a force field, that you can see crackling and glowing at intervals. You can feel the force and energy of it as you get nearer and you realise that it is the depression you have felt at times and the dark, inner emotions that have on occasions gripped you. As it is a force, you realise that you can beat it with an equal and opposite force. Focus on what this may be within you and allow yourself to picture this in some form. Now focus the form of your positive force through your hands and blast this at the force field of depression and sadness. See it fizzle and crack and then it will collapse, sparking and hissing on the floor until all is quiet.

Now you come to the last wall, which appears to be the tallest and strongest of all. It is completely black and seems to cast a shadow over you as you approach. You become aware that it is made from the object of your fears and seems to threaten you greatly. Be encouraged as you get to the wall and summon all your love and strength from within. Now search this wall for the door that you sense and know is built into it somewhere. You will need to touch and even lean against the wall to find your door, but with a little effort you will do so. Open it and step through.

110

You will now find yourself in a wonderful environment that seems to appeal to you in a deeply fulfilling way. This may be anywhere or indeed any time at all. Simply spend a little time here, in your land of emotional freedom and peace. Let your emotions be expressed and when you are ready let if fade away, bringing back the feeling of joy and release as you return, grounding fully before you open your eyes.

If you find that you feel a blockage as you progress through this meditation, take note of where this is and whilst still in meditation, consider why. Try to accept whatever you come up with and then return from your journey. Work on this emotional blockage for a time, in your own way and when you feel ready, perform the meditation again and see if you are able to destroy the wall now. Blockages will always come and go and this exercise allows for you to clear them from you inwardly.

Exercise 4 - Meditation of Universal Love

This meditation is simply to try and give yourself an experience of the love that always lies at the centre of yourself and all things. It is helpful to have become proficient at Exercise I of this Chapter before trying this one, but you will find that the depth of feeling you experience through it, each time it is performed, it akin to your level of 'centredness' in life at that time.

Begin as usual by grounding and connecting. Now visualise yourself, where you are sitting or lying in your room or area where you are. Let yourself drift upwards a little, so that you are looking down on your body from above, hovering just a few inches above your physical body. Become accustomed to this and then raise yourself up a little more, perhaps as you breathe in you feel able to rise up. Now you can see your room beneath you. Rise a little further then to see the house your are in, or the immediate area if you are outside. When you have become used to this, you then rise some more.

This time you can see the whole street your house is in and then you drift up again to see the village or town you are. The next stage takes you to see the surrounding countryside and then again until you can see the outline of the land you live in, with the water of the sea or ocean around it. Now move up, adjusting and letting yourself become comfortable with each stage before moving up.

Now you can see your whole country. Soon you rise again and you can now see more countries. Take yourself up still further and see the planet below you. You are out in space now, quite alone, yet somehow connected to everything and all things. Give yourself time now to feel that connection and consider that the force that animates this connection is love. Feel that Universal Love within you and also within the stars that glow and twinkle around you. You may reach out and touch the stars and feel their power of love entering your being. Spend as long as you like out in the stars, experiencing Universal Love in whatever way you wish and when you are ready, return.

To return, bring yourself back down gradually, through each stage that you went through to get up there. This is vital, as this meditation can leave you feeling, literally, spacey and ungrounded if you are not careful. The experience can be very deep and profound on occasions, once you have become used to it. So you must ensure that you take your time to return. Put your hands on the floor or Earth about you before opening your eyes and then adjust to where you are and the solidity of your body before you move.

One final tip with this meditation is that to make it a truly amazing experience, it is best performed lying on your back outside on a clear sky with the stars above you. The effect when you open your eyes is to allow you to recall that Universal Love and realise that we are indeed 'star stuff'.

Chapter 5

The Needs of the Mind

We must now consider the needs of the Mind, as a vital and all too often dominant part of the human psyche and condition. With the advent of an automated, logical and reasoned world, the need for individual thought and planning of our lives has diminished, as we are able to (we are told) make our lives easier and more comfortable, since machines do much of our thinking for us, principally by computer.

This is not to say that all computers are bad or even all machines, but some may certainly be. The field of robotics is an ever expanding one that offers some exciting prospects for humanity as a whole, but in this field, as in that of all automated mechanics, from the potential of the smallest Personal Computer, to the largest multi nationals system, we must be sure and certain that the freedom of the human individual to think for themselves is not lost.

Of course it can be argued that such computerised technology can free us to do just that, taking away the need for much of our routine activity, yet we must also remember that it can often be precisely such activity that allows for the mind to roam free, taking advantage of the requirement of the body to engage itself in such mundane activity. A portion of the human mind is engaged in what the body is doing, but since such simple tasks require very little of our mind's capacity, the deeper levels of our mind are able to explore items filed away for such times. These valuable delvings into our depths can often provide us with much of our learning. What may be construed from the outside as daydreaming are often a form of conscious dreaming, where the symbolic language of the mind is freed by the body's distraction to communicate what it has learnt from the symbols it has encountered.

The yardstick we must measure our technology by is a principle that we have already touched upon, that of marrying our mechanical and scientific achievements with the power and workings of nature. Far from limiting our use of technology, the power inherent in nature provides for massive advancement in the energy and achievements possible. Occultists, esotericists, witches, sorcerers and healers have long known how to tap into and utilise the power in wind, wave, storm and water, to name but a few, so we need only embrace some of the esoteric principles that have been proven and know for thousands of years to begin to learn how to develop technological blending with nature. Happily, the highly regarded field of quantum mechanics and physics appears to be doing just that, albeit without saying so, so we are offered some hope.

The mind is likened in such esoteric thought to the Element of Air. It should be mentioned here that some practitioners put Fire here, Air being seen as belonging to the needs of the spirit. I can only offer that which I have been trained to do and work with myself. If you wish to, explore and experiment and find what works for you; this is what is then correct.

As the Element of Air, the needs of the mind can be seen as like the nature of wind, sometimes welcome, often not. Without Air, we would of course perish, for we need Air perhaps more immediately than any of the other Elements for life. Starved of air for just a short time, we die. Starved of individual thought, we become little more than physical machines. It is the ability to think and make choices and decisions that gives us our individual character and expression. Of course we must ensure that we do not rely solely on our minds for who and what we are, instead as we have seen, blending and amalgamating our thoughts and logic with our emotions and needs of our heart. Now we combine to become more complete.

We require a free flowing and plentiful supply of fresh air for the well being of our minds. If you have ever been in an environment where you have been deprived of this for even just a few hours you will easily recall the drowsy, drugged-like state that results and the welcome lift when you step outside to gulp down what passes for fresh and clean air in a city. I make reference here to the artificial environments we find ourselves increasingly in today, from air conditioned offices, restaurants and shopping malls to complete holiday cities under domes for stable temperatures.

Remember that each Element is seen as a vital and necessary part of the sacred human condition and must be cherished as such if we are to embrace ourselves as a truly and wholly spiritual person. Air conditioning usually recycles and recirculates the same air around its system, meaning that the airborne germs and bugs are able to thrive and find plentiful new hosts in the tower block or shop. Should you work in such a place, it is wise to learn a protection technique, as well as a deep breathing method, to guard against such likelihoods. For this, please see Exercise 1 for this Chapter.

With our cozy and safe environments we have become somewhat afraid of 'the Elements' or the weather, cowering beneath our coats and scarves, we scrunch our bodies, and often our minds, up against the North wind that would chill our bones to the core. Whilst it may be true that such a wind is an unpleasant experience, it is also necessary and can be used in a beneficial way. To stand atop a hill, stretch out and let the wind blow through your body and symbolically your mind is an exhilarating feeling and one that I highly recommend if you are feeling lethargic, sad or trapped. Face the wind, close your eyes and feel the wind blow. Imagine it blowing away all the cobwebs and ripping out what restricts you. Imagine the wind reaching into all the dark and dusty corners of your mind and washing a clean burst of new air there. Reach your arms out and yell into the air and let this be carried away on the wind. Feel the release and refreshment that follows and celebrate the force, power and life giving properties of the air.

As we see those tense folk with shoulders hunched, bent into the cooling air, with an expression of pain on their faces, we may see too that such people are those that are unable to let thoughts come and go easily too. Our mind needs new ideas to fuel it, some of which may challenge us and make us work harder. Mental energy is a strong force and it is quite tiring to think. Physically we may feel strong and able to keep going after a hard day's work in the office, yet there is a strange feeling of apathy and stupor, that is the result of the mental strain and focus of such work. To such people I say drop your shoulders as you walk and you will find it is not so bad, not as cold as you expect and rather easier to walk and think too. Relax into your work and let it flow. You will find more time to do things if you flow with the demands of your mind and you will end the day more refreshed, physically better and mentally stronger.

Consider then the nature of the Element of Air. We see here the vital flow of life force contained within it. We know that it can be a refreshing and welcome breeze on a hot day or the icy blast that makes you shiver on the coldest day. Each of these extremes has their function and role to play in the body of nature, which could be viewed as the breath of Mother Earth as she exhales and inhales. As we have seen we must learn to flow with that breathing, adapting and turning as best we may.

One of the most significant features of the Air is that it is viewed as containing within it the life force energy that exists throughout all living things and the whole Universe and indeed is life. As such, each time that we breathe in, we are taking in a supply of that which keeps us alive. Each time we exhale, we expel that which we have used and need no longer, which is returned to the Universe to be recycled. With this in mind that state and nature of our breathing becomes paramount to our well being and condition. An Exercise (2) is given at the end of this Chapter to explore and utilise this.

The practice of Yoga recognises this fact and so gives many breathing techniques as part of its practice. It also advocates breathing through the nose, since, apart from the sense of smell, this is what the nose is for. Filters within the nasal passages are able to filter out some of the pollutants in Air at an energy level and we are better able to direct and control the energy and air we receive when we breathe through the nose. One of the main principles to be aware of in your breathing is the depth to which you breathe in your body and how this affects you. Do you breathe from your chest or your stomach? The Exercise mentioned above will help you with this.

Since we know that the air we breathe contains the stuff of life itself, it follows that the quality of our air is all important in providing quality of life. Many of us breathe precious little real air in today, existing in cars and trains on our way to work, rather than walking part of the way. Consider your average day and how much time you spend outside. Look at this as a percentage and see in what ways you are able to increase this. Provided this time is spent away from car exhaust fumes or other pollutants, you will feel and be better for it.

It also follows here that we need to do a great deal before we can return the real quality of air back to something like it should be, not just for ourselves, but for all animal and plant life on the planet and indeed the planet itself. Consider too then, the various materials and resources you use that might have been damaging in their manufacture as well as their use, in what they put into the air. Air is sacred, this much is obvious, since it contains the blue

116

print of life itself. How much damage this can cause if we clog it with the chemicals we are currently doing remains to be seen, but already the thinning and breaking of the ozone layer is having startling and threatening consequences. This message is now a familiar one, but we must not become complacent in this familiarity, It will take longer than your lifetime to put this truly right no matter what, so it is for your children's sake that you must act, and perhaps (accepting reincarnation) yourself in another time and place.

We must now turn our attention to the mind itself and explore and examine its workings and effect on our complete being. As mentioned before, the mind is often that which directs and controls the logical person, often at the expense of the heart. We have also mentioned that there is the need for a balance to be struck between the two. Of course at certain times there is the need for one or the other, but neither should ever be completely ignored. To achieve this balance, we must first identify if we are a person of the heart or the head. To do this, please see Exercise 3 for this Chapter, where you will find a series of questions designed to illustrate which you are.

Having ascertained if you are a head or heart person, you now need to be aware and alert as to your responses in specific and challenging or demanding circumstances. A good way to do this is to spend a few moments towards the end of the day reviewing the major happenings that day and seeing how you responded. If your response was primarily an emotional one, then you need to try and think before you speak a little more. Your feelings are of course perfectly valid, but do not diminish the needs of your mind. Equally if your response is primarily mental, there is the need to take account of your feelings more and listen to your heart.

This is also illustrated further in the workings of the human brain, traditionally considered of course to house the mind. A further point of interest to make here is that the head is thought by many to contain the soul, illustrating for us the importance of 'correct thinking' and addressing the needs of the mind.

The human brain has two lobes or spheres, each corresponding to part of our way of thinking. The left side of the brain relates to the logical, common-sense, everyday functional way of thinking, whilst the right side relates to the more intuitive, receptive thought processes. This can be seen as masculine and feminine respectively. These two spheres are seen as

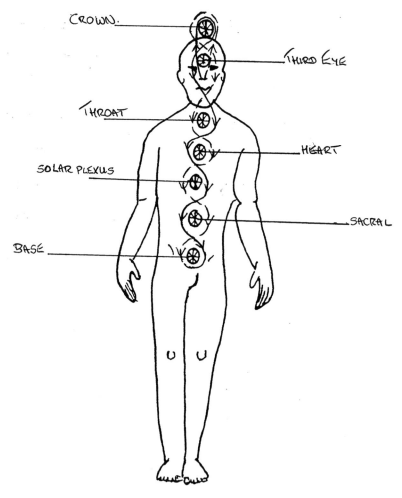

The Energy Channels

communicating cross-wise to the opposite side of the body. That is, the left brain to the right body and vice versa.

This goes some way to explaining why left handed people are often thought to be more intuitive and psychic and in older times was seen as justification enough for accusation of witchcraft! It should be mentioned here that in some people, for reasons still largely unknown, the correspondences between the two spheres of the brain and the related side of the body, reverse. With our view of integrated balance described above, perhaps the ideal to aim at here is that of being ambidextrous!

We can extend the symbolism and view of the human brain to that of the complete skull. If we take the right brain as the intuitive, internal, feminine and so feeling side, we can see it as belonging to the Element of Water, linking it to the heart, as we know. If we view the left brain as logical, external, masculine and so thinking side, we can link this with the Element of Air, thereby it governing the province and functions of our mind. This means that in the Native American view of the Medicine Wheel, the right brain belongs in the West and the left brain in the East. This leaves us the Element of Fire, the direction of South as being located in the forehead, our forward direction, where we are going and that which indicates much of our overall facial expression. The back of the skull is therefore the Earth and the North, the foundation on which we are built, the supporting role of the neck and top of the spine.

A further point we must make here is that the centre of the skull is seen as the centre of the circle of the Medicine Wheel, a microcosmic reflection of the Earth and wider Universe as the circle of all existence. Here lies the Pineal Gland, known as the Master Gland, being viewed as governing the response of the other glands, located as we know at the areas of the chakras beneath it.

The Pineal Gland is know to secrete a substance called melatonin which triggers breeding cycles and as the gland is sensitive and reactive to light, which itself contains life force, it also governs and controls, from deep within us, our sleeping and waking patterns and so our direct level of energy flow.

It is thus we come to see how the clear and balanced inhalation of both breath and life force has a direct influence, through the energy channels, chakras system and thence physically through the glands, on our overall being and so we see its importance.

One last point to make here in our study of the skull and its link to the energy system is that many people of centuries ago viewed the human soul or spirit as existing in the head and it is perhaps easy now to understand why. The gruesome picture of the Tarot card of Death traditionally shows the 'Grim Reaper' harvesting heads that appear to be growing out of the ground. The symbolism aimed at here is that he is the 'gatherer of souls' not the harbinger of that which we seem to fear so much.

The practice of meditation should also be mentioned here as it is known that when the brain wave pattern switches to the alpha state, as it does in the altered state of consciousness that is meditation, synaptic or nerve joining responses are caused to flow between the two spheres of the brain. Meditation thus causes something of that integrated balance we are aiming for. It has become known through recent research and development that such practices actually cause soft brain tissue to establish more of a link between the two hemispheres, so we literally are building bridges within.

In our earlier study of the needs of the body we explored the Chakra energy system of the body and we can now link and integrate this with our two halves of the brain. By referring to the Energy Channels picture, we can see that the life force energy enters our system as we breathe through the nose. It then travels up our nostrils and follows the two main currents over the head and down the spine.

As the picture shows, this energy flow follows two separate yet linked paths that repeatedly cross the spine. These are viewed as the masculine and feminine energies and therefore these different aspects of ourselves. We have already seen the need for a clear and deep intake of breathe as the ingestion of life force and here a deeper reasoning for this becomes clear.

We can see that the path of this energy flow criss-crosses the spine, crossing at the points of the chakras. We can therefore see the chakras as points where the male and female within us are balanced and integrated. We can work with our breath to clearly circulate the flow of life force through these channels (See Exercise 2) and also with the Chakras (See Exercise 4). When we combine this approach with the symbolism of the skull outlined above, we can see how basic and vital the breath is to a healthy and harmonious mind and body, since all life exists first as energy and the breath draws this energy to us.

There are other methods of achieving the altered state of consciousness required to cause the responses between the spheres of the brain, such as hypnosis or the use of drugs, but meditation gives us absolute control over what is happening and so we learn a greater degree of personal responsibility and potential through its use.

Each sphere of the brain has a different language by which it communicates to the rest of the body and indeed to the outside world. The left, analytical, logical brain communicates in words and by dissecting and destructing what it is given in order to arrive at an understanding of the material. This is the basis of humanistic philosophy, that the human brain is capable of understanding all by mental learning alone. This function is used by all of us to some degree, whether we are philosopher or not. In the course of our everyday lives we each rely on 'mundane' tasks such as consulting a timetable, reading a newspaper and exchanging gossip. Every piece of information presented to us in this fashion is analysed and filed by the left brain, for use when it is deemed appropriate by the deeper levels of the mind where it is stored.

The right, intuitive side of the brain has as its language more abstract images and symbols and it is to this that we must now turn for an exploration of the part of the mind that is all too often ignored and ridiculed in our logical, divided world.

Symbols however, do play a massive part in the world around us, occupied by the apparently logical businessmen and politicians that have so much influence over us. Partly because of the advent of the global multi national business and the inherent language problems this creates, we are finding that we must resort to symbols for our communication. The English language, despite being the most used in the world, is limited to those who can understand its complexities. Now that technology has enabled us to communicate across the world to peoples speaking with a different alphabet, we need to find ways to communicate without language. The happy truth here is that such systems have been used for thousands of years in cultures across the globe, albeit independently. The most obvious example of this is Egyptian hieroglyphics.

That such corporate giants understand the role symbols play is demonstrated for us in the use of company logos, used in a most powerful way via advertising. The subconscious mind, a deeper level of the brain than the everyday, conscious one, notices and remembers everything it comes across. This means that everything you are told, everything you read, hear and see is retained in the mind. This may sound incredible, but not so when we realise that it is thought that in all our lives the majority of us use only approximately one third of our mind and brain power.

When such exposure to a piece of information is repeated and then in symbolic form, the subconscious effectively becomes flooded with the same information, which it logically accepts as important. When we see the same adverts on television, billboards, newspapers and so, we come to recognise a product with a particular company and it becomes almost an instinctive urge to respond, prompted by our subconscious mind telling us it is important to do so. Advertising can become little short of brain washing unless we are strict with ourselves and find a means to control what is allowed into the subconscious.

We will return to the subconscious and other levels of the mind in due course, but for now we will look at symbols a little more. We have seen how a symbol can work its way into the very fabric of our minds and selves and lodge itself there, feeding and prompting our desires and often finances too. But symbols can also play a vital educational role in our quest for learning and personal growth and as such form an important part in addressing the needs of the mind through understanding its function and so developing its use, potential and power.

One of the prime ways in which the mind understands and processes these symbols is through our dreams. Our dreams provide us with an excellent means of accessing that which is in our subconscious. This is a level or layer of the mind that is deeper or more buried than our usual, everyday logical and conscious mind. As such some link it with the right brain activity we have examined previously.

It is known that the human mind has the capacity to retain all that it encounters. If this suggestion seems incredulous to you, I would remind you that we use only one third of our minds power in the course of our lives, so the remaining two thirds have a potential far greater than we at present realise. It is not far fetched to suggest that those two thirds can consist of information that is a record of all that we have experienced and encountered since birth. Such is the subconscious.

This information must be processed and ordered and a point of understanding reached in order to achieve this. To be able to understand or integrate the information it has received in the course of any one day, the subconscious must communicate the information to the conscious. However, it cannot do this while the conscious is engaged in everyday activity, for the conscious has the limitation of being able to concentrate on only one piece of information at a time (try listening properly to both a conversation and piece of music at the same time!). The subconscious must therefore wait until the conscious stops thinking and functioning. This usually occurs only when we are asleep or deep in meditation.

In meditation we are able to slow and eventually stop the chatter of conscious thought and so access what lies beneath and process and learn from it. However, except for the most advanced of practitioners. this blissful state is rare. Usually when we do still the mind for even a moment, it fights back and the release is lost. So the subconscious must resort to other, more devious means to communicate what it knows. Devious it may be, but its sole intention is to assist the complete being to grow, learn, develop and expand and so we should and must not fear what our subconscious may know and tell us about ourselves. We cannot escape from it after all, for it is within us.

Its deviousness comes in lying in wait until it is presented with a suitable opportunity to let go with its information. This is usually at the end of the day in which it has received the information. Such are dreams.

The means by which the subconscious gives its information is in symbols. Words and numbers are logical (or at least should be!) and as such are the province of the conscious, logical mind. The deeper levels of our mind cannot relate to this information as they work on a more abstract means of communication. By processing all the information, together with the emotional responses it observes as a reaction to that information, it comes up with a suitable symbol to represent a particular feeling, thought or piece of information.

These symbols are arrived at over the period of time one has been alive and occasionally from previous lives. As such our dream symbols are individual, rather than universal in their meaning. Whilst it is true that certain symbols at a more surface level may have collective application and meaning, at the deeper, therapeutic and developmental level with which we are concerned, the subconscious symbols become an individual and personal method by which we can learn of our deepest emotions, fears, blockages. In this way we can use our dreams to remove such pitfalls on our path to integrated wholeness and freedom from pain.

This really means that the ubiquitous dream dictionaries are useful for only the most surface of applications, or at best as a starting point for adapting what they give us to our personal response. The best interpretation of our dreams comes from our own analysis of them. This requires that we be objective and honest without fault, which is not easy to achieve.

To begin an interpretation of a dream, look at what the content of a particular dream says to you. Ask yourself how you feel about what you dream and where and how you have encountered such a symbol before in your life. Perhaps try through meditation to glean further meaning, by re-entering the scenario of a particular dream and letting the images well up before you once more. This allows for a better contact with conscious understanding, since you bring information up to this level as you return with it from your meditation. You might also utilise the services of a trusted friend who knows you well enough to be completely honest in their view of what the symbols may mean - for you.

If having followed the above methods you are unable to interpret a particular and apparently significant dream for yourself, you might consider the services of a qualified dream therapist, or perhaps a hypnotist, or one experienced in working with guided imagery. The role here should not be to give you a cold interpretation of what your dream means, but to assist and guide you in working the dream through at a practical level, so that the meaning is made clear as well as allowing you the opportunity to put into practice its message in your self and your life, or at least to begin that process.

We should not take the view that we are at the mercy of whatever our subconscious has in store for us however, though this can certainly be appropriate some of the time. The point here is that we are able to programme our dreams and learn to work consciously with them. This is done by much the same means as that described for programming ourselves

124

to wake up at a given time. By focussing on our area of need or that which do not understand or sense a blockage with, just prior to sleeping, we can then relax and know that the subconscious mind will respond to our conscious request. Prior to sleep we are tired and both body and mind are relaxed. This allows us to form something of the bridge between the two spheres of the brain and so our conscious thoughts, when focussed for a short time, are easily received and dealt with by the subconscious. This activity also helps us to learn to exercise a greater degree of control over our mind and its needs.

If you find problems in remembering your dreams, firstly see if you can do without the alarm clock, as this is a sure fire way of destroying the natural method of waking and in the shattering instant that the alarm goes off, you are catapulted back from wherever you are in your dream to conscious, outer reality. This is a shock to the physical and mental system and is truly a rude awakening. It is no surprise that your dreams are lost, for you are, to all intents and purposes, in shock for a while on waking.

The human system does include an in built clock that will allow you to set your own alarm. This may take a little while to get used to and to trust, but once you have become familiar with your body's way of working, you can throw the alarm clock away. Whilst in the transition phase, you might like to have the insurance of setting the alarm for a little while after your programmed time of waking by natural means, to avoid getting a reprimand at work!

All that is required to set your own body clock is to tell yourself when you NEED to wake. It is the energy of your emotional need that will trigger the responses in the mind at the appropriate time. You could repeat the time of waking over and over a few times to yourself as you first lie down and shut your eyes or you might like to picture a clock in your minds' eye. Then have enough trust to forget it and drift off to sleep. The result is that you wake slowly, the deeper mind letting its hold go gradually and so enabling the retention of much more information in the conscious mind, making the interpretation and understanding of your dream easier too.

The old advice of having pen and paper beside the bed is endorsed too, for whilst you may think in your slumbering and pondering state of 'wakeful sleep' that you will remember your dream when you are 'up', you will not, particularly in as much detail. The sooner it is written down and recorded, for later dissection, the better. This will also enable you to be much more objective, which is a necessity in dream interpretation.

As such when we listen and learn from our dreams, we are able to integrate the deeper learning and understanding of our sub conscious mind to our everyday existence and so shape a little more for ourselves the reality of our beings and who we are. In this we become a little more whole and a little more complete.

The mind is also able to use symbols and symbolism in general in far more ways than this. Chief among these are the various systems of divination, such as Tarot, Numerology and the like. However the popular use of such oracles has been largely for the purpose of future prediction. Here we must make a distinction between this accepted use and that of the deeper and therapeutic application of what is really a method of consulting the Divine, as the very word 'divination' implies.

That we have such psychic abilities is beyond doubt, especially when we consider again that we are only making use of a minor part of our brain's capacity. Psychic ability is not a special gift, available only to a privileged few. Rather it can be seen as a natural part and function of our mind, since we are born this way. It is said that small children have a much more open intuitive and psychic sense, that is only closed off, in most children, when they begin to be educated and logical. Twelve or so years of this way of thinking is enough for most people to lose the use of their psychic muscles, but in some, for whatever reason it seems and manages to stay open and working. These people are the so-called 'natural psychics', as indeed we all are.

Divination systems make use of abstract symbols to switch the mind's functions over from the logical to the intuitive, or from the left to the right brain. This is done by the same way that we relate to symbols in our dreams. If we take arguably the most popular and wide spread of divination systems, the Tarot, as an example, we can see how it can be used as an individual tool for therapy, over and above future prediction, thereby restoring something of its undeniable sacred nature.

Most interpretations of individual Tarot cards rely on accepted universal application of a symbol, which as previously mentioned, only tells us half the story. If we then apply and investigate a clients reaction and view of the collection of symbols that is any one Tarot card, utilising counselling skills in a consultation, we can enter a therapeutic and developmental realm into the traditional Tarot reading. This takes their meaning much deeper than the 'tall dark stranger' type of reading to an individually tailored guidance for the now, rather than the hope of what might be.

Such deep methods can then form essential guidance to the person wanting to discover their sacred nature and develop and evolve themselves to the best of their ability, which are much more in keeping with our aims here.

This can also apply to the other divination systems such as Runes, Numerology and even the much ridiculed crystal ball and tea leaf style of reading. Symbolism, being an individual thing, has the ability to be part of our personal sacred life, if we regard and approach it as a sacred tool, given to us from antiquity for this use. A knock-on or side-effect of such use also enables us to regain the intuitive and psychic faculty which can be such a vital and eminently practical means of simple, direct guidance and knowledge as we live our daily lives.

A linked area here is that of scrying, whereby we are able to form a deep link with the natural world. The aforementioned crystal ball is one such method of scrying, but is a relatively modern invention. Prior to its introduction, a simple bowl or pool of water was utilised, to provide the apparently empty surface in which the vision and mind is cast, to allow images and symbols to merge.

With a relaxation or meditation technique that allows for the necessary switch in brain wave patterns that takes us across the hemispheres from the left to right brain, we are able to open our minds to perceive such abstract information and with practice, experience and skill, apply this to ourselves or our clients if in a consultation. Again it is the individual, therapeutic approach that counts.

There are many methods of 'natural scrying' that we can utilise, which we can see simply by looking around us. We can watch the flames or dying embers of a fire to peer into with a relaxed but steady gaze to see symbols and images, as we can look up at the waving patterns of the branches and leaves of a tree, or at the clouds and the patterns they make in the sky. Perhaps with the addition of a prior request to be shown that which we need at that time, we have direct communication with the kingdom of Nature that instils a deep respect and honour for the natural world. A more simple and sacred form of interaction with our planet we could not hope for. It is making perfect use of the natural, sacred ability of our minds and can save us a fortune in fees!

The whole field of 'extra sensory perception' as it is known has been much criticised and undervalued in recent times but we can now see something of its deeper use that demands respect. With the establishment of therapeutic uses by qualified and skilled practitioners we can now hope for a return to the acknowledgement of the sacred nature of divination and psychism, not as a freakish method of predicting the future but as part of our natural ability. If you wish to avail yourself of your ability in this manner it is necessary to seek out a good and respected course in the discipline of your choosing and commit yourself to serious study for some time, a minimum of one year's study really being required before you begin to consider using your abilities for others. Such study should also include a good deal of work on the self. Here we are able to apply the old and very true maxim that when the pupil is ready, the teacher will appear.

Through the therapeutic use of divination systems and psychic ability we can go a long way to addressing the deeper needs of the mind and learning a great deal about ourselves in the process. Many people have trouble applying spirituality to an intelligent and active mind, since the 'proof' that the mind naturally looks for (the conscious mind being a somewhat insecure creature) does not exist at the conscious level. Rather we need faith and trust in what we are experiencing, especially in the early days of its use, but an experienced practitioner of symbolism, in whatever form, will tell you that you know you are right, because you know. Rather than trying to attempt to persuade or convince any other of psychism or divination, I can only exhort you to convince yourself by whatever experience you choose, for this is the only way you will truly come to accept it.

In todays world we are presented with a great deal of information, from a wide range of multi media applications. We must be careful in all these technological advances that we do not lose sight of the power that exists in our imagination, to form and shape our own realities. This was largely done in the past by the use of storytelling, much truth being encoded in the mythological and folk stories that have been handed down verbally for centuries in cultures the world over.

It is a well known truth that all myths have their origin in fact, but the reality may in fact be more than that. Telling and re-telling the myths of the land one lived in for centuries formed the basis of ones education. In certain cultures, such as that of our inherent native spirituality through the Druids, such story tellers were highly regarded and sometimes feared, for their stories were recognised as having power and effect in their performance.

This gives us a clue to the use that we can still put our own stories to today. The Bard of old would undergo strenuous training in order to memorise a vast store of poems and stories derived in origin form myths that have been in their turn shaped down the years by countless re-tellings, each one subject a little to the interpretation and imagination of its teller. The story, like the myth, is alive and in this lies its power. That it is alive tells us that it is imbued with vital essence, that same life force that interpenetrates so much of our lives. When we expand and increase our awareness of all aspects of our lives to account for the existence of this essence or energy, we can learn so much, regain a vast amount of our power and establish control over ourselves and our lives.

Following the tried and tested principle that 'energy follows thought' it is easy to see how, with continual use over hundreds or thousands of years, a story derived from a myth becomes a powerhouse of stored energy, ready and waiting to be tapped into by any with the focus, concentration and imagination to explore its meaning. Each time a Druid would teach the Bard a particular story, the energy from their focus and concentration on it, flows out into the 'ethers' and gives it a little more power, depth and meaning. There it lies, sapping up more energy each time it is accessed and told, just like a computer programme.

This analogy also tells us that stories do indeed move with the times. As humanity evolves through its generations, each learns to adapt to the changing, growing and evolving world it finds itself in. As each generation of Bards learns the stories it is given, it become necessary to adapt it to the current time. This is not done by changing the setting of the story, for the power lying there is more subtle than that. Rather it is achieved by opening one's deeper subconscious to the story, by meditation and trance, and letting what is stored there come out through the individual telling of a story. Such is a Bard's power and so it was that if the Bard choose to ridicule you in their story, so was your fate sealed. As such Bards were deeply respected and paid for their trouble and 'entertainment'.

This may seem a long way from the parent sitting on their child's bed making up a story about princesses and dragons, but they still tap into the same root. This type of story telling serves so many valuable functions and surely is preferable to dumping the child before the television to soak up its output, seen and unseen.

The conjuring of a story encourages and develops the imagination, at the subconscious level, of both teller and listener. It also helps to train the mind at the conscious level for concentration, but in a relaxed, unforced way. A deep and intimate bond can be developed between parent and child this way and if the parent or teller is clever, a child's troubles can be weaved into the story and solutions shown, that encourage the child's self responsibility and power. Done last thing before sleep, it also enables the mind to be relaxed and open, thereby enriching the dream life, in which we have seen the therapeutic power.

It is not only parent to adult scenarios in which stories can be used however, for groups of adults have traditionally gathered around the fire for telling and learning in the dark half of the year, between Samhain and Beltane (November to April). The bonds spoken of above can be quick to form, for each is also traditionally expected to contribute in some way or pay a forfeit deemed suitable by the others in the group. Perhaps you might consider forming a group that meets each time at the Full or New Moon for an evening's storytelling, nominating a story teller each time, the rest bringing food and drink. Perhaps softened by a jug of mead or some such who knows what wonders can be dredged from the depths of your subconscious, gently brought up to the light where the monsters turn out to be heroes and the frogs turn into princes! Truly our myths and fantasy heroes are still alive and well, breathing their essence into us for our edification and evolution each time we open the pages of their stories in our minds.

This brings us to the power of the word, both written and spoken. The use of affirmations has now become widespread in the 'New Age' community, but is often mistaken for 'positive thinking' In truth affirmations have been around for a long time, in various forms, and their power and effect goes much deeper than the power of positive thinking sought by forcing the conscious mind into focus. Such concentration loses much of its power and therefore effect by the use of force and persuasion. If instead we are able to relax into the deeper sub and unconscious levels, we find there the real force of the mind.

The conscious level comes into play in the repetition and recitation of a pre determined statement that hones our intent down to one or a few sentences. In this the deeper levels of the mind are able to communicate with a focussed intent that forces nothing but subtly blends and adapts our reality in accordance with our statement. If you are thinking that this sounds like magic, then you are quite right, for this is exactly what it is and we see the use of affirmations in the traditional village witch or cunning man and more modern ritualistic magician.

The traditional but much maligned spell uses as its focus an affirmation, or statement of fact that pulls the power of the emotional intent and mind's concentration, out and into the higher levels of unseen energy that exist all about us. This is why witches and magicians are often portrayed as pointing a (usually gnarled and wrinkled) finger as the direction in which their power travels. This helps to focus the conscious mind to a specific point that the words will follow. From here the spell is recited and the words, invisibly (to most of us) float out, cloaked with power. They settle and reside in the world of energy and slowly take shape and form into solid, tangible reality and the spell woks. The inner concentration and focussed intent are all important and the words express these inner forces.

It is important that the spell or affirmation is seen as a positive statement of fact, as if the intent has already happened. Otherwise we slip into trying to persuade and force and the Universe cannot be forced, for its nature is that of love, which is patient, gentle and kind. Here we must also make mention of the responsibility of using spells and affirmations, that should not encroach on another's free will, for again, this is not in the nature of love or the Universe and so goes against the grain and cannot work. The principle that applies instead here is that which you put out into the Universe, returns to you, multiplied three fold (in accordance with the nature of creation).

To construct your own affirmation, it is necessary to first be sure of what you wish to achieve. Let us say that you wish to become more accepting of what life gives to you, rather than reacting from a point of view of anger or resentment. Now you must put this into an objective perspective, detaching your self from any emotional consideration you might have.

The next step is to put this objective truth into a statement that reflects your intent in the present tense, as though that state is already a part of your reality. Thus, with our chosen example, we might arrive at something like "I

131

openly trust what the Universe gives me. I accept the working of grace in my life with humility, love and honesty".

The use of this affirmation now follows. The mind as a creature of habit needs continually reminding of something before it accepts it inwardly at the deeper level where its power resides. It is to this level that we must get with our affirmation. It is therefore good to write the affirmation down and display it where you look frequently - a mirror, fridge door, bathroom cabinet etc. This has the effect of the conscious mind being reminded often of the statement and so it slowly and almost surreptitiously creeps down to the subconscious, where little by little the conscious trusts it and so programmes your whole being in the light of this now factual information.

It is also very beneficial to repeat your affirmation to yourself when in a relaxed frame of mind or in meditation. Here the real power can be unleashed, for as we have seen, the relaxed focus of the mind accesses all its levels and when in meditation we form a link between the levels, as we now know. The slow, deliberate and preferably daily use of an affirmation is a powerful way to achieve its statement and intent, without strain or exhausting yourself in the process. I would recommend repeating the affirmation three times in meditation, as three is the number of the force of creativity.

Through this chapter, much mention has been made of the levels of the mind and we have seen in some detail the nature and working of the conscious and subconscious layers. What remains unexplored to us at this time is the still deeper unconscious, where that which we choose to try and ignore, pretend does not exist and truly fear resides. This dark place must, with gentleness and love, be infused with the light of creation and be nurtured into providing us with its deep and powerful lessons.

The subconscious in its receiving sense very often acts as a filter between the conscious and unconscious. It notices all things and then chooses where to file it. If it is deemed too threatening or horrible to recall, it pushes such information to the unconscious, the bottom drawer of the mind. Here the monsters lurk, dormant but affecting us still, for try as it might the mind cannot throw away the key to that bottom drawer.

Over the years we can however become convinced of certain facts as we see them programmed by our unconscious, and so we have seemingly in built

132

fears, irrational prejudices and opinions, that have their origin in the subconscious giving unpleasant information to the unconscious.

Do not fall into the trap of thinking that the contents of your unconscious must be avoided because it is all unpleasant however. If it is in there, it must one day come out and since the nature of the Universe is love and expansion, this cannot be denied forever. However harsh and hard your present life may have been and however cynical and cold your resultant view, the Universe and all within it is love and one day must unite in that love. If you have cut yourself off from this constant and never ending flow of love, it is your choice, for we have the free will to do so. There is always love available to you, but you must find it for yourself, for this is the way we evolve.

With compassion, grace and a little help from our friends, the coldest, walled heart can become soft and yielding and so does the unconscious offer up its secrets and release its dragons and monsters. When set free this way, we see that which we feared and cowered from so is not so bad, and before us the frog is transformed into the prince, for such is the analogy.

Of course such work is not easy and needs to take time and it is here that the trained therapist has a role to play, in whatever form you choose. The field of counselling is important here, but its fees are sadly beyond many of us. Do not underestimate the value of what you receive from a counsellor however, for its value is estimated in the charge with deliberate intent. I would also like to mention here that the physical therapies can also be of great help in helping to release the secrets of the unconscious. The body also absorbs all that it experiences and comes into touch with and over time our joints become stiff as we lose trust and our organs become clogged with fear. Do consider aromatherapy massage, yoga. shiatsu and all the other bodywork treatments and methods to help you in your quest for freedom and the sacred. You are sacred; body, mind and soul.

The subject of meditation can answer a great many of the needs of the mind and is here mentioned only very briefly for it is a big subject that I have previously written about extensively (see 'Practical Meditation', Published by Capall Bann, 1996). Suffice to say that meditation allows for that subtle but so powerful relaxed control over the mind that switches us from the automated robotic thinking we can so easily fall into in the modern world and allows us to capture our innate and natural sense of freedom. Through meditation we can process the workings of the mind and preserve its open and fluid nature avoiding the pitfalls and blockages outlined above. Meditation can go a long way, with practice and perseverance, to uniting body, mind and soul and so arriving at the full knowledge and awareness of our own sacredness.

The needs of the mind are then many and varied, as are the needs of all our aspects. The scientific and industrial age has seen a revolution in the thinking and functioning of the human mind and this is still undergoing massive transformation, with the advent of the computer age. In all the benefits this has brought us, we must ensure that we do not lose touch with the power and ability of our minds as naturally intuitive and instinctive creatures, able to travel between worlds and talk to each other without opening our mouths, and able to visit places and see things without opening our eyes. Time travel, telepathy and untold mental bliss are all natural and achievable if we allow our minds their full scope and power.

Perhaps the first step on this seemingly impossible journey is to focus on identifying our intuition and becoming familiar with its workings. This is perhaps best done by blending the feelings and emotions of the heart, with the logic and thoughts of the mind. Intuition can be seen as a mixture of the head and the heart, of thought and emotion. As such we take ourselves up a level and into what is known as the 'thinking, feeling mind'.

The coming Aquarian Age has as one of its principles intuition, received teaching telling us that this will be of paramount importance to our communication and understanding. It is interesting to note that the symbol for Aquarius is two pitchers of water. The view here is that one is full of water, one of air. When they are both tipped and poured, we arrive at the blend of the symbol for feeling and the symbol for thinking - the thinking, feeling mind.

Let your intuition, your inner tuition and teaching, that which you know without having to be told, guide and direct you through your life and you will recapture your control and sacred nature of the mind and take yourself into the next age of humanity.

Exercise 1 - The Protection Breath

This exercise is for use as protection against the invisible but nonetheless harmful pollutants that it is hard to avoid in our modern artificial air environment. It uses the breath coupled with the power of the mind through visualisation for its power and is easily learnt and performed in a matter of minutes.

First find as quiet a place as possible to sit for a few minutes and make yourself comfortable. Relax your mind and body by taking a few deep breaths, focussing on the breath coming from the stomach or abdomen rather than the chest. To help with this, place your hands lightly on this area of your body.

When you feel relaxed in mind and body close your eyes and continue with a deep breath, ensuring that you maintain your sense of calm. Now add to your inhalation a visualisation of a strong golden flow of colour and energy that pervades every part of your body. Draw this into you on your in breath and circulate it round your body on the out breath. Try to feel the strength and power of the golden force and feel the resistant flow through all parts of your body and being.

Continue this process for as long as feels necessary, until you feel refreshed and revitalised. This technique will strengthen your lungs and the golden energy will fortify your system with its protective qualities and you can continue your day with this added knowledge and power.

Exercise 2 - Life Force Breathing

This technique comes from the Yoga practice known as Pranayama and so will be familiar to Yoga practitioners. 'Prana' is the yogic term for the life force, with the remainder of the word meaning to master, so here we are mastering the breath as the focus of life force. It is important to be clear here that this force and breath is viewed as life itself and so this exercise should be performed with an attitude of reverence and humility, for you are controlling and focussing the very essence of life.

Sit comfortably without crossing your legs and become relaxed. Perhaps take a few deep breaths in the manner described for Exercise 1 and when you feel calm and composed, begin. It is good here to read the section in this Chapter on the twin channels of male and female energy that enters our body through the nostrils as this is the focus for this technique.

Place your thumb on your right nostril (the male energy channel) and inhale as fully as possible without straining, through your left nostril. Any noise created by this breathing is irrelevant. If you are able to without inducing any sense of strain or tension in the stomach or chest, hold the breath for just a few seconds and then release your thumb and instead place your ring finger to close the left nostril (the female energy channel). Now breathe out through the right nostril and exhale your lungs fully. Hold the breath out for a moment and then inhale through the right nostril. Hold once more, change fingers and exhale. Inhale again and so on.

The exact number of breaths does not matter in itself for this purpose, but I suggest a cycle of scvcn full breaths (inhaling and exhaling through each nostril seven times), so that you can imagine and feel that you are energising each of the seven main chakra energy centres of your body. Try as you breathe to feel the flow of life force circulating to each chakra in turn, starting with the base and working upwards to the crown.

It is then nice to pause when you have completed your breathing to say a few words of thanks for the life force you have received and continue to receive freely and abundantly, whether silently or aloud, in whatever way suits you. This exercise will reenergise you if you are feeling tired or lethargic and will clear and calm your head. Try to aim for an even and equal breath through each nostril and on inhalation and exhalation.

Exercise 3 - The Head or the Heart Questionnaire

The purpose of these questions is to identify if you respond first in life in general with your feelings or your thoughts. Neither one is preferable to the other, they are just different, so there are no right or wrong answers. They are purely for observation purposes and do rely on your honesty and truth for their effectiveness.

Sit quietly and calmly and have pen and paper ready to record your answers. Try to neither think or feel as you answer the questions, but let your instincts flow form a deeper level inside you, onto the paper.

1. You are standing on the kerb, waiting to cross the road. It is busy and you are late for where you are going. A gap in the traffic opens where you might run across the road. Do you run or wait for a longer gap?

2. You are given a large bunch of keys and asked to unlock a door, but you do not know which key is correct. Do you start at one end of the bunch and work your way through or trust to luck and try them at random?

3. Which colour do you prefer, red or yellow?

4. You are playing in a sports competition and your team is losing, to what is obviously a better team. When, at the end you lose, do you get angry and apportion blame to whatever factor or accept defeat and see what you can learn?

5. You have been studying hard for a year to sit an exam, which you take and do to the best of your ability. While waiting for the results do you worry about it or do you put this aside and get on with life in the meantime?

6. While listening to music, of any kind, do you listen to individual instruments and marvel at the expertise (or otherwise!) of the playing or sit back and let the effect of the whole piece take you away?

7. Do you prefer team games or games of individual achievement?

8. You see that one of your house plants looks neglected and you think it might be dying. Do you throw it away or water it, put it in a better position and try to nurture it back to life?

9. Do you have photographs of the people you live with (or your immediate family if you live alone) on display in your home?

10. Do the needs of the many outweigh the needs of the one?

Obviously these questions are only intended to illustrate if you are a head or a heart person and need to be taken in context and applying common sense to your situation, without taking them to extremes.

By using the answers given below, see if you have more head or heart answers, and so this is the kind of person, in general, that you are. Whichever is the lesser, try to be more aware of the other in your decision making and through your day generally. If you have five of each, congratulations, you are an intuitive person, letting your deeper thinking, feeling mind guide you!

1   - Run = Heart, Wait = Head

2   - Start at one end = Head, Random = Heart

3   - Red = Heart, Yellow = Head

4   - Apportion blame = Heart, Acceptance = Head

5   - Worrying = Heart, Put aside = Head

6   - Individual instruments = Head, Whole piece = Heart

7   - Team games = Heart, Individual achievement = Head

8   - Throw it away = Head, Nurture it = Heart

9   - Yes = Heart, No = Head

10   - Yes = Head, No = Heart

Exercise 4 - Opening Chakras Meditation

Begin with grounding and Connecting (see Exercise 1, Chapter 1) and become centered and calm. Now focus your attention on whichever chakra you are intending to open and breathe life into. Begin to count each time you breathe in and count comfortably, without straining for a count of four. Do the same for your out breath and let this fourfold rhythm establish itself.

Now imagine a closed flower at the chakra you are working with and each time that you breathe in, without changing your rhythm, imagine that the petals unfold, one by one, with each breath you take. When the flower is fully open, continue with your rhythmic breathing and let a flow of golden energy move into that area and chakra, until you sense that it has become charged and alive. Let this feeling and awareness wash over your whole body and being and when you feel ready, let your rhythm relax and spend a little time in peace, feeling the benefit of this energy flow through you.

When you feel ready to finish, spend a few moments grounding yourself once more and bring your breath and awareness back to their usual level. Open your eyes and stretch ensuring that you feel balanced before you stand up. Do not be tempted to rush around if you feel particularly strong as you will soon undo the good you have done with this exercise. Instead continue in a calm and balanced way.

Chapter 6

The Needs of the Spirit

In one sense, we can see the needs of the Spirit as those that we have already explored, which when addressed and heeded give us a healthy, open and balanced body, emotions and mind respectively. We can see that these three areas interlock and integrate to form a healthy Spirit. So we have the image of the three 'human' levels as we shall call them, at a lower level than that of the result of their combination, the Spirit level, if you will forgive the poor pun!

We must then come to realise that the needs of the Spirit, as a result of blending the lower level, must be addressed and heeded throughout life as well. This allows us to maximise the opportunities the attention paid to the three human levels of our being affords us and enables us to progress from the human to the Spirit level, and beyond. Since the human levels combine to produce a higher result through their combination, we can also assume that the full freedom and outworking of the Spirit aspect to our beings results in a further evolution, to hitherto unknown and unexplored levels. It is perhaps to this level that we need to address ourselves, individually and collectively, in the coming Aquarian Age.

Before we can achieve these lofty heights, the expression of which will result in a more harmonious existence for all humanity on Earth and so a clear and unhindered practical spirituality, we must turn our attention to the immediate and pressing needs of the Spirit.

It should be made clear that the human levels spoken of should not be seen in a lower, meaning lesser level, or to assume from my use of this word that they are not worthy of the spiritual person or need not be viewed as having spiritual significance. It is vital that our individual conditions, as shown through the body, emotions and mind are addressed as the first and ongoing steps on the spiritual path through life. Only then can we achieve true integration and freedom for ourselves. To miss or ignore any one of these, is to be only part of a person and never truly whole and complete. You are body, emotions, mind and then Spirit.

The Element of Fire is likened to the Spirit, as the internal aspect of the human being. As such we will first explore this inner side, before putting it into context of the above, higher Spirit level, or layer, as they can be better and more accurately seen.

As the inner side to the human being, Fire describes it very well and tells us much about our nature. Like Fire, we can be consumed by the heat and intensity of ourselves if we let ourselves rage indiscriminately, never paying attention to the demands our inner drive and ambition gives us. The plight of the workaholic is all too common in today's competitive, achieving world, trapping all too easily those that seek to climb the corporate or financial ladder, under the illusion that this will give them contentment, security or status and power. True power of course, as well as the contentment we really need, comes from within, where the will to continue and further ourselves in terms of character and understanding, must be carefully tended and fed, like the safe and purposeful fire.

As such, we become protected, as by a fire, from the danger of those that would steal away our power and energy, for the competitive outward manner we see so much of also exists on the unseen energy dimensions of existence. Psychic vampirism is very common, but this dramatic sounding term simply shows us that if we are unprotected and let ourselves be used and abused, there are always people ready to suck away our energy, absorbing it for their own ego or power fulfilment.

This should not be taken as meaning that we need to close ourselves off and hide our inner beings, trusting that in this protective tower we are safe and secure. The Tarot shows us that if we seek to hide in the Tower, the external forces of life, be they fate, destiny and chance, are bound to send it crumbling to oblivion about our ears, pushing us on, a little older and a bit more wise than before. Perhaps the best form of defence is an openness, a softness of heart that gives us empathy and understanding of our fellow beings and their circumstances. We cannot judge another, for to do so is to assume much, but we can come alongside another to share their pain, glory, sorrow and joy. As such we become stronger than ever, the sharing of such inner, fiery energy leaping like flames from one to the other, creating a unified, altogether bigger and stronger fire that expresses something of the higher layer of Spirit already.

Consider the nature of Fire for yourself then and examine what you are presented with by your understanding of its character and nature. Do you see fire as a threatening, wild thing that given the chance will devour and put to death all it encounters? Perhaps you see fire as a warm, secure and life saving and giving thing that offers some light and safety in the darkest of cold nights, able to shed its power into the shivering bones of the wet, downcast and dejected. See Exercise 1 for this Chapter to do this.

It is an interesting thought to reflect that the above two extremes certainly exist in our world, in the hearts of many people, each lacking the balanced energy that, utilised properly, fire can offer. Fire is within our nature and therefore must be recognised, tamed and tapped into to utilise its enormous power and energy for the further expansion and evolution of our beings and for the integration of our holistic selves.

Your reaction and content of the notes you could make regarding fire and its nature can tell you much about yourself and your inner needs of this aspect. If you have a tendency to look upon the destructive aspects of fire as being paramount to its nature, this may tell you that you have tendencies in some situations and circumstances to be destructive, to yourself and those around you. Equally, if you tend to see fire as the safe and protective creature, this may suggest that sometimes you are apt to hide away from the truth and do not confront life and come to be in control and charge of what it gives you.

The key to integrating the inner Fire of ourselves and so our direction, inspiration, ambition and will is of course a balanced and measured view. Fire can be both the destructive and positive force that we require and can utilise as the situation demands. As such if we look within, we can realise first the truth of our inner nature and come to make friends with it, rather than leaving it like a wild beast in a cage, ever threatening and pacing from end to end in boredom, frustration and aggression.

Sooner or later the beast must be set free, be it lion, tiger, or of course, wolf. When this is achieved, we take possession of our selves, of the beast within, the fire inside, We have then at our behest a source of enormous strength, that we know now can no longer destroy us or gobble us up in its work.

142

Rather it can be something we can apply as the need arises, turning us into the spiritual warrior, the fighting monk of old, the "wise and savage old man".

If we do not have such a proud and noble existence then we stand at all times to lose our power. This can creep up on us and take us unawares. When we come to see life as the sacred thing it is, we consequently take a more precious view of our inner power and the energy that underpins our selves and the quality of our existence.

We can lose power as energy chiefly by being uncontrolled. This may occur in a moment's unimpeccability, but do not take this to mean that you must be a harsh judge to yourself, rather that you need to focus yourself on what you are doing in that moment implicitly. Do only one thing at a time and focus on this only and do what you do to the utmost of your ability and will. This applies as much to making a cup of tea as to running a marathon.

In this way you maintain an optimum level of power, consistently drawing a supply to yourself, since you become open, letting a through flow of life force move in and out of you. You move and exist like the waves of the ocean, free and natural, expressing what you believe is in accordance with your life. In this, you rise above anger, despair or out of place love.

The unchecked expression of the three mentioned areas, as well as many more can be a drain on our reserves and power. A moment's anger truly takes more power away from you than a good physical workout. The key here, as mentioned before, is to regard life and its constituent energy as sacred and to treat it as such, enabling you to tap directly into a limitless supply.

This direct access to inner power is a big challenge, that the human potential movement and the likes of Walt Whitman, Robert Bly and books such as 'Iron John' and 'Women who Run With the Wolves' have done much to assist. With the tapping of this inner resource, we can take the quantum leap into the higher levels of our potential and existence. Here we must look upon ourselves as sacred, full of power and energy, indeed as the beings of energy and interchangeable matter that we truly are. Only then can we seek to free ourselves of all that constrains and limits us, turning instead into the creatures that we were intended to be. Here we must now address the needs of the Spirit.

The Sacred Birth Ceremony

In this we can see much of the outworking of the inner nature of our beings, as shown in our lives. We can come to see ourselves, as body, emotion and mind, as the outer reflection of the inner energy, will and consciousness, as expressed and symbolised by Fire. We need to work on and increase our awareness of ourselves as beings of energy, will and consciousness. Please see Exercise 2 for one way in which you can achieve this. The more we realise and exist in the knowledge that what we are physically and what we experience in our daily life is but a reflection and direct result of the focus, power and force of our energy and will, the more free and complete we become.

We are told that we are never given more than we can cope with, though it may feel that way at times. Always there is help available, even in our darkest, most despairing moments. We are never so alone in the Universe that we cut ourselves off from a force of love, or simply the energy of life.

What we must realise here is that it is left to us, as creatures of freewill, to make the decision to ask for the help. If we ask, it is given, unquestioningly and unconditionally. But if we choose to turn our backs on life and others and/or the world, ultimately we must accept responsibility for it. As such, the knowledge that we possess the power to achieve great things must be nurtured and cherished, as must the power itself. The chief expression of this power is through our will, energy and consciousness. It is left to each individual to make the effort and dig deep into their beings when they are faced with circumstances, feelings or thoughts that may appear to be overwhelming. The force and power of the human will is one of the greatest miracles of life.

It is in this working that we achieve much of the deeper sacred nature of existence and life. As such we can trace the journey of the sacred life, bringing the needs of the spirit to the fore in various rites of passage.

Such rites of passage have come to take a sad and pale place in our current society. Today we have only the all too often inconsequential Christening and marriage ceremonies and the tired funerals to mark our passage through life. In former times, the stages of life were marked in flamboyant and celebratory, sacred rites, ceremonies and rituals that provided a focus for the recipient at the particular event in that stage of their life. If we turn to see their inner, sacred nature we can learn much from them that is still relevant and practical in today's world.

Our life begins with a slap and a cry - not a very glorious way to enter life. A few months later, many babies are christened, almost because it is the done thing and the meaning becomes lost to all but a few. This is often because all that appears available seems to offer little in the way of personalised and relevant ceremony and celebration.

Recently however, books have become available supporting the individual's right to celebrate and mark life in ways of their own, giving guidance on the construction of their own rites of passage. I would recommend readers to William Blooms book *Sacred Times* (Findhorn Press 1990). This approach is to be much encouraged, for in it we can recapture that which was lost - the sacred celebration of life thereby being the most direct form of practical spirituality we can find.

The construction of individual ceremony is no less spiritually powerful than that conducted in a church. Many consider their 'church' to be the Mother Earth, the creator and taker of life and it is to her we bow our heads in respect, gratitude and awe. Consider then, taking your child and holding them up to offer thanks and request a blessing of the Mother upon their life. Give thanks for their life blood and the energy that flows in it. Declare their chosen name loudly and proudly, as a reflection of their character and offer it to the four winds, the four directions and Elements. Herein lies power, old as the hills and capable of great feats, as is your child.

Construct for yourself a ceremony that includes the words you want. Express how you feel at the birth of your little one and what your chosen name for them expresses, for in names there is power too. Hence we arrive at the classically portrayed names of the American Indians, Grey Wolf and the like. In such names are the expressions and characteristics of the owners. Should you choose a name that reflects the child, bear in mind the practicalities of this, perhaps reserving this for use between the family or when you are alone, or for special use, in further ceremonies and rites of passage. Such an 'inner name' serves to hold its power more effectively, given the sacred regard suggested.

Beginning education can be a scary time for any child and marks an important stage in their integration into life. We are here presented with another opportunity for a rite or ceremony, that can serve to show the child they are loved and respected for who they are. Such a ceremony can also instil confidence and a sense of achievement in the child.

146

Again, at the end of education, at whatever age this occurs, an important and significant stage is reached, which requires more than the trip to the pub, though this can be something of an initiation in itself. This may be part of your chosen ceremony certainly, but also take care to include a sacred time of reflection and contemplation, a time to reflect on what has been achieved and where the future direction lies.

The next stage of life is often marriage, where the energy of one's life is shared fully with another. Such a wondrous thing as love surely deserves some recognition, perhaps more meaningful to the participants than the muttered but not understood vows of the standard church ceremony. Consider the full expression of the depth of your feelings before your family and friends, towards your chosen partner. This may make some recoil with embarrassment, but for those that like the idea, it can be a glorious, beautiful and liberating experience to take part in. Perhaps exchange a token, ring or otherwise, to symbolise your union and joining and make your pledges, with intent to stand by them as sacred vows. Receive the blessing and perhaps gifts of your supporters with pleasure and grace, for in them there is love, the greatest power open to us.

The end of the working life also marks a stage of liberation, when we become free from the need to continue the sacrifice and giveaway, in order to continue gathering. Now we can be more free to pursue our dreams and develop our wisdom and experience, to be passed on to those that may come to us and to prepare at length for death. Use this time to see opportunities and chances and reflect on what you have achieved so far and what you would still like to achieve. Make promises to yourself in your ceremony and set out to fulfil them. Make your life a continual expression of your accumulated learning so far and celebrate this in your rite of passage. View it not as retirement, but as release.

Death is a subject much misunderstood in our society, yet slowly we are coming not to fear the supposed icy hands of the Grim Reaper. Death, as inevitable as the dawn, is our only certainty in life, which is as it should be. Now our consciousness is slowly beginning to turn to the sombre funeral ceremony and adapt it to one of a celebration of the individuals life and all they stood for. If through your adaptation of the sacred life, in whatever manner, you find a healthy and vibrant spirit within your skin and bones, you will also find the knowledge that death is not the end and that life endures all. With this knowledge comes an indescribable peace that cannot be explained, only experienced. Fear of death, uncertainty and worry about it, then disappears.

Of course there is a place for grief, which needs to be expressed fully. But there is also a place for fond remembrance, and of the happiness and the person's progression through life, as they move on to their next stage. Wish them well and celebrate their power, energy and life, however 'active' they may have been. Thank the Mother Earth and Father Sky for their qualities and energy and tell them of your feelings, as you perform what can easily be a quiet and private ceremony as much as a noisy and public one.

We can of course prepare ourselves for own death, internally and externally. The internal preparation is a matter for personal preference, but it can help our transition and passage a great deal if we are willing to relinquish our fight to hold onto life, when we are really going against the grain of our energy flow. This is to embrace the fullness of life, at the proper time, not to acquiesce to it.

Externally, we can leave specific instructions for our belongings and perhaps our death ceremony. You may like to write a piece to be read at such a ceremony, or ask for particular music to be played, poetry to be read etc. For some suggestions for this, see Exercise 3.

As far as practical suggestions for your rites of passage go, this is largely to be decided by the participants and their preferences. You might consider the location, perhaps your local sacred site outside, or your own garden, or atop the nearest hill. You can choose the dress you like and feel befits the occasion. You can of course choose who is present and the words to be recited. You may like to open ceremonies with a prayer or affirmation to your chosen god or goddess.

As the ceremony progresses you may pause for silent meditation or thought, the exchange of gifts or symbolic objects, the recitation of prepared pieces of poetry, prose or statements. You might include some shared sacred, specifically prepared food or drink and then close with another prayer, of blessing and thanks. You may then choose to celebrate outwardly in the more traditional 'partying' form, but do not forget the sacred nature of the reason for the party, no matter how drunk you might get!

There are occasions and times in our lives when we may feel the need to focus ourselves and our direction in and through life. Such time may also require a rite or ceremony to be performed, to dedicate yourself anew to your quest or to show and mark that you have reached a certain stage upon it and are moving to the next. This is more in accordance with the initiations of old, where the initiate is led through the stages of the order to which they belong, each one being a point of transition, an achievement and recognition of knowledge and power, studied for and achieved through diligent effort.

These initiations are open only to those who belong to such groups, as should be the case. For those outside of these inner working groups, it may be that a privately constructed and individually performed ceremony or time is more powerful. For direction with this, we can once more turn to the Native Americans, from whom we could have learned so much about practical spirituality had we not been so fearful and slaughtered the majority of them.

Many Native American tribes had the custom and practice of the Vision Quest, in which the person concerned took themselves off, for a specific period of time and often to a specific place, to seek and cry for a vision. Such a vision was often achieved only after many offerings were given, of sweat, tears and blood. One's whole being was offered with dedication to the gods and Great Spirit. With fasting, chanting and drumming, the vision may have been given. This granted sure and certain knowledge, which the future of a whole tribe may have been awaiting and depending on.

Today, there are few with the will to perform such a feat, but we can at least find a day, perhaps to coincide with the New or Full Moon, or perhaps a special birthday, where we can spend some time alone, in the wilderness (where you are never alone!) to seek our future, our knowledge and our truth. There you can make your dedication, speak your own sacred words, maybe dance to your own inner rhythm and set yourself free. This can be extended to form what can become an aptly named Retreat, both from the outer world and the outer self.

These Retreats, for contemplation, rest and spiritual focussing and work are becoming more and more popular, as the move to live simply gains momentum. The Retreat can become a time of re-establishing one's vital connection with the natural world and of realising who one truly is, within the mad swirl all about you. An annual retreat, rather than a 'two weeks in

149

the sun' holiday will be of considerably more benefit to all. The Retreat can then be seen as an alternative to the Vision Quest, not necessarily any less powerful or meaningful, for in quiet, peace and withdrawal can great and profound truth be realised and obtained.

This Vision Quest should be a significant time in your life, whose precise nature is never repeated, for it is unique to the moment, time and circumstances in which it is performed. It therefore needs to be treated as a sacred time for you, in which you encounter the very depths of your being and the essence of who and what you are. A Vision Quest can act as a time of adjustment to a new phase in your life, whether physically or otherwise. It is a time of examination and sometimes hard decision.

It is deliberately taken in the wilderness to give you an objective viewpoint and also to place the focus of your entire being on what you are doing. The actual ceremony may be only a small part of your overall Vision Quest, wherein you put the essence of what you have learnt into ceremonial form. By this you receive your guidance and receive your vision. Receive it with grace and thanks, for this deep and direct interaction with beings of a higher order of life is sacred and calls for your response as such.

This brings us to the oft thorny subject of guidance and guides themselves. We can see the need for guidance in the sacred life, but it can be difficult to trust our own intuition, meditation images and the like. It is all too easy for us to place wishful thinking in the place of true guidance or received teaching and strategy, the demands of being in a group or known as a spiritual person can put a pressure on us to always know what our guides are telling us, or for the ego to flatter itself by giving a wondrous piece of 'channeling' in the meditation group. Human nature is such that it puts a pressure on us to perform when required.

If you are diligent and disciplined in the true nature of your meditation however and request humbly and sincerely, you will be safe in your intuitions. True spiritual teaching is always practical, does not go against the principles of respect for life and always adheres to love. It does not flatter, attempt to persuade, blame, judge or destroy; it simply is. Be on your guard against such words that do not conform to the above for they come not from the higher levels to which you aspire. Rather they originate from your own mind, imagination or what has become known as the astral plane, wherein dwell the focus of our small, human ego.

True guidance will offer help to the whole, not the benefit of one individual. It is empowering and inspiring, not challenging. It holds no conflict, but grace and love. This is the voice of the still, small one within; it is a whisper not a shout and in this way can make itself heard above the noisiest din. These principles may help you to discern what is positive and what is not among the myriad voices of guides we hear today.

The majority of guides that we hear about in the plethora of New Age groups and teachings are those of the American Indian, Chinese sage and ethereal nun. This is often met with understandable ridicule, for there seem to be an awful lot of them about. However, when we consider that the human source of these guides are usually the most spiritually accomplished and evolved of people, it seems more reasonable that they would progress to become guides. Ancient wisdom teaches us that when we have evolved to no longer require the necessity of physical, earth bound existence, we have the choice of taking up a role as a guide, or guardian.

As such we become responsible for our chosen human 'subject', requiring our guidance to ensure that we encounter such circumstances, situations and people in our lives that will afford us the opportunity to teach us what we have chosen and need to learn in our current lifetime. The actual learning of such things is a matter for us and us alone. A guide cannot interfere with our freewill, this being perhaps its main purpose. A guide in this sense is rather like the 'Prime Directive' from *Star Trek*, if you will forgive another illustration from the 24th Century! Here, the 'Prime Directive' dictates that intervention in another race's situation such that it would not have been possible to acquire by natural means is forbidden and so it is with our guides.

There are different levels or orders of guides, in which we can include what have become known as Guardian Angels, Angels and Archangels. Each has a succeeding role in this spiritual hierarchy, each having risen through the ranks according to its evolution. Much New Age teaching tells us that at the present time in the evolution of humanity, we have a unique opportunity to evolve both individually and as a race. It is up to each and every one of us to do what we can to play our part in this evolution. Just as the best way of helping another truly is to help ourselves, so the best and most effective way we can assist the advancement of the human race is to focus on our own beings and attempt with all our will to develop and grow as best we are able.

With this hierarchy comes the different levels of existence in which guides move and have their being. As such, each successive level has a faster and lighter form and speed of vibration of the particles that constitute its existence. As such, those who have outgrown the need for earthly life such as we know it, have no need for a physical body. Instead they have become beings of energy, that is interchangeable with matter. It is this that allows them to take on the form in which they appear to us.

This assumed form may be one that the guide knows will appeal to us, since we are told they have access to our innermost and deepest thoughts and knowledge, which we are often ignorant of ourselves at the conscious level. Therefore, the fanciful images quoted above become again more acceptable.

It is often said that there are an awful lot of American Indians/Chinese sages/ethereal nuns about for the numbers that were known to exist physically, but this may be because that particular race, or the others that appear as guides, have appealed to something deeper than the romantic 'Hollywood' style image of the Indian we have become used to recently. Perhaps it is that these spiritually based, sacred cultures have reached an identity in which those whose guides are from that culture, appeals to them, offering them the chance to recognise their own sacredness and to outline a life style more in keeping with their deepest, tribal longings.

The point should also be made at this stage that it is equally possible that a guide be a small child or a person with whom we have no tangible connection or romantic appeal. It may be that we have a connection to such a guide from a previous lifetime that we consciously know nothing about as yet. The guide that comes to us, when we have approached with sincerity and humility, we must accept.

If you find you have a sense of disappointment or disillusion having met your guide, you are really insulting someone who has chosen to help you. Apologise and become humble, for they have chosen you, not you them.

In time and with repeated meditation or ritual exercises, you can learn to have a close connection with your guide and they will become an intimate and prized friend and companion as your life undertakes its sacred quest. Your guide can show you the way to learning far beyond what you imagine you might achieve in your present circumstances and with your present knowledge. This is true of all of us, no matter what our academic level or professional standing. There is simply no discrimination that exists at this higher level.

Many guides have lived physical lives prior to taking up their teaching role in life. As such, they have the capacity to understand and empathise with the human condition and the sense of separation from the Source or Divine that leaves us with the in built and instinctive longing we all have, whether recognised or not. It is this longing that allows us to create and appreciate great art, in whatever form, since true art conveys something of the sacred and connects us more closely and consciously with the bittersweet sense of longing and pain we feel.

This is also why so many of the great artists lead lives of great suffering, for such despair and pain fuels the longing and gives rise to the most profound and moving forces the human spirit is capable of, expressed in the individual's particular medium, whether music, words, pictures or movement. This is another reason why we should strive to increase the arts in our society and recognise the value of the Bard, musician, artist and dancer as, at best, an expression of the sacred. Such art gives each of us, who experiences it, the opportunity to come a little closer to and to touch consciously, our own sacred nature and person.

From their 'higher' vantage point, guides can acknowledge our pain, reassure us and love us unconditionally, for they have none of the human traits of jealousy, possessiveness or insecurity that plague and limit us. They exist in a medium that is not limited by the gross physicality that we must adapt ourselves to.

Guides can be of real value to us in this sense, offering us companionship, understanding and wisdom, of both this Otherworld and our own. An exercise to enable you to begin the process of meeting your Guide is to be found at the end of this Chapter.As mentioned many guides have been physical people just as you or I, but we should not fall into the trap of assuming that just because they are a guide, they are all knowing creatures of infinite wisdom. In truth, they are dead people. When we die, we die with the hang ups, hates, prejudices and so on that we have when we are alive. It is true that we can acquire knowledge and awareness of other dimensions when we die and that this can assist both the guide and their subject, but we should also maintain discernment in our dealing with guides and what they tell us.

When you receive communication with your guide, check it against your personal ethical code and consider if the information you receive is practical and of use to you. You do not have to follow advice given in this manner and there is no recrimination if you do not. Your guide loves you as indisputable fact and reality, irrespective of what you do. Whilst we should not abuse or dismiss all they say, nor should we blindly accept everything if we do not want to.

There is a great deal we do not yet know, but hopefully will discover, as we develop the techniques and practices available to us, about guides and the Universe we all inhabit. We have at our disposal a vast store of knowledge and information accrued over thousands of years of human existence and exploration. We would be foolish to dismiss out of hand the abilities and practises of our ancestors, simply because they lived in a different age. Many cultures across the world have demonstrated much that is of great use in our modern society.

Chief among these is the oldest science of all, astrology. The origins of astrology as we know it are thought to have come from the Chaldean race, several thousand years before the birth of Christ. Surely information that has survived so long has something to offer and teach us, the more so because of its antiquity. It is well known that many of the greatest figures and thinkers of our history embraced astrology, including Confucius, Aristotle, Shakespeare, Alexander the Great, Francis Bacon, Caesar, Napoleon, Pythagoras, Hippocrates, Isaac Newton, Galileo, Goethe and Carl Jung. An impressive list and one that cannot be dismissed.

Astrology teaches us a great deal about where we live and who we are. From a universal standpoint we can see that the solar system we live in consists of different planets, each having a different level and speed of vibration of the particles of their own particular matter. As such, those vibrations spread out through the Universe, each affecting the other. We live on a 'small, blue/green planet' nestled in that system, with its own distinctive rate of vibration, that serves us by creating and sustaining life. From here we absorb, as do all the other planets orbiting the same Sun, the energy influences of those planets.

Astrologers have for those thousands of years interpreted those influences in a personal manner, enabling us each to understand our place, not just on the Earth, but in the Universe. The subject of astrology is a huge one that it would be foolish even to attempt to explain here (not that I have the necessary expertise!) and there are countless authors better than I who have already done so. For the dedicated Seeker living a sacred life, it is perhaps a necessity at some point to seek out the services of a qualified and affiliated professional astrologer to explain and explore the mysteries of who you are, by the construction of your birth chart.

This chart, a map of the Universe at the exact moment of your birth, will tell you a great deal about the lessons you have decided to learn by living your life in the time and place you find yourself. You can also, with the aid of the expert, plot the movement of the planets to see how they will affect you at specific points in time, to ascertain the direction you will be gently directed towards (and away from) by the Universe.

The more we view astrology in this light, the more we can see that the Universe, like our Earth, is a living being, like some kind of master computer, that does not dictate or compel, but guides and teaches, precisely by allowing us our freedom.

The nature of the human I believe, is to explore, discover, grow and learn. This 'pointless optimist' view may go against the evidence of history, but we must have belief both in ourselves and our brothers and sisters that form the rest of humanity, perhaps even if we are to survive our present environmental problems. By allowing us the freedom to pollute and ravage her resources, the Earth has made something of the supreme sacrifice and showed us that we must learn to harmonise with Nature if we wish to survive. What she also shows us and what we are perhaps at last beginning to learn is that if we give her the chance she will also provide for all of us through her materials. What we need to learn here is that our technology must blend with the power already in existence in nature. This power has the ability to destroy us if we threaten its existence but if allowed will demonstrate an awesome ability to provide for millions upon millions of people. If we can harness our own increasingly awesome technology to utilise that natural power in non-harmful ways, we can make achievements that will enable us to learn more than we can imagine.

Astrology also shows us an aspect of the sacred passage through life for each and every person alive, by giving us an annual reminder of who and why we are, that is often ignored now in favour of a few hours of hedonism.

Our birthday allows us the chance to recapture that same energy that existed at the moment of our birth. On our birthday we can take some time to reflect on what this is, how it feels and how we are harnessing the power of the Universe that seeks to guide and help us. If we perform a meditation to explore our innermost selves we can connect at this time with the very essence and core of our being in a unique way. If we open ourselves, through meditation or ritual, on each birthday, to the incoming energy of the Universe, it will have special meaning and power for us each successive year.

Our birthday is then a sacred time during which we experience a pull and movement forward in our individual evolution. If we remind ourselves here that by helping ourselves we are helping humanity as a whole, we can come to see our birthdays as a chance to push not only our own evolution forward a little each year, but by so doing we are helping the 'plan' if you will, to unfold a little more in keeping with the original intention.

If we also realise that we are still discovering the existence of planets in our Universe by the use of our technology, we come to see in truth how little we truly know of where we live. With the advent of the Aquarian Age however, we are told that we are being given opportunities to make great advancements in knowledge and make important discoveries. As our awareness expands, so does our technology and knowledge. Through these, it may be that knowledge of other planets will come, that will have a great bearing on our development and evolution. It is but a short step to make the assumption that one such planet will inhabit some form of (extra-terrestrial) life that we can establish contact with. It may be that such contact will only come when we are able to take the responsibility as a race, that it would bring.

With the damage being done to our atmosphere currently it is unlikely that another species would seek us out as a good contact to make, unless through pity. The sooner we can learn to accept responsibility for our own planet and its workings, the sooner we are likely to make contact with those from other planets. The quantum shifts that are taking us into the Aquarian Age may make this possible and I hope I am here to see it! In the meantime, we can best achieve this contact by looking each to ourselves individually and to the planet that gives of herself to allow us to live. It is to this wondrous and awesome being that we must now turn our attention.

156

Exercise 1 - Recognising Your Fire

Re-read the section in this Chapter concerning Fire so that it is fresh in your mind. Put aside some time when you will not be disturbed and when you are able to focus on yourself. It is good before this Exercise, as with all the Exercises in this book, to perform the Grounding and Connecting meditation, so that you are in touch with your inner being. This is necessary so that what you conjure up through this technique will be real for you, and not just the product of the flippancy of your imagination.

Now take a sheet of paper and in it draw fire. This is the only instruction you are given for this part of the exercise. Simply let whatever image comes to mind come on to the paper, or let the first thing you think of be drawn. Do this now, before reading any further.

The type or kind of fire that you draw will be indicative of how you perceive fire. If you have drawn something being destroyed by fire, it is perhaps telling you that you have a need to embrace your inner spirit more closely or that you are fearful in some way of what the spiritual life might entail for you. This itself is a subject for further exploration and meditation.

If you have drawn fire in a warming or protective form, it may be that you are connected with that inner spirit and have some recognition of what it is for you. If it seems a somewhat extreme form of protection, such that it precludes others, it may that yours is a solitary spirit or that your spirituality separates you in some way from others.

The interpretation of what you draw or depict in any form is best done by yourself. You might ask those who know you extremely well their opinion of what it says about you, but you are your own best judge. Look at your drawing in a symbolic manner and see it as an expression of your inner spirit. Be honest in your interpretation.

The second part of this exercise is to take your drawing and meditate with it. Go into meditation and then bring your image to mind. Focus on it and see it clearly. Hold the image and see how you feel. Be open and let your feelings rise to the surface. See what you make of those feelings and see if anything spontaneous happens to your fire. Try to form and establish a link with the sacred spirit within you and that IS you, with the fire you see and have drawn.

Now realise that you can change that fire. Feed it with whatever materials come to mind and adapt it so that the fire is a more pleasing form to you, if that is necessary. You can then use this fire as a focus for the condition and nature of your inner spirit at regular intervals, to see how it has changed, if there are different colours visible within it, if the flames need fanning and so on.

Exercise 2 - Self Recognition

This exercise utilises the practice of affirmations, which were explained in the previous Chapter. It may be useful to read this section again before you begin to use the type of affirmation suggested here.

The object of this exercise is that we increase our awareness and knowledge of ourselves as beings not only of physical body, emotions and thoughts, but of the energy and power that underlies those outer forces. Since our perceptions and indeed our reality changes daily, we need to instigate the use of such an affirmation on a daily basis too. For the serious Seeker of the sacred, it becomes a necessity at some stage to contact the inner sacred spirit on a daily basis, whether through meditation, ritual, martial art exercise or other form. This affirmation is ideally suited to be included with what should by now by a daily practice for you.

It is obviously best if you arrive at your own specific affirmation that best describes what you are in terms of power and energy to you, using words that appeal and are comfortable for you. The affirmation given below is therefore a suggestion only, but may be used as it is given if you feel it pleases you. The affirmation need not be recited aloud, but requires only a specific focus and concentration whilst it is said.

The affirmation I use is as follows:

> *I dedicate my life to the power within and without me.*
> *I am a being of pure energy, consciousness and will.*
> *I am eternal, immortal and infinite.*
> *So let it be.*

This short wording allows for easy memorising and for focussing. It encapsulates a great deal for me and the more it is used, the more it is effective. Once recited it is put aside for the remainder of the day, for the power used during its recitation is dispersed into the ethers to do its work. Its daily use at very least serves as a reminder of what and who I am, which is of infinite value in today's rushed, hectic and noisy world.

Exercise 3 - Facing Death

The subject of death brings with it much fear and this exercise will require a good deal of courage if you are fearful of your own, inevitable decline!

The objective here is to ensure that you express what you wish at a ceremony designed to mark the end of your life. Since this is a unique thing to each individual to each person I have merely listed below some suggestions for you to work on that might help you to end your life with responsibility, sacredness and not a little style.

Make a will. In today's world this is the only sure way to carry out your wishes after you have gone. Include in it all that you wish to do or have done for you, including everything listed below.

Write a letter to each important person in your life that you have anything to say to - be honest, it's your only chance!

Write a list of your favourite pieces of music/poetry/pieces of prose/quotes that you would like to be read aloud at your funeral or death ceremony.

Make a list of all your possessions and decide who you would like to give what and include any relevant explanation as to why you are giving it to them.

Consider how you would like your body to be disposed of and where and appoint someone whom you trust to carry out your instructions.

Review your life and what you have achieved. Look at your successes and failures, pleasures and disappointments. Have no regrets for we are all compelled by our own nature to progress within the constraints of what is, but all too often we do not stop to take account for them. This serves to tie up any loose ends within that might restrict you.

Prepare a statement to be read aloud at your death ceremony detailing absolutely anything you like.

There are doubtless other actions you will think of for yourself to prepare and carry out prior to your death, but this list may get you started. It is good to construct these things at any age, for your life may be over when you least expect it to be. Should you prepare this at age 30 and live to 90, then you have an excellent means of taking stock of your life and the way that you change and what you achieve, by using this as an annual review as you go.

Exercise 4 - Meeting Your Guide

This exercise takes the form of a guided meditation journey, that will usually require many repetitions before success is achieved. It is also to be found, with more relevant information, in my previous book *'Practical Meditation'* (Capall Bann, 1995) and is reproduced here with kind permission from me!

Begin by Grounding and Connecting in the usual manner and then take your focus to your Third Eye chakra and opening this by imagining the petals of a flower unfolding. This aligns your awareness with the optimum energy flow for the higher perception necessary. Spend a little time in this, ensuring that you are in the best position possible for meeting your guide.

Begin now to visualise a place that will act as a Sanctuary for you. This may be any place, real or imagined, that you would choose for a Sanctuary (More information, and a journey to find and establish one is also in the same book mentioned above).

Acclimatise yourself to your Sanctuary and take time to explore the reaction of all of your senses as guides may communicate by any one or more of them.

Now find a comfortable place to sit in your Sanctuary and await your guide. When you feel ready, always progressing in your own time, mentally request that your guide come to you in a clear image. Do this in your own way, using words that you do usually, being simple, direct, clear and polite.

Look now into the distance and you will see a glowing light, small at first but growing larger as it draws closer to you. Remain as you are, patiently watching this growing light come to you. As you wait the light grows until it is before you. See it shimmering, perhaps one colour, perhaps many. Allow the light to hover where it is.

Soon you will find that your guide will appear to you. They may step clearly out of the light, or the light may dissolve to reveal them standing there. It is at this point that you must pause and allow events to unfold. Your guide may be able to communicate in some form straight away, it may not. Accept whatever happens as correct for they know best

You may of course speak to your guide, possibly hearing responses in your head, as if you hear a delicate whisper just inside your ear. You may for a time only see them, or even a part of them. There is, in most cases, a distinct knowing that accompanies the guide, that tells you that this is precisely what they are. It may be that all you receive for now is a light touch on the face or a stroke of your hair. This may be all that is possible to begin, but this will increase and progress to a full, moving image and communication in subsequent visits.

When you have spent as long as you wish letting communication take place, it becomes time for you to leave and your guide to depart. Give them your thanks in a simple and sincere way. Always do this, even if you think nothing at all has happened, since it is impolite not to do so and guides do not take kindly to this - give them the recognition they deserve. Whilst they are never malicious, they have 'put themselves out' (literally!) on your behalf and your thanks is extremely little to give in return.

You may then see the light surround them once more and they will leave in the same manner in which they arrived. The light will drift from you until it is but a speck and then disappears completely. It may be that you will sense that your guide will wait for you to depart. Whichever applies, you must leave now, but know that you can return when you wish to communicate with your guide, when you have need.

Let the image of your Sanctuary fade from you gently and slowly and return your focus to your breath and your body and where you are. Bring your breath back to its usual level and ground your energy to ensure you are fully back and present in everyday reality. This also ensures that you bring with you what you have experienced. When you are ready open your eyes and make some brief notes regarding your experiences.

Chapter 7

The Needs of the Earth

We have looked within ourselves and identified the needs we have at each level of our beings and turned in all directions to orientate ourselves through life. We have also looked up to the everlasting Sacred Spirit that exists within all things and indeed, within ourselves. We must now look down, to identify and learn to love the planet upon which we live and which supports and nurtures every life upon it. We must learn how to live in harmony with this planet and discover how we are each and all a part of Her and She is part of us. This can best be done by following the pattern we have established previously and now by examining the needs of the Earth and in so doing recognising what we need to do to bring about the state of peace that is living in harmony with all things.

For this, our objective can best be achieved by looking to the numerous indigenous tribal cultures that throughout history have spread themselves across the surface of the Earth. These cultures knew and cherished, in each individual, the necessity and secrets of living in harmony with the earth, often coaxing life out of the most barren land. Patience, trust and honour were chief among their values, not only to each other, but to and with the Earth.

Whilst we cannot hope to return to a way of life that our ancestors knew in this sense, we can re-learn what has been forgotten and bring forth the wisdom they knew, the wisdom that the Earth controls all, has power over life and death and as such must be honoured, loved and respected. Then may She look favourably upon her guardians and bless them with sunshine and rain, each in their turn, thus granting a plentiful harvest and food for the beasts.

The Sacred Mother

Knowledge that the beasts and birds are also a part of that creation was instinctive and understood amongst these fabled peoples. Respect for them was therefore a natural part of their daily life. This did not mean that they were never eaten or slaughtered however. Rather that the animal was honoured for its sacrifice, was humanely and swiftly killed and nothing wasted. The skin was used for clothing and material, the meat for food and some of the organs for making bags, rattles and other objects. Tribal peoples knew and indeed still know, that life, all life, is sacred, something that is essential for us to recapture in the very deepest places of our hearts and minds if we are to live the spiritual life. So how can we set about relearning the wisdom of the ancients, when they are for the most part no longer here to teach us, having been wiped out in many parts of the Earth, by the spread of 'civilisation'.

If the Earth needs and wishes to care for and love us as her guardians and custodians then She must teach us how to do it. This is what the ancients knew and with patience, commitment and determination sat and listened, to the Earth and to their hearts. Also, by observation they learned what the Earth was telling them, through the patterns of the clouds, actions of birds and beasts, the changes of the Seasons, cycles of growth and decay and entering into deep and sacred communication with unseen beings all around them, in the trees, in the waters, in the air and beneath the ground. These beings of course still exist, though must be approached again with still more patience and understanding and not a little humility, for they may well have become angry or defensive, having seen what we have done to their beautiful Mother.

So we must sit, take time to smell the flowers, lay our bodies on the ground and feel the pulse of the Mother surging and pumping through our very essence. We must, each of us, contact the Mother directly, by coming to her workers, the nature spirits, elementals and devas or whatever name may be given to them in any tradition. These beings are that which exist beyond the scale of human existence. Just as do guides above us, so do the nature spirits around and below us. Each exists in perfect communion with the Mother Earth and so must eventually approach her.

Taking something of a leap now, we are reminded here that modern science has purported the theory of the Earth as a sentient being, alive of herself and with consciousness and awareness. This again, was known and understood by our ancestors, but we are learning it anew and in so doing

The Chakras of the Earth

1. CROWN – TIBET, MOUNT KAILAS
2. HEART – ENGLAND, AQUAREAN TOHANG
3. THROAT – JAPAN, MOUNT FUJI
4. SACRAL – BALI, GUNUNG AGUNG
5. SOLAR PLEXUS – AUSTRALIA, AYERS ROCK
6. SACRAL – AMERICA, MOUNT SHASTA
7. BASE – PERU, LAKE TITICACA

casting a bright ray of hope to each sunrise, for with this awareness comes respect and a healthy fear of Her power from that respect. It is this that will give rise to the connection we each must find with the Earth and her beings.

As with all matters of the spirit, they are most practical in their essence and so it is here. It is helpful for you to read these words and for me to write them, but without action they are empty and dead. Action is required to breathe life into the mental knowledge the words give you. Each must make their own connection with the Earth and feel Her pulse within themselves. See Exercise 1 for a suggestion as to how you might do this for yourself.

There is such a vast amount that the Earth can teach and give to us that I can only hope to mention but a few things that I have gleaned, to encourage you in your own discoveries and purpose. There are thankfully, many books available now that turn their attentions to the specifics of such techniques, but again all these require action on your part if they are to be of real use.

Chief among these is the inner acceptance and recognition that the Earth is alive. James Lovelock has explained the science behind what has become known as the 'Gaia' hypothesis, but to turn that hypothesis into practical reality, we must listen for Her heartbeat. If you attempt the grounding and connecting meditation, preferably outside and in a non-polluted, natural place, you may well, if you are still and patient enough, feel this heartbeat, a deep and vibrant pulsing that seems to connect with your own. Here you touch your basic instinct, your bestial urges and wild drives. Your senses become alive and you know within yourself that you are part of all that is around you. This truth changes you within and you instinctively recognise your sacred nature, just as is the bird singing near you, the leaves that rustle, the animals that run and hide and the rain that soaks you while you sit.

Gaia is a benevolent, maternal being, but like all Mothers, she has her limits. It would seem from the 'natural disasters' as we ignorantly choose to call them, that are happening across the world, that we have reached those limits by our actions over the last two hundred years or so. Since the industrial revolution we have polluted our Mother's body and she is choking and spluttering for air. However, we have polluted this too and infected her life blood in the waters of her body with all manner of poisons. Like every body, the Earth is doing what it must to reject that poison and to purify herself again. Hers is not revenge or anger, it is survival. Yet still, as we continue to pollute and attack her body she provides for us as best she is able. What wondrous love there is in this, surely that demands not just our respect and love in return, but the very essence of what and who we are.

To this you may be called at some time on our sacred quest and we are reminded of the Sundance ceremony we learned of in Chapter 1, involving the giving of the self in this way. What are you truly able to give up of what and who you are, for your Mother the Earth?

Prior to that inglorious industrial revolution life was able to be lived much closer to the natural order of life, where the turning of the wheel of the year dictated what happened. With machinery that carved and cut the land and left destruction, not growth, in its wake, we shifted our perspective to one of domination and control, instead of blending and harmony. Now we are seeing again that being at one with nature is not some hippy, unreal ideal but a practical necessity for the survival for the vast numbers of people that machinery and technology has allowed to be created.

Again a reminder should be given that this does not mean we remove the technology, for that is futile, but that we learn to blend it with the natural power around us. We cannot hope to ever fully dominate and control nature. It would take but two generations for nature to recover a city without maintainence and you have only to look at the cracks in any pavement of wall to see nature bursting forth against the most incredible odds. Her character and whole being is to grow and expand and so must we, with Her.

Even if you live in the most grey and soulless of cities, no matter what the acid rain content or level of humidity created by what that city is doing, glorious natural creation is all around you. We have lately begun to create artificial environments now for recreation and holiday and when we get there we find nature - running streams and flowering plants. We can never dominate nature, for this is not in the scheme of things, it is not how and why they were made and this cannot be changed.

So we are left with the conclusion that Nature or Gaia if you wish, is in charge. We must therefore bow to this power, acknowledge and respect it and learn from it. This can be done by a variety of ways and through various means, some of which we will now explore.

We have already seen how we can contact the Earth herself, taking us directly to the source as it were. There are however, many other forces and beings that can lead us to the Mother's breast to suckle and be nurtured. Perhaps chief among these is the identity that you can establish with where you are, the spirit of the place you are in. Such a powerful connection can be made with a specific place and through this relationship you can come to meet the Mother in a full and profound encounter.

It is perhaps obvious to assume that the place to do this is in the centre of your nearest stone circle, burial chamber or other ancient, sacred site. These places do indeed provide a special kind of atmosphere or energy about them, that certainly helps to establish communication with the deity you are aiming for, but they are by no means the only places where you can do this.

These ancient sites can act as focal points for power, almost like chakras upon the surface of the Earth and as such maps have been produced to show these particular 'power points' on the body of the Earth.

Study of the map may well reveal some significant information for you, perhaps showing a link between the places you have visited or feel drawn to, without really knowing why. It seems that certain, more sensitive, people are drawn instinctively to be at a certain place at a certain time, without ever consciously knowing the true purpose. Something draws them there and that is all that is needed to 'know'.

If we are able to respond to such an instinct, as it seems we are, then it seems logical to assume that when we are in that place, we can and should deepen that instinct to something more tangible. It is known that places such as Stonehenge did act as theatres for ritual and ceremony and so it is that we are now seeing echoes of that distant past enacted once more in modern day Druid celebrations, weddings and birth ceremonies. By this practise those involved are able to contact the Guardian spirits of the place they worship in, as well as the Lord and Lady of Nature themselves, in whatever form they deem fit.

However, do not assume that such worship and communication is reserved only for those be-robed Druids and witches you see on your television each Summer Solstice. Far from it, for the very people may be your neighbours, for they are all quite sane and rational people living lives of the daily grind like all of us struggle to do. The difference of course is that for these noble folk there is a sacred centre to themselves and their lives that finds its outer reflection in the sacred sites and the land and sky itself.

If you feel yourself wanting to be able to visit the sacred sites of our Isles, or those all over the world, then it may be that you are feeling the first stirrings of your Pagan heart, finding its own rhythm amongst the discordant barrage of sound that daily echoes about our ears. Be still and listen within, to the still, small sound within the ear and you may hear the whisper of a place or even a deity calling you to a particular place.

Do not however, expect a vision of a lady clothed in samite and jewels to reach out her hand and beckon you. For the most part these things happen subtly and quietly and you may be drawn somewhere completely unexpected. Follow your instinct and intuition and you will not go wrong. I have before found myself quite alone, wet and cold, walking along the side of a road at some obscure hour of night, outwardly aimless and insane, but inwardly quite joyful and blissful at the communication I was experiencing with the Goddess.

An excellent aim is to find and then establish such a sacred centre near your home, or where you visit regularly. This can be any natural place, whether in your garden or elsewhere. It may be the top of a local hill, beside a tree in the nearest woods or just an area in your local park. If you visit often and take time to sit and relax there, in time declaring your intentions, whilst in meditation, to the local spirit or Guardian of the place, you can establish a contact that can be as powerful and profound as that in any ancient site.

This can be developed over time in many ways. You can set yourself the task of looking after your power spot, tidying any litter, planting flowers there, feeding any birds or wildlife and caring for it on the unseen energy level too, by offering healing, sitting in meditation beneath a tree and simply allowing a focussed flow of life-force through you and to the place, using yourself as a conductor to amplify and increase what the place is receiving. Soon you will find that you care deeply about this particular place, it can become a retreat for reflection, meditation and peace, it can be a place for you to resolve problems and commune and learn from nature.

Remember whilst forming your connection that the beings there, whether the spirit of a particular tree, the spirit of that particular place or the God or Goddess themselves, that just as you receive in energy, knowledge and love from them, so should you give. This, as said, can be at the energy level, but it is so helpful to both involved, if you also care for it in an outer, practical way too.

Wild places, or natural spots, generally will have a Guardian spirit and it is good to acknowledge these beings, whenever you visit any such place, even if just visiting to walk the dog. Silently, you can tell the Guardian why you are there and what you will do whilst there. This may be just walking the dog, but the Guardians we come across now are often protective over their places, because of harm being done to so many.

When you leave, remember to thank the Guardian too. This can be done by the same form of silent communication between you and can be in words of your own, whatever you feel moved to say. It may be you find that a simple bow of the head as you leave is what you feel appropriate or perhaps some other ritual gesture, such as bending forward and opening your arms, or holding them aloft and intoning a brief chant.

Be mindful too, of the details around and in your power spot. Consider which Elements are present in any form. Is there a presence of water in any way? Consider what types of wildlife may visit or live there and why. Get to know their habitats and take care not to alarm them. It may be even that you are able to establish a link with a power animal for yourself through your link with your power spot.

Look at the kinds of plants, identify them and learn what they need to flourish and do what you can to provide it. When left alone, plants will find the best spot then can to flourish and they grow where they do for a good reason. Learn, through direct inner communication or from books, the topography of the place and be aware of the kind of soil and rock that lies there. Examine stones and perhaps find a little something you can remove, to maintain the link with you at all times. If granted permission for this, give thanks and make some form of sacrifice from yourself, plant food, water or if all else fails, a hair from your head.

Find out what trees are there or near and again the reasons why. Discover what these trees need and try to provide it. Here powerful links can be made for trees can teach us a great deal about ourselves and our lives if we are patient to learn. The different types of tree can teach us different things as each tree has different qualities that it represents and is able to give off.

Your own home and its contents can also take on a sacredness, from the nature that you take within and from the atmosphere and energy you can create. Do not fall into the habit of neglecting to water your plants as so many do. If you work in a place with plants, take the responsibility for their care, as so many wilt, neglected and forgotten in the dusty corners of offices and the like.

Remember that your house stands on Earth and that you live on her and as part of her. Maintain your home as a sanctuary for you, a place of love and communication with the natural world all about you. Consider what you have in your home that is sacred to you and why. Use these things to deepen your links with the Earth and of course, be extremely mindful of the things that you use, their sources and what you can give back to the Earth in compensation and thanks for Her free giving of them. If humanity is to continue it must learn to renew the natural resources it uses, in whatever form, and to return something in exchange. You can assist this by 'doing your bit'. In reality every piece of paper, every bottle and container is vital to reuse if possible, then recycle. See this as part of your sacred duty of giving thanks to the Earth and make the effort.

The Order of Bards, Ovates and Druids, the largest Druid group in this Country, operates a 'Campaign for Individual Ecological Responsibility' and the name here serves as a perfect reminder of what is needed, with regard to our attitude and conduct towards the Earth. Set yourself the target of becoming such an individual and make a list of whatever is required to achieve this.

This does not have to be joining the local British Trust for Nature Conservation Volunteers and giving your time and energy to undertaking work in your area some weekends (though do not let me put you off this!) but can be just adding to your home recycling efforts those of your workplace. Most people are willing to help if someone will take the responsibility of the trip to the recycling centre and collecting the bags together. Make yourself that person and stick diligently to your task and take pleasure from it.

If you are artistic or creative in any way, you might consider the use of natural materials to demonstrate your feelings regarding your link and connection with Nature, that can inspire others to do the same.

All the above tasks and a great many more besides, can add to and instil deeper, your awareness of who and what you are, as part of Nature, the Earth and the living Universe. You are a cosmic being, a 'bag of mostly water', a physical reflection of a focussed energy. You are unique and perfect just as you are. Realise your own sacredness and that of the Earth upon which you depend and live and ask yourself what you can do to bring these two closer together. Just as we need the Earth, the Earth needs us. Above all, maintain an attitude of respect and develop your love for the Earth. Let this be demonstrated in your actions and the way you live and with patience and time, the inner beings, Devas, Goblins, Elves, Fairies, Tree Spirits, Guardians or whatever name you choose to give them will recognise you not as a threat, but a glowing being of love, with whom they can communicate and in whom they can trust. It is a truly wondrous world that we are part of, so do please open yourself to this wonderland, enjoy and love it.

Exercise 1 - Contacting the Mother

There are may practical things suggested in this Chapter and you may wish to re-read the above taking the suggestions at a practical level and see what you can begin to do to start your links with the goddess of the Earth, Mother Earth, Gaia or many other names. I would recommend that you allow time to pass enough so that you feel some kind of response within your being from the Earth, before you try this exercise.

If performed, perhaps many times, with an attitude of respect and a little awe or even fear, you will receive a beautiful and timeless feeling within the very core of yourself, that is inexpressible, but very real. This will soon establish itself, if you keep up your practices and actions you will come to know the love of the Goddess in your heart.

Set aside a particular time for your Contacting the Mother' exercise. You will need to be outdoors, preferably in your power spot. At the very least you need to feel comfortable and relaxed and familiar with your surroundings. Ensure that you are safe and that somebody knows where you are. Go, whatever the weather, for this is a promise to yourself and the Earth.

Now find a spot where you can lie down on the Earth, grass or whatever looks inviting to you. You could have your back against a tree, but it is good to actually lay your whole body on the ground, to let the Earth support you.

Feel the Earth or soil around you with your fingers and toes (bare feet are required!). Feel its temperature, if it is dry, wet, has pebbles in etc. Let in run between your fingers and toes and feel the life force within it. Perhaps hold a stone loosely in your hand. Lay your face against the soil, smell it and become conscious as you do so of the life force and energy flowing through it and through yourself.

Now close your eyes and relax. Let yourself sink into the Earth and be aware of the body of the Earth supporting yours. Let your energy move downwards into the soil and Earth. Imagine that you sink down and take root, blending and merging with the Earth. Your limbs become heavy, like branches and it grows darker about you.

Now open your inner sight and see what is around you. At first all may be dark and gloomy but soon you begin to pick out movements and flashes of light around you. Let yourself follow these and gaze steadily about you. Soon you will distinguish distinct movement of light and this is the energy of the Earth. See if you can discern colours and be aware of how it feels to you as you lie there, deep within the Earth.

Realise that what you are seeing and feeling is the Mother Earth, the workings of her body and being. Let yourself become part of that identity, Relax and drift. Call inwardly to the Mother, as words come naturally to you and ask her to make herself known to you in some way. Declare your feelings for her and say whatever occurs to you to say. Lie still then and wait.

The Mother will come to you, but when she is good and ready. This is not a test necessarily, for the Goddess loves you, but you may find that nothing happens for your first visit, or even for a month of visits. If you come back here often and wait, at some stage the Mother will show herself and you will know it. You may see a being of some kind. it may be an animal nearby, or perhaps just a leaf that falls onto you.

When you do so, it is largely a matter for you to decide what, if anything, to do or say. Follow your instinct and you will be fine. Remember to give thanks and then bring yourself back when you are ready. To do this, begin to be aware of your physical body, lying on the surface of the Earth. Listen for the sounds around you and draw your energy back up into your body. Bring your breath back to its usual level and stretch your fingers and toes.

174

Open your eyes when you are ready and sit up. Give yourself a little time to adjust and with a word or two of thanks to the place you are in and its Guardian for protecting you, leave with no trace of your visit behind you.

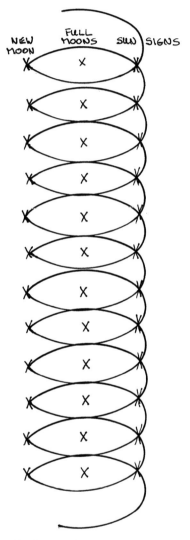

The Spiral of the Sun and Moon

Chapter 8

The Sacred Calender

Now that we have learnt of the needs of the Earth as our Mother and provider, we widen our vision to take in to account the planets that form the remainder of our Solar System. This allows us to orient ourselves around our Universe and provides for us a system of marker points through the year that give us a Sacred Calender to follow.

Our present calender is man made, constructed by logic and giving us a precise means of measuring the passage of time by the marker points of years, months, weeks, days, hours, minutes and seconds. Nature however, does not conform to any form of logic, simply flowing instead with its impulses and instincts that are given and brought about by the existence and interweaving of all the planets of which it is part and here on Earth, chiefly the weather systems that result from their movements and the tides of energy that cause trees to blossom when they do, flowers to open and close, rain to fall and so on. All these things, whilst scientifically caused by chemical reactions to other chemical constituents (that I cannot explain!), are in their turn caused by the flux and reflux of life force.

As human beings we are part of that same pulsing of energy and can feel its movement within us, at all levels of our selves - physically, emotionally, mentally and spiritually. It is necessary to pause and be still to contact and become aware of such energy, but our whole being is intrinsically bound up with the same energy that causes the sun to rise, the wind to blow, the seeds to scatter, leaves to unfold and us to stay awake or fall asleep. By inwardly contacting the energy at the marker points nature gives, we are able to make our lives immeasurably more comfortable and cause an optimum effect by the actions we choose to make from day to day. Thus we have a natural rather than man made calender that we need to adjust to, to live easily in the new millenium and all that symbolises.

This calender is based on three different, but intersecting movements. The first is the natural flow and working of Nature, following its annual cycle. These times have been recognised and celebrated for thousands of years at eight main points around the year. The ancient Celts of Britain are the chief source of inspiration and this is quite correct for those of us now living here, for by using these same times, we tap into the natural force created so long ago by our ancestors.

This does not mean however, that we must revert to ancient historical practices alone for our celebrations of these Festivals. Recent times have seen a revival of interest of the festivals and we can see their effects all around us in our present society. The various Mayday festivities all carry a memory or shadow of the ancient Celtic methods, the doings of what we know as Halloween, Easter Eggs, even Christmas trees and presents all hark back to former times. Whilst it is vital not to see these celebrations as an excuse to party and give way to blank hedonism or material gluttony, it is important that we adapt our celebrations for modern times and views.

Whilst it is true and quite correct that traditional or hereditary witchcraft has precise and definite wording, action and format for its ritual celebrations of these times of natural power and focus, these are not suitable or applicable to the majority of us in our everyday lives, uninitiated as we may be. With an increasing acceptance of their role in our current world it is now conceivable that the festivals can reclaim their place as times of community wide sacred worship and celebration. Perhaps it is, that the ceremonies performed unceasingly by the aforementioned witches have kept alive the life force and energy surrounding the festivals and it is now time that energy thus created, works its way outward into the everyday world once more. This is the nature of all life force, to flow and grow, ever expanding and increasing, like the love we can have for each other. It falls to each one of us to make this a reality in our life.

The main principles and qualities of these eight Festivals are outlined later in this Chapter, but there are now a great many books giving much detail concerning their significance and practices to choose from. Please refer to the bibliography for some of these, if you wish to undertake a wider study.

The two other movements we are concerned with in the Sacred Calender are those of the Sun and Moon as they make their way, or we make ours, through the heavens. Here we must realise that it is the energy we receive from this Star and planet respectively that is important. We can view the Sun and Moon as embodying the masculine and feminine principles of life respectively, or of the outer and inner. As such, the energy that we receive from them allows us to form and shape our basic identity, since each one of us is a combination of these building blocks of life, in energy form.

We have already seen some of the relevance and significance of the Sun and Moon through this book and now we are able to put these into practice. As the basics of our identity and being, the times when the Sun and Moon move into new phases are the times when we can take advantage of the energy given to us and ensure that we are moving and living in phase with the natural order of things. The effect of this can be likened to swimming with, rather than against, the tide.

The link with the Sun is made when it moves into a different sign of the zodiac, at 12 points of the year. Each zodiac sign gives, as we know, different properties to us and astrology tells us that those born while the Sun is in a certain sign will exhibit certain basic traits and behaviour patterns according to the principles of that sign. This also means that the Sun is emitting and sending us energy in accordance with those same qualities and patterns as it passes through that sign each year. Since the Sun is the symbol for our outer selves, actions and masculine side, we can link this with the principles of each zodiac sign and concentrate on these, as a means of personal awareness and development, rising in a spiral as our lives progress.

As can be seen from the diagram the points of intersection mark the times of transition of the Sun from one sign to another. These are mirrored and balanced by the Moon, as she moves into her New phase, every 28 days or so. Now we focus on our inner, feminine side, looking to the inner impulses we have and focussing on the New Moon as a time of peaceful contemplation of the new energies coming to us. These grow through the ensuing two weeks or so until the Full Moon, where they build to a peak. At the Full moon our focus should turn to the integration of what the Moon is giving is inwardly, with what we receive from the Sun outwardly.

In our spiral diagram, the Sun and Moon integration creates a natural hollow, or rather fullness, in the centre of the spiral, when the Sun and Moon are in alignment, opposite each other in our sky, These are the times of maximum power when we are drawn together to heal, pray, worship and celebrate in groups, or individually.

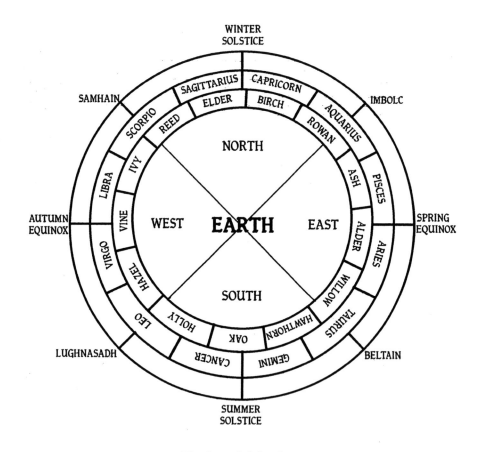

The Sacred Calendar

Since we get 12 Moons some years and 13 others, the spiral is seen to be in a state of constant flux, expanding and contracting as the movements of the Sun and Moon dictate. This is also in accordance with the nature of energy, since its basic impulse is to grow and expand. Nature abhorring a vacuum. Of course, the New and Full Moons will sometimes occur close to the time the Sun moves to a new zodiac sign, but this is again as it should be, for the Universe is expanding in all directions, up and down, in and out, not just one way. Our natural, sacred calender is thus complete and so we have a means of universal orientation, a method that guides us around our Universe and self, the one reflecting and interacting with the other in a beautiful dance.

It is vital to realise, in working with the Sacred Calender, that it is the underlying energy that the marker points I will explain carry, rather than the position or movement of the physical planet itself. As with all things in life, the actual reality exists at the unseen energy level of what happens practically, that dictates its particular quality and form.

It therefore becomes necessary to contact and feel that energy within us at certain times of the year and to align ourselves with it, chiefly by opening ourselves to it by some method, whether that be meditation, physical movement such as Tai Chi, ritual, or whatever occurs to you. This allows for the energy to flow into the fabric of our beings and so we become aligned to the frequency and type of energy flowing naturally all around us. Once within us in this way, we are able to let the energy flow out once again, so that our actions take account of and indeed utilise the natural life force and its resultant preferences. This makes our life less of a struggle and allows us, quite literally, to go with the flow.

We therefore need to be aware of the qualities and principles of the festivals, Sun signs and Moons in order to make ourselves aware of what kind of energy we are receiving at these particular times. These are available in a great many other books and many readers will no doubt already know the basic properties of the 12 Sun signs. However, I will list below the very basic and general qualities attached to each, drawn from a wide selection, for the sake of ease of reference and the sake of those who do not know.

In reality and to be perfect with this, what is needed is for each person to draw their own conclusions as to what they get from the Sun and Moon and how they feel about and wish to celebrate each of the Festivals. This needs time, patience and study on the part of each person. The point should be made here that this does not necessarily mean buying a myriad of books on astrology and Celts, though this might help, but chiefly by experimentation by DOING things at each of the marker points mentioned. Bear in mind that with books you may choose to read, including this one, that what you are reading is chiefly that author's opinion or approach. This may be agreeable to you or not and as such, have the attitude of taking what you need and leaving the rest (remembering that if you take nothing, this does not make the book or author 'bad' - just in case you get nothing from this book!).

As stated before, the Earth and indeed the Sun and Moon are able to teach us all that we need to know, if we are still and quiet enough to listen and take heed. The Sacred Calender is a natural one and that Nature, whether on Earth or in space, is alive and so able to communicate its needs and methods to us. Make notes as you go as to your feelings and responses to your practices and over the years you will build up an invaluable source of material and knowledge about yourself that will enable you to become a powerful, efficient being.

Festivals

Listed below is a very brief introduction to what the eight ancient Celtic festivals are about, together with their dates. The year of course continues around itself in an endless rhythm annually. Astrologically the year begins with Aries on March 21st. Since we are dealing closely with the Sun and Moon, we will therefore begin at that point of the year.

Spring Equinox - March 21st

Face the East at this time of year and take your focus to your mind, with the Element of Air, letting the fresh winds of the spring blow through you, to take away the winter's rest. The dawn of the year, when spring takes hold. Rise and greet the dawn, of a new day and a new year. The Light of the Earth has risen and the Sword is raised to greet it.

The path of Opening the Way has begun, the way to growth, and receiving wisdom and enlightenment. New inspiration can flow, ideas, hopes, dreams.

Throw off the winters cold and run anew in the open fields. Reach out for what you want, make things happen for you and create what you will.

Work with your Base chakra as the gateway of Earth. Ground yourself on the Earth, feel her growing warmth and energy flood your being from the base of your spine and throughout. This can be linked to the time from 7 to 14 years of our life. Think back to how you were. Recapture those childlike dreams and fulfil what has been left. In nature the sap rises and the mists rise too. Be amongst that mist and see your way clearly through to a bright future. Feel your metabolism quicken and the pace of life pick up a beat once more. Explore the sensation of touch, move and celebrate your being and your life. Feel the equality between the day and night and find that balance reflected within you. Sense with your Etheric body the energy in all living things. Live your existence and be deliberately alive.

Beltain - May 1st

Turn to the South-East, taking your plans and ideas within to your Spirit. As you begin the journey of the Summer seek a blending of the Elements of Air and Fire. let the winds fan the flames of your Spirit. In the mid morning the Sun shines and sheds its warmth to all. Stretch out and open yourself to its healing, life giving rays. The Festival of Expectation is nigh! Consider what you expect from life and from yourself. Seize the day and reach out and grasp what is yours. Celebrate your potency and fertility. Run and dance amidst the newly blossomed hawthorn. Dance the maypole and intertwine the male and female, red and white strands of life. Polarities come together and so do we. Spend a night in the woods and follow the natural impulse of nature at this time! Wander a maze and find yourself and all of life at the centre. Celebrate the woodland marriage of all, wear green, celebrate the beginning of Summer. See what you labour for and use your power wisely.

Work with the sacral chakra and its orange energy. Flood your being with the Sun. Feel your power grow and put it to deliberate use. Take yourself back to aged 14 to 21 and capture again your wondrous inner being, full of excitement at the world and a future in it. Feel emotionally what and who you are. Celebrate and explore your feelings. Build a sacred fire and jump the flames in exuberance. Be part of all that grows, lives and is maturing to fruition.

Summer Solstice - June 21st

Now we turn to the South and the heat of the Element of Fire, when we embrace all that we are with full force. The noon Sun is hot and burning. Cast your eyes to the horizon at dawn and pause in awe at the majesty of the Sun as it reaches its highest point in the year. This is the time of fullness, the time of Fire and heat. Raise the spear to direct the power you feel and be part of the Festival of Attainment. At noon, shout and yell for the power of all life is there. Scale new heights in yourself, of power and understanding. Use your potential and be the best you can. Use drive, determination and focus.

Work now with your Solar Plexus chakras, where you drink in the abundance of the Sun. Take yourself back through your 20s and feel the thrill of discovery and attainment once more. Have one pointedness of mind and step forward proudly and boldly on your path. Own and control your power and make decisions. You are a unique being, eternal, immortal and infinite. Celebrate this and proclaim it to the Sun.

Lughnasadh - August 1st

The wheel turns, to face South-West and the end of the path of Fire, with the beginning of that of water. Let the water soothe the burns and temper the heat. The harvest begins and so the work of gathering in must begin in you too. Make a sacrifice of that which has passed its prime and no longer engenders respect from you. Give thanks for what has been given until now and reap the rewards of the bountiful harvest the Earth bestows for all. In the afternoon, pause amidst the heat and reflect a little, before continuing with your work and your path. The Festival of First Fruits calls you to the altar to offer your fruits and give account of your previous deeds and plans. Bite deeply into the fruit and feel its sacredness flow into you. Be mature in outlook and listen well, to the spirit within you and that of nature, which lays down and begins to die at this time. What greater sacrifice can there be, but of the self. Do not allow ego to cloud your awareness. Cut its tie and hold on you with the sickle and own your death too, for surely it will come.

Work with the heart chakra and let the healing green into you. Hold a wake for the dying King of the Corn and what you must leave behind too. Be thankful for your life and through the focus and intention of your 30s. On the Path of Insight be wise. Let the Gateway of Winds open wide and blow away the chaff. Love others for what and who they are and have compassion. Accept your own karma and seek to find balance in it through your actions and decisions now. Maintain your integrity and serve.

Autumn Equinox - September 21st

Face West and take rest within after the labour of the Harvest. The life giving power of Water comes into its own now, and so you look to the needs of your heart. All is drawn together and so begins to take root deep inside. Plunge yourself into the Cauldron and become renewed through your rest. Dive into the Light of the Water and drink the sacred wine that flows now. Day and Night are equal once more and a deeper balance is found. At the twilight and setting sun find peace and stillness. Find your healing and be the spiritual warrior. Dream and purify yourself with the smoke of the sweat lodge.

Look to your Throat chakra to teach you now. Open the Gateway of Time and Space and find clear speech and expression. Communicate who you are and what you are. Know this as truth, accept it and take strength from it. Listen too to your inner voice and express your deepest desires. Look inward to your deep mind and know thyself. Let the sound of your voice ring true and hear the echoes coming back to you.

Samhain - October 31st

The North-west beckons as we leave the Element of Water behind and turn ourselves to the needs of the body, which the water has refreshed. Here we enter the time of dusk, the dawn of the dark half of the year when we turn within, casting a glance over our shoulders at midnight to bid farewell to the old year. Thank what and whom has gone the previous year and look at your achievements and failures too. The Festival of Remembrance calls us to look back and recall, with tears and laughter the life of the old year, now passing away. All is gathered and stored for the winter now and so it should be with you. The Cleansing Path begins, the attention is taken to your inner self where you can learn from your suffering and trauma. Use the power of your inner sight and see clearly within. Recognise and accept any weakness you find and resolve to turn it into strength through the coming darkness of winter. Tell the story of your previous year around the fire, lit by candlelight, with ale and food.

Look from within through your Brow chakra and perceive yourself clearly from there. Attune yourself with the source of wisdom and then turn to darkness in Nature. Sow seeds within yourself that will be nurtured through the winter, full of potential. Open your mind to your own inner teacher and gaze into the Otherworld at this time as the doors to the Otherworld open. Seize what you see and act from your vision.

Winter Solstice - December 21st

Turn to the North, the direction of the sacred Earth and focus your attention fully on the needs of your body. Now the quiet heart of magic is at rest and all sleeps soundly. Those that will hibernate and we too can retreat to the very core of our beings, spending long hours beside the fire, dreaming. Find in wonder the birth of the Star Child and make a quiet celebration of thanks at your hearth. See the eternal evergreen in nature, promising eternity to you.

The Festival of Rebirth calls you to be reborn anew, as the days begin to lengthen from now, increasing a slow and gradual, gentle experience of emerging into the new year. Kiss beneath the mistletoe as a symbol of fertility and rebirth itself. At midnight, find this time in yourself and feel its qualities, quiet, restful, potent. Burn the Yule Log of the year and follow the cleansing path onward, seeking purity from the fire.

The Crown chakra opens and we enter the void. This connects us to the eternal directly and so we experience the gentle blinding white light of the Divine. The Sun is reborn and the Earth and its inhabitants bow to its being once more. Giveaway what you can and celebrate the eternal brotherhood in humanity. Find the mastery of your being now and discover your life's purpose anew.

Imbolc - February 1st

Take the wheel of the year full circle now and turn to the North-east, embracing the new air that lets you breathe anew once more. The Festival of Renewal begins quietly, with a pure spring bubbling forth from the green hillside. You can emerge too, from your winter clothes and your slumber. Stretch and greet the dawn again and take delicate steps forward on your journey. The Spring begins and the ewe's milk flows. The young are born and now is the time for nurture and gentle love and care. The weak finally go to an eternal strength so the rest can feed from the meagre supplies during this 'hunger gap'. Purify yourself with fasting and cleanse your system. Let yourself be inspired by the new growth about you and let words of poetry come. Clean away the dirt of the winter and sweep out the dust from your depths.

Focus on the soles of the feet and feel the ground beneath you. Take firm root and draw strength from the rising tide of the Earth's energy now. Light a white candle as a symbol for your purity of intent, thought and purpose and be sure to remain true to what you tell. Move onward through the year to take possession of your life and let it grow with the Spring.

Sun

Since the Sun personifies and symbolises the outer and active in our lives and selves, the energy that we receive from the Sun as it moves through the signs is to be used and directed towards those parts of ourselves and our lives. The indications given are to help you maximise the use of natural energy we receive from the Sun through the year.

Aries - March 21 - April 19

Use the qualities of energy and enterprise to push ahead with your projects in life. Consider how you are using your impulses in life to direct yourself. Focus on your self and your interests and ask if they serve you in a manner to increase the fulfilment of your potential. Assert your freedom and use willpower to achieve your goals. Be assertive and pay attention to detail. Examine how your active energies are used in your life and resolve to correct any faults that you find. Be aware of aggression and look to see the causes of your temper and how this affects you. See what you can do about this. Have courage and persistence on your path.

Taurus - April 20 - May 20

Now is the time for practicality. After the initial rush and surge of Aries, Taurus takes a more steadfast approach and so must you, in all you do. Consider your fixed opinions, ways and habits and how these affect you. Resolve to extract anything that is not beneficial to you in some way. Focus on your needs for security and see what you have that provides this and what detracts from your material sustenance. Be productive in what you do and ensure that this is done in the most efficient manner possible. Develop a love of what is beautiful to you, this sign being ruled by the planet Venus, goddess of love, femininity and all that is beautiful. Be aware of your body and its sensuality and yield to your softness.

Gemini - May 21 - June 21

This is a good time for communication, with others and your self. Look to the masculine and feminine within yourself and see how you relate to each one, as the twins of this sign. Ensure you are not being 'two-faced' in any area of your life and look for inconsistencies in your behaviour. Adapt yourself fully to your circumstances in life, whatever they may be - try to accept what you have as correct for you and resolve to change it if it is not as you would wish. Ensure you have a variety of things in life to stimulate you and give you pleasure. Do not become fixed into one thing in any area of your life. You may be incessantly on the go as is the urge now, but remember that part of being 'on the go' is to know when to relax and let go. Cease the endless chatter you may have now and instead learn to communicate your deepest self with those you love.

Cancer - June 22 - July 22

Ensure you are protected now, against sudden misfortune or change that may unbalance you. Stay in touch with your soft interior, beneath the hard,

188

protective layer on the outside, like the crab of this sign. Ensure you are protected and see where your protection comes from in life. Move carefully towards your goal, with diligence and taking nourishment along the way for what you need. Cling to what you know is real and what you strive for and truly you will achieve your goals. Look to your sensitivity and see in which areas you are vulnerable and easily hurt. See if you are being too easily influenced by others. Use your inner resources to bring more security to yourself. Collect and gather what you need to prepare you for the path ahead.

Leo - July 23 - August 22

This is the time for extroversion and for being outside, both physically and of yourself. Be active and wild, like the lion, intense and demonstrating your power. Take authority over yourself, roar and assume control. Celebrate your primary power and instincts. Be the leader of your pack and lead yourself too, fearlessly to where you have not gone before. Organise yourself and your life as you would wish and take pride in your achievements. Be warm of heart to others, leading them on by example. Be true to your principles and but do not be overbearing.

Virgo - August 23 - September 22

We now enter into a time of restraint and passivity. You have worked hard, so now take stock and withdraw a little. Look to see if you are criticising yourself unfairly and take heed of any real shortcomings you find. Analyse your self and your life and weed out any pieces that do not fit the overall picture you would like. Look for small details that may have a larger significance, that may have been there for a time unnoticed and unheeded. Remain conscientious in your approach now. You may feel the need to stick to convention and what is safe and familiar to you. Ensure you are not suppressing any emotions and worrying unnecessarily and take action where you can to resolve these worries. Avoid wasting your energy now and from your analysis of self find what is positive.

Libra - September 23 - October 22

Bring yourself into balance now, between the inner and outer, mind and heart and action and rest. Resolve any conflict between you and others now, and indeed, with yourself. Restore a balanced attitude in all things and avoid over indulgence on any level. Be romantic and enjoy the peace that comes with this love. Cooperate wherever you can, again with yourself and others. Look for what is good in others and see if you are receiving what you need from others as Librans have an instinctive urge to find this from those they interact with. See what throws you off balance and do what you can to bring it back. Make sure that the environments you live and work in are acceptable to you and do what you can to improve them, to make them more of a place of ease and balance for you. Anything out of balance, in any way whatsoever, can be brought back into alignment now.

Scorpio - October 23 - November 21

Look for the sting in the tail of your own scorpion now. Do you have anything left at the back of your mind and deep in your heart that waits to creep or dash out and sting you with its hurt and pain? See what you can do to gently face and embrace that pain and you may find it is not so fearful after all. Look to your sexuality and ask yourself what you express about yourself through your actions on this level. See if you are resolved to the certainty of your own death and if you feel you are truly alive now. Focus on your spirituality and have full and honest intent on this level. Regenerate anything that has quietly withered and that you feel you still need. Uncover anything that is a mystery to you, either in others, your life or of course, your own being.

Sagittarius - November 22 - December 21

During the time of long nights and much darkness, sharpen your arrow, of ambition and aims. See that furthest you can ahead of you now and aim your arrow true. See what your ideals are and examine them to see if you are moving towards them and if they are achievable. Look to create the space around you that you need. Aspire to the highest that you can achieve, mentally and physically especially. Take time to travel if possible and gather more experience and learning to you. Explore also what you already know and see if your truth still fits the person that you are. Discover new truths for yourself and accept and integrate them to become a part of you.

Capricorn - December 22 - January 19

Now is the time when you must practice discipline with yourself and be prepared to make steady, perhaps small progress, plodding on as best you can. It is a time for restraint and to experience the cold facts of life. This can teach you much however, so take time to chew over what you have available to you, within your identity. Bring into order that which is not. Find the essential warmth of your character and energy and construct protection as it is needed. Make plans using your powers of logic. Be persistent and patient and remember the strength that comes from a good sense of humour. Ensure that you have not allowed yourself to become inconsistent and believe in yourself as a perfect being, for your needs now. Spend long nights at home, safe and warm, nurturing yourself.

Aquarius - January 20 - February 18

The blend that the water bearer of this sign achieves is between logic and intuition, so look to see how you use and manifest these in your life. Find the middle point between feeling and thought and seek to maintain this awareness in yourself at all times. You may find yourself attracted to areas that are unusual for you, so push ahead and explore the unknown around you now. Ensure that you are not carrying fixed ideas or opinions as to how things should be. Synthesise into your own being that which is for the good of all, such is the communal urge at this time. Celebrate your individuality and do something that is different to you, that gives you a sense of the uniqueness of your being and so come to celebrate being part of the whole too.

Pisces - February 19 - March 20

Now is the time to transcend the material and mundane in life. Look to higher matters and the highest in your self. You may feel especially sensitive, emotionally and psychically. Develop your natural psychic awareness now, to help you on your path. Break down any barriers that you find you have constructed and that may be preventing you from sensing what you need. Cleanse and purify yourself in water, ready for the year ahead. Break free from limits and restriction imposed by others that you do not need too. Realise your strengths and weaknesses and be sure that your otherworldly feelings are not answered by using artificial means only.

Moon

As the equal and opposite to the Sun, the Moon brings to us the inner, passive qualities we need and can adjust to as it too, brings different natural qualities through its passage of the year. Take these principles within you as we move into each New Moon, building them up to a peak at the Full Moon and then releasing what you have learnt into your being during the waning Moon, of each Moon of the year. The qualities of these Moons are taken from the trees that are ascribed to each Moon, from the ancient Celtic yearly calender, secret language and method divination known as Ogham. You can easily set yourself the target of learning about the trees as you go too. We begin at the same place as the Sun. Exact dates cannot be given, since the Moon does not have fixed dates, owing to the length of time taken between phases, so you will need to adapt the months given below to the actual Moons. Of course some times there will be 12 in a year and at others 13.

New Moon in March - Alder

Bring a quiet resistance into your being through this Moon. Turn this into a positive energy within you, to protect against corruption, as the alder protects itself against the effects of water. Calm yourself with the power of this tree and reduce your anxiety by meditation and attunement beneath it. Get in touch with your anima, your inner woman and get to know this aspect of yourself. This tree gives powers of prophecy, so use these to discriminate clearly between what is false and real.

New Moon in April - Willow

This is a water seeking tree that will enable you to come fully into touch with your femininity and your emotions and feelings. Absorb this energy and experience the fullness of your emotions. Let sadness, joy, anger and love show and find the sacredness of all of these and more feelings that you will discover within you. The gift of fertility can be given, if you are seeking this now. Seek inspiration from the muse, as the Moon and create poetry from your dreams. Have trust in yourself and the Universe to unfold just as it should. Ask for help with this from the Moon and the willow. If you have lost things, on any level, realise that in the loss, new growth can begin, from the space it creates and the energy it takes.

New Moon in May - Hawthorn

The hawthorn gives protection with its thorns; and beauty, cleansing and purity when it blossoms. Find these qualities in yourself and draw to you what you need. Build up inner power and see this as a fertile force, ready to be used when needed. Do not rush ahead, but remain patient and accepting of the promise of things to come soon. Take shelter beneath the Hawthorn and nourishment from its energy. Do not be frightened or dread what is ahead, for as you find the inner strength that comes to us now so you relax into the future. Your purification can be achieved now, through this energy and so depression can be lifted.

New Moon in June - Oak

The oak is often recognised as the king of the trees and so now is the time when you can draw in the strength, energy and power that you need for your basic self and being for the whole year. Oaks are said to grow on power spots on the Earth, so sit against one and draw on that strength, once permission is given. Draw security to you and open a doorway in yourself to a realisation of your sacredness and spirituality.

Boost your physical, mental, emotional and spiritual power during this Moon, by drinking in all that is given. If you feel drawn to, channel and focus this energy out to others too, giving them what they need to help them on their path, as equal to you. Realise that you can subsequently manifest your goals and dreams and look to doing this with the Sun's outer energy.

New Moon in July - Holly

The Holly is regarded as the best in the fight, so make sure that what you attract now does not threaten or spike you. Instead draw towards you defence as needed and ensure that you are not spineless. This is a male tree in its energy and is regarded as strong and potent, so draw these qualities into you through this Moon. Be assertive, but not aggressive with yourself. Build a fire within that does not consume, but nurtures, warms and strengthens. Become the warrior within you, as you build up this energy. Become your own guardian and protect yourself from vulnerability.

New Moon in August - Hazel

This is the tree of wisdom and now you can link with the salmon and feed on the nuts of wisdom that come from the tree. Draw wisdom, knowledge and intuition to yourself and use these to look ahead and 'divine' your way forward as you see it and as it is revealed to you. Focus and study yourself and clear away unwanted energy within you. Open your channels of creativity, be inspired and meditate with this tree to create what you need within. The wood from this tree is the most flexible, so ensure you can bend and sway with what life gives you now, by drawing in its force and power to do this.

New Moon in September (early) - Vine

Since at the end of the month of September, we reach the end of the year for the Celts, turning towards the dark half of the year with the onset of Samhain, this is the point at which we include two moons to the one month, traditionally. This may not be the case in any one year however, but again, adapting the guiding dates here is needed.

Now is the time when the fruits of the vine can release you from your inhibitions. Let your subtle intuitions surface and guide you now. Let the

194

natural lunar energy now connect you with your deepest feelings and let these gently and lovingly rise to the surface. Place your trust in the place of your deepest emotions. Ensure you remove any falseness or unfaithful attitude to your true self. This tree can also give great joy and liberation, so find this energy within you too, for we all have the capacity of it, if we choose to find it.

New Moon in September (late) - Ivy

The Ivy connects you with your inner resources, so now is the time to draw this energy towards you, to connect with what is within you that serves and feeds you. Encourage these aspects of yourself to grow by drawing more in of what you need inside. Anything within that has been hidden may come to your attention now, so try to face and embrace these as they arise, using the natural energy to help you deal with them. Turn inward and find your spiritual strength and depth and on the outward phase of this moon, link this energy with others. Nourish yourself within using the power of the Ivy.

New Moon in October - Reed

Now is the time for finding your most basic truth and self, of what and who you are. Draw conviction of belief and attitude to yourself. Bring order rather than chaos to your inner self and let this exude out to others too. Discover your own royalty and reflect on this within yourself. Find the arrows of your desire and aim these truly and clearly and you use the natural energy now to sharpen your wits. Consider your dreams and ambitions and draw power unto them.

New Moon in November - Elder

The Elder is the tree for regeneration so draw into you a power which will do this for you, on whatever level you need. Now is the time to remove and be rid of the old from the previous year, so release any outworn energy you are clinging to for security. Instead find anew security in the stability and forgiveness that comes now. This is a good time for transformation and change and this must happen on the inner to be truly effective on the outer.

Draw energy and force for such change to you now. Achieve a balanced image of yourself and let this inner state be reflected on the outer.

New Moon in December - Birch

The tree of renewal brings this quality that can be a deeply needed energy now. In the starkness of winter the white bark of the birch stands out, so purify yourself with a pure white light. Consider where you are going within and move into a new cycle of activity that begins inside you now. Plant the seeds of new ideas within you and nurture these, feeding them on the natural energy from the Moon. Allow light to flow into you and experience the beauty and calmness of this tree, that in time gives knowledge and fertile power for others.

New Moon in January - Rowan

Use the magic of the Rowan to protect yourself against losing your way in the enchantment of your dreams and plans. Instead inspire yourself with your spiritual strength, drawn from this tree and the Moon now. Distinguish positive from negative energy and power in your life and let the Rowan cleanse what is impure at this level for you. This tree grows in places of height so aspire and grow to reach the highest point you can, in yourself and your power. Prepare to give birth to what you have conceived and nurtured within yourself over the last few months of winter and be ready to release it out when the time comes. Ensure you are connected to your lunar self to do this.

New Moon in February - Ash

The Ash is the World Tree we have met before. Use this Moon to connect with the Under, Middle and Other worlds. Be a part of those worlds in your inner life. Look backwards and forwards and come to a point of rest and focus on the now, living fully present and alive, deliberate and conscious in the present moment. Now you can become the young warrior within by conserving and using your power wisely, aided by the Ash and the Moon. Thus you can establish the inner strength and control you need for your preservation and development now. Draw courage and dynamism to you and all will be as it should within you.

Chapter 9

The Sacred Life

Having dissected and examined ourselves, facing the four directions and meeting the Elements there, we must now concentrate on putting those four components together. Traditionally, these four Elements when combined give the fifth Element of Spirit or Aether (that which is between energy and matter). This fifth Element or Quintessence, is looked on as the end product of the other four combined, and is holistically, greater than the sum of its parts.

In turn this represents the whole and complete human being, to which we now turn our attention. By working on the Elements in turn we are able to integrate their properties and energies into our beings and so we arrive at our overall spirit, our sense of identity as a sacred, spiritual being. The practical, daily aspects we have so far examined must ultimately be transformed or transgressed into a higher, spiritual form.

We have identified many areas in which daily life can be taken and lived as a sacred act in and of itself. When this is done, the natural product or result is to look to higher realms, to cast our eyes to the edge of the Universe and beyond. Here we find that all-encompassing spirit that pervades all things, including ourselves. We must now learn to deal with this and to identify our own particular and individual spiritual principles and beliefs and learn to live by them, with deliberate intent. It is this that ultimately makes for the most profound spiritual life, one that sets you apart from the mundane and the apathetic. Apathy can rightly be identified as the great blight of the modern industrial world. With governments taking responsibility for our decisions and the people naively trusting them to do so in their best interest, the end result is the masses become victims to an energy sapping apathy that comes from the ease of life that industrialisation gives.

Once begun, the spiritual life, embracing and integrating the everyday, has the effect of causing the very foundation of your existence to alter, away from the career achievement or bank balance as the highest goal and to the development and progression of yourself, coupled with a close awareness or relationship with, the Divine.

Wherever you live in the world, you are able to identify your own particular God or Goddess as the representation of that Divine. Once identified, this becomes the highest target for you to aim at, not as some distant, ethereal being, but as a real person who lives close to you, but just unseen (for the most part!). The Divine is able to interact with you as much and as normally as any other living being.

To help you identify which particular principles and beliefs you wish to make your own, we will examine some of the most popular and relevant to our times now. This information is not intended to serve as a 'pick your religion' guide, but simply an overall look at tried and tested spiritual ways of living in the everyday world, in keeping with the aims of this book. One is not put against the other and those given are the ones I have become intimately aware of, through my own practices. What I practise is a hybrid and merging of many of these, which constitute MY principles and beliefs.

I have not provided a detailed commentary on each of these principles as the way in which you choose to apply them to your life, or not as the case may be, is a matter for personal consideration. Any commentary is therefore limited to my own perception, as they apply to me. What is required for their successful implementation is a deep and personal integration by and for yourself of any principles you choose to adopt.

The task before you now, as an Exercise for this Chapter, is to examine what is presented here, as well as whatever other methods of spiritual living you choose, and construct your own list of principles and spiritual, or sacred, codes of conduct. This will result, over time, in your becoming someone who has as their central focus, a sacredness that sets them apart from those living for the profit they can make out of life. As we shall see at the conclusion, it is the continual and determined movement towards the goals you identify here, that allows you to fully integrate into yourself and your life. This in turn, is done by ensuring on a daily basis that your acts, intents, feelings and thoughts do not stray from the sacred principles you have taken as your own. You could perhaps perform your own dedication ceremony to begin this process, reciting sacred vows as a part of your dedication to the Divine. Remember that this is also a sacred vow to yourself too.

If you find this task a daunting or complicated process, I would suggest examining your life as it stands now, to see what things you do, say, think and feel, fit and contribute to the principles you want to live by, and which things detract and take you away from that path. Then examine the information given here (and others) and see which applies.

To bein our exploration we will look at the practice of Yoga, which is often seen as a purely physical practice, but in actuality is a very ancient and profound form of spiritual living, with strict principles and guidelines for how to live that life. These are split into eight areas, or limbs, and as you will see, these cover every aspect of what life contains. As such, these eight limbs provide a comprehensive means of assessing and adjusting our lives to meet the sacred standards we set ourselves.

The word Yoga means to unite or to join, and this is meant in the context of joining the individual with the Divine. The first limb is known as Yama and contains what can be viewed as Universal moral commandments, detailing how you look at life with regard to others. These commandments are looked on as ethical disciplines that transcend age, creed, country of origin and time.

The first of these principles is Non-violence, which includes both physical and mental, meaning intent of harm from your thoughts or speech to others. Violence is here seen as residing in the mind and working out to the body in the form of physical violence. The definition and limits to violence is for you to decide.

Honesty is the second principle of the five Yamas. The direction here is to live in accordance with your deepest beliefs, which we are about here. Truth is also important, being true to yourself and your true emotions. The third commandment is to not steal, avoiding hoarding material goods and abstaining from unnecessary things. Again, the point at which this occurs is a matter for your own conscience.

A fourth principle here is that of chastity, which is not necessarily taken to mean abstaining from sexual activity (before you put the book down in horror!). If it were, how could our species continue and evolve? Nor does it mean that sex is only for the creation of offspring. The direction we can take is that sex should not be greedy or for pure indulgence, but the sacredness of the act takes precedence. It is, as with many such things, a matter of attitude, which you must find your own limits with, accepting those of your partner too.

The last of the principles here is that of not coveting. This is again of material things and of harbouring a self centered attitude, putting the ego first. The direction given is to reducing craving by reducing need.

Greed, desire and attachment are the enemies for these principles so look to see how these apply with you. If they are not obeyed we are told that violence, untruth, theft, dissipation and covetousness result.

The second limb of Yoga is called Nayama and the five principles of this limb give us rules of conduct for individual discipline. As such, the first of these is Purity. This is taken as meaning cleanliness of the physical body, internally, by means of the Yoga postures and externally by washing, including clothes worn on the body. Purity of heart is also important, requiring kindness and generosity to the self and others. Warmth, decency and pure food are also included here.

Nayamas second principle is that of Contentment or Tranquillity. The guidance given here is to be satisfied with what you have. This is meant at all levels of our being.

The third principle is personal asceticism, requiring the relinquishment of all things that detract you from your path. This requires purification and self discipline.

The fourth Nayama principle is that of study and education, at the level of study of the self and the exploration of the spiritual journey. The last principle is that of surrender and dedication, requiring the acceptance of the wider view of life and the Universe and its meaning. We are given the guidance of trusting processes of change as they happen in our lives and to let go and surrender, to the beneficent Divine, within and without us.

We come now to the third limb of Yoga, called the Asanas. These are the physical postures Yoga is famed for. Attention is given to the full use and development of the physical body, as a vehicle for the Divine to operate in. The continued practice of the postures, coupled with attention to the breath, results in the healthy and developed body thereby allowing the spirit within it the maximum possibility to function to its full and highest potential.

The fourth limb of Yoga is Pranayama and here we encounter the various breathing techniques included as part of the physical routine of the Asanas. The breath is seen as the method by which the sacred energy or life force enters the body. Therefore, when this is focussed and directed in certain ways, the maximum intake and regular flow of that energy, from which comes all life, again releases the best possible function of the spirit within the body. A regular and equal rhythm is seen as being all important to achieve this. The importance of the breath cannot be underestimated.

The fifth limb is known as Pratyahara, directed as being the withdrawal of the mind from being subject to the desires and demands of the senses and external objects. The point at which your senses seek to control you is one that you must establish by yourself, by consistent self examination and objective viewing. A useful method of achieving the required objectivity can be to enter into meditation and from a central, balanced point observe your self.

The sixth limb of Yoga is Dharana meaning concentration or contemplation. The idea here is one focus, pouring your whole being and existence in the one task you are engaged in at any one moment. By this you achieve a purity of intent and an excellence of standard. You are decisive, clean and clear. Your flow of focus in uninterrupted and complete and so you become the thing you are focussing on. It is likened to water taking the shape of the container it is in. It is made clear that this is a natural process, that cannot be forced.

The seventh limb is Dhyana and is the practice of meditation. A great deal is made of this in Yoga and this principle flows on from the previous one. Detailed instruction are given for the development of practice of meditation in yoga and I would here refer readers to my previous book '*Practical Meditation*' (Capall Bann 1995) for a method of meditation that embraces the everyday life.

The eight limb of Yoga is Samadhi and marks the end of the quest, and being in a state of oneness and bliss. This takes you beyond consciousness

202

and achieves the full realisation that all is Divine and that you become at one with that Divine. There is no longer a sense of ego or individual identity as the one is blended with the Divine, who is all, with bliss and profound silence. This is seen as coming in a single flash of illumination.

These eight limbs can be viewed as progressive, working from one to the other. Indeed, each can be seen as the result or product of the previous one. These eight limbs can also be grouped into specific areas. By this, the first two teach control of the emotions and how to be in harmony with others and with Nature. This makes the body a fit vehicle for the spirit. They cover our outward quests in life.

Principles three and four teach regulation and control of the breath and the mind. This leaves one free from objects of desire. These two govern the inner quests we undertake in life.

Principles five, six and seven reach to the innermost, deepest parts of the soul. Here we can find the Divine within us and integrate it to our complete being. These three principles cover the quest of the spirit itself. The last three stages of the eight limbs can also be looked on as the three stages of meditation, leading to what can be termed enlightenment.

The product of adhering to these eight limbs also stretches to the four areas of physical, emotional, mental and spiritual we have examined in turn through this book. Thus, the active or physical person achieves the completion of the eight limbs by finding the Divine through work and duty.

The emotional person seeks and finds the Divine through their own personal love and devotion for them. The mental person finds the Divine through the intellect and the spiritual person by meditation and control of the mind. When each of these areas is conquered by adherence to its disciplines we are ready for the royal path of life, known as Raja Yoga. Such is the yogic code for the sacred life.

The approach of Buddhism, so famously promoting enlightenment as its goal, shows many similarities to the path of the yogi. Indeed it is true to say that when a deep analysis of the major religious and spiritual approaches to life across the world are studied they reveal many overlapping areas and offer us similar goals and principles, even if the method of achieving them may be different. In the midst of this, there is room for each individual to find their own, one true way of the sacred life. For there is indeed only one true way of living the sacred life and that is your own.

In Buddhism, certain virtues are extolled as the means to achieve union with the Divine. This is known as Metta, meaning friendship, but of a deep and profound, sacred nature, that extends far beyond just knowing someone as an acquaintance. Indeed the purpose echoes that of Christianity in its principle of loving thy neighbour as thyself. We are guided to relate to others by a disinterested friendliness, rather than need. By this is meant a detached place of warmth and openness that ensures a truly helpful position to be in, for the sake of the friend. We are required to see our friends and others generally as free from any conditioned predispositions they may have, offering goodwill to any conscious being. We are implored to respond to the potential of each person and so achieve unity with the virtuous.

Another principle of Buddhism is that of morality, being another area of overlap with Yoga. This requires a sensitivity to others and requires civilised behaviour on our part. We are needing to be polite and dignified in our behaviour and movement. We are also told that causing no harm to living beings is required as is not taking what is not given, freedom from sexual misconduct, false speech and drink and drugs that disturb the minds' clarity.

Patience is indeed a virtue in Buddhism, requiring that we overcome our hatreds and cravings. We must blame no other for our own misfortune and harbour no ill feeling to those who may cause us harm, directly or indirectly. We do not seek vengeance against others and instead are receptive to them. We listen and learn and so are able to absorb truth. Thus we are able to care properly for others.

The above feminine principle is the balancing counterpart to the masculine one of energy. This balances our patience and gives us initiative and vigour. We are able thus to actively seek the good and so transcend the self, meaning that we no longer have our own selfish desires at our depth of heart, our main focus. Instead the focus is raised to what has become the sacred for us.

Meditation is vital in the Buddhist path too, being looked upon here as the method of training the mind to experience more of that which is positive and good. This raises the consciousness and brings a mindfulness, or full awareness of breathing and its effects. This has the result of developing the loving kindness spoken of previously.

We then reach the path of wisdom in Buddhism, seen as the most critical virtue. For this we must be aided by others, taught and shown. Here we are able to convert all the virtues into perfection, so bringing the spontaneous expression of insight, into any given situation, able to recognise the true and the good.

In Buddhism it is commitment to our higher evolution that makes the sacred life possible and the virtues to be fulfilled.

Many of these Buddhist principles are echoed in a sacred way of life that is physically a long way in historical terms, that of the Lakota Sioux American Indians. It is known that Sitting Bull, together with his Mother, Her Holy Door, sought to pass on to his children the four principles of life in their tradition. Their way of life may have been being forcibly removed from them one hundred and forty years or so ago, by the white man, but the approach to that life was important to this great example of practical spirituality, and idol of many, to pass on to his children, in the midst of the conflict and poverty they faced.

The four principles are bravery, fortitude, generosity and wisdom. These can be divided into the four areas we are familiar with, that of the physical, spiritual, emotional and mental respectively, becoming broad guides for our attitude and behaviour by doing so. Bravery was considered the first virtue. Whilst this may have been much needed in Sitting Bull's time, it can still have many applications to the fearless and free attitude we require now on our own sacred road, with its twists and turns, leading to the unknown and the depths of the forest.

Fortitude was practised in the Lakota Sun Dance ceremony and sweat lodges, as the capacity to endure physical pain was a demonstration of the attitude required. There was also a call to preserve dignity and reserve in emotional situations that applied here, something quite rare in many people now.

Generosity demonstrated an awareness of the needs of the whole tribe, over and above that of the individual's needs. In our times of material greed and hoarding this is of great value in its teaching. People are seen as mattering more than individual prosperity. There was honour and prestige in giving away property 'belonging' to you and any thing that you possessed more than one of, was given away for the old, crippled or orphaned.

This led to wisdom, each virtue succeeding the other in turns. The experience of age and insight was necessary here, the regard with which the old were seen putting our current attitudes to shame. The old were entrusted with judgment in matters of war and the hunt, vital to sustain life for the tribe. They also had much say in matters of human and the tribe's relationship, since the old were viewed as having a close interaction with the spiritual and natural worlds.

The acquisition of the first three virtues came about through hard work, persistence and practice, giving the result of wisdom. The point of adhering to these virtues was to attain a practical, spiritual life, giving one the personal power required to make that life a successful one.

Moving to the other side of the Pacific Ocean, we encounter the ancient and highly regarded disciplines of the East. Legends and tales abound here of the warrior monks, expert in the martial arts that in their highest evolution become a spiritual practice and dedication. There are many branches amongst these, offering different forms of martial art and the disciplines accompanying them. The famous 'Book of Five Rings' gives much detail about some of those principles, from the Samuari's point of view. This sets out the warriors way, 'the way' being the method of living the sacred life to best effect. The 'Way' as taught some 2,500 years ago by Lao Tsu, is detailed in his fascinating book 'Tao te Ching', the natural law, which he gave us in some eighty-one beautiful verses. Study of this book, easily available, is highly recommended.

The practice of Zen is also very well known from its meditational puzzles or 'koans', set to train the mind to dimensional thinking to aid meditation. An example is 'what is the sound of one hand clapping'? Focus on this unanswerable question takes the mind beyond its normal logical restrictions and to the transpersonal level, wherein truth may be discovered, realised and experienced by that individual. Explanation and teaching are not enough, but the truth must be experienced by each one. Followers of the Zen path also had fundamental teachings, being summed up as: the truth does not depend on words or texts and must be sought within the mind, for 'one who has not seen into their own mind cannot be called wise'. This leads to enlightenment, being here the direct and clear understanding of truth, escape from unreality and entry into true being.

We can see already that it is left for the individual to discover what 'truth' is for them, just as in our method of 'practical spirituality' it is your own sacred self and life that you must find in your own way. this is echoed in the oft quoted dictum applied to many Pagan practices, being 'do what thou will shall be the whole of the law, lest it harm none'. This follows the idea of personal responsibility, required in all spiritual approaches to life and following a principle applied in magic, but also having meaning in the everyday world, that whatever you put out, comes back to you threefold, or with three times as much power and force. The more you give, the more you receive.

There are four guidelines given to us for the practice of successful magic, which can also have meaning in the way we live our lives on a daily basis. In many ways, these echo the four virtues expounded by Sitting Bull. The first of these, 'to know' tells us we need to be able to discern the need for magic and have a practical reason for performing it, just as we should any action in life. The second, 'to dare' is to have the bravery and fortitude to carry out our intentions, to the best of our ability and for the highest development of all concerned. 'To will' means having the attitude and focus to achieve our ends, to apply one's inner, more primal self to the task ahead and the last 'to keep silent' shows us a dignified approach and the power behind the spoken word and the energy attached to our actions, which as we know, dictates and shapes our practical circumstances. There is a prayer used in Druidry that also gives us several guiding principles, which is interpreted in many different ways by those following the Druid path, in which we can see much of great value to the everyday life, again showing how life itself is sacred. The prayer is as follows;

> 'Grant O God/Goddess your protection
> And in protection, strength
> And in strength, understanding
> And in understanding, knowledge
> And in knowledge, the knowledge of Justice
> And in the knowledge of Justice, the love of it
> And in the love of it, the love of all existences
> And in the love of all existences, the love of the God/Goddess and all
> goodness'.

Yin, Yang Symbol

Here we can see the principles leading back to the Source from which they came, in other words, leading to wisdom or enlightenment, in much the same way as have seen the principles apply in Yoga, Buddhism, or Zen. This gives us an endless spiral of existence, forever moving onward and upward as the principles once adhered to, move us up to a continually higher level.

The modern and comparatively recent method and approach of the Spiritualist, adhered to by some famous figures (such as Sir Arthur Conan Doyle, author of the Sherlock Holmes stories), carries with it seven principles that outline their approach and belief. The first of these is the Fatherhood of God, which may cause some problems among many people who accept a Goddess as equal to a maternal God. The Brotherhood of Man is the second of the Spiritualist principles, echoing the regard for others seen in many of the beliefs looked at so far.

The communion of Saints and Ministry of Angels comes next, showing us the natural ability to communicate with beings of a higher order than our physical selves, something that gives us the natural acts of psychism as an aid to our lives. We may not be able to see such things as nature spirits and deities but it does not mean we cannot communicate with them in a natural way.

Spiritualism does much to promote the evidence for human survival after physical death by their use of mediumistic contact. This shows us that we are not simply here one day and gone the next but that what and who we are, in matters of attitude, belief, achievements and feelings, lives on and we must learn to accept these and evolve in this and further lives to the best of ability and potential.

This requires the next principle of spiritualism, that of personal responsibility, seen as already central to the sacred life, whatever way it is lived. There is also compensation and/or retribution for good or evil deeds. This is not dished out by some vengeful God, but brings us to a level balance in our selves and our lives, teaching us, by our mistakes as is so often the case, to live a life that balances our karma if you will, as all things must be brought to balance, beginning with the heart and mind of each individual.

Lastly Spiritualism carries the principle that the path to eternal progress is open to every soul, irrespective of their standing in the world, or any other circumstances or beliefs. This again guides us to treat all others as if they might be angels, for we do not know in our limited view of things at what level our neighbour, family, friend, boss or acquaintance may be operating and so we cannot judge another. This means within the heart and mind as well as the bitchy gossip that seems so prevelant at the workplace in our society. As such the approach of spiritualism can teach us much, perhaps to our surprise.

A system of 'religion' that brings with it many great volumes on its teachings across the Western world is that of the Qaballah. Chief among these teachings are seven principles that we are told were dictated by Hermes, the God of Magic, amongst many other things. This received wisdom has led to associations with many other spiritual paths and such things as the Tarot being in its Major Arcana as some say, a pictorial diagram of working one's through the Tree of Life, the Qaballah in diagrammatic form. Thus the Qaballah gives us its code for life.

The first principle states 'the phenomenal Universe considered in its Unity, reflects the spirit of the all', showing us how the energy and life force brings the apparent world into being and as such must reflect the inner with the outer and vice versa. This leads us to the maxim 'as above, so below', again showing us how, by virtue of the fact that we exist, we are sacred.

Secondly the Qaballah gives us the principle of correspondence, which allows humanity to deduce the unknown from the known, much like the discernment of the truth in the Zen approach. We are also told that 'everything vibrates, everything is rhythm'. Spirit, we are told, vibrates so intensely that it appears as motionless to us. This tells us that all things exist at an energy level, irrespective of its physical state and that all things must adhere to this Universal law. Science now agrees, telling us that nature abhors a vacuum.

Hermes goes on to tell us that 'everything is double' and that the apparent opposition of duality is only the double aspect of one reality. Here we can see an overlap with the ancient Eastern symbol, now so ubiquitous across the world, reproduced below.

This shows us the above Qaballastic principle in symbolic form, detailing how in the light there is always a little darkness and vice versa, just as in the celebration of the Summer Solstice, there can be a little sadness, for the days begin to shorten after the Sun has reached its point of highest power and force in the year.

The fifth Qaballistic principle we are given is that 'everything manifesting the movement of life has a beginning and an end'. This is followed by 'every cause has an effect, every effect has a cause', which has similarities to the yin, yang symbol in its interpretation, the dark causing the light and vice versa. Each moves and has its being in and as a result of the other, just as we cannot live truly alone, needing the interaction and exchange of love to and from others to feel secure and at peace.

This interaction is echoed in the last Hermetic principle, which is that the 'masculine and feminine are found in everything physical, psychological and spiritual', though this obviously goes much further and has far greater implications than just love of others. We would do well however, to always remember the Biblical principle that 'love is the law' and that there is 'no greater law than this'.

The Muslim religion gives us Five Pillars for the practice of its approach, from God and his apostle Mohammed. These are: Witness or the Confession of Faith, Almsgiving, Fasting and Pilgrimage. As can be seen we have met these before, in the Zen application of 'truth', the Giveaway ceremony of the American Indian, the yogic practice of fasting and its subsequent purification, also practised in sweat lodges by American Indian and Celts, leaving pilgrimage to be taken either practically or symbolically. Many people practice a form of pilgrimage in their regular visits to certain places, that hold for them a sense of the sacred, because of the place itself. Certainly amongst the Pagan community of Britain, people 'pilgrimage' to the ancient sites and standing stones and circles or the land about them, to worship and celebrate.

The Hindu religion, often historically at odds with the Muslim, gives us the way of devotion, knowledge and karma for its guiding principles. The way of devotion is highest here, to a 'personal God', since it is apparently 'easier and nobler'. In the end, we are told to come to our God with all our being, showing us that what is sacred to us must be at the centre of our selves and the way in which we live our lives.

The last of the sacred approaches to life we shall explore is that of, as far as we know, the oldest. Shamanism is thought to have first been practised by those living in Siberia, thousands of years ago. Its practise has been followed in many countries and in many different ways, according to the laws and beliefs of each particular tribe, the tribal culture seeming to be where we have always found Shamanism, whether it be in North or central America, Europe and Britain.

The first principle we encounter is that there is an 'ordinary' level, that must follow the laws of the physical and chemistry. The inference here is that we must accept this and learn to deal with it as best we may. This takes us to the second shamanistic law, that there is a 'non-ordinary' world that works to different and 'more flexible' laws. we are given three levels of this spirit world, the Under, Middle and Other worlds, to use the Celtic terminology. The Underworld contains mystery, challenge and a confrontation with our fear. The Middle world is the everyday, practical one around as, seen as an inherent part of the spirit world and giving us the opportunity to learn balance by integrating with it. The Otherworld gives us inspiration, guidance and cosmic or Universal knowledge, for use in the Middleworld.

Shamanism has provided us with maps to guide us around this spirit world, being found in the Medicine Wheel of the Native Americans and the World Tree of many cultures, that grows at the heart of the spirit world and interacts with all three 'branches' of it. It is a shamanic principle that the Middle or ordinary world is dependent on the Otherworld for its existence, since all material things come from the life force and energy that constitutes the Otherworld. This includes every living thing, be it human, animal, plant, vegetable, rocks, minerals and so on. All have life and therefore energy, just as with the Otherworld.

Since power flows from the Otherworld to the Middleworld, the secret to the shaman's ability lies in directly accessing the Otherworld and the Underworld, bringing back the information necessary by communion with the inhabitants of those worlds. The shaman (or feminine shamanka) learns how to open doors into those worlds and must learn the laws that apply there in order to correctly and safely function whilst in them.

It should be stressed here that this is not for the purpose of an escape from the ordinary world, or to 'be spiritual' for the sake of being so. Rather it is because a cure is needed to preserve life, information is required for the decision and policy of the tribe in a particular matter, or for requests to be made; things that have a natural and eminently practical application in daily life.

Imagination, concentration and the will are required in order to gain access to be able to journey to these worlds, utilising many of the principles we have met before in their working. Ceremonies, drumming and the use of a rattle are all useful tools to enhance this ability, whilst the shaman often utilises helpers or guides from other worlds, in the form of animals or birds. Amongst a great deal else, this gives us an equal footing and therefore necessary respect for all living things, since we are just a different form of the same energy from which we all derive.

Whilst the whole of Earth was a sacred place to the shaman, certain places or spots are seen as being particularly powerful. These 'power spots' would be cared for on a practical level by the shaman as part of his regard and respect for it. The same also applies to certain objects, often reserved for use in ceremonies and shamanic practices.

The shaman also had to learn and abide by specific attitudinal principles. Among these are that personal and Universal limitations must be dissolved and abandoned in order for expansion to be possible. Expanding and growing means facing and embracing change, which must be done step by step, as they occur, without any hint of regret or sense of loss. A sense of honour and the ability to play, to dance and to laugh are seen as increasing the flow and force of life force through the shaman.

This gives us four sacred laws that apply to the shaman. These are:

1.   Everything is an inseparable part of the One that is All.
        Everything is linked with everything else

2.   Everything is born of woman. Life is born of the feminine.Tthe
        Earth is our Mother.

3.   Children are innocent and so must not be harmed. To harm a child
        is to harm oneself.

4.   The law of energy given motion is 'maximum efficiency with
        minimum effort'.

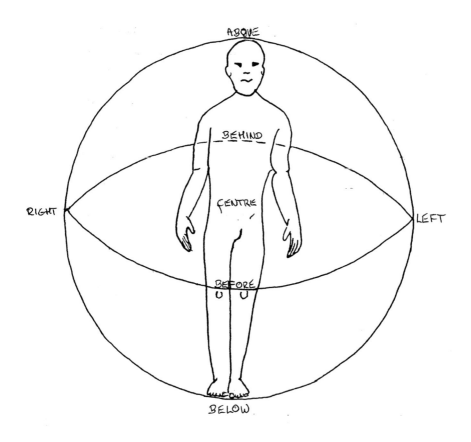

The Seven Sacred Directions of Universal Orientation

Just a cursory look at these four laws will show us that the beliefs that shamanism is grounded upon, as the oldest 'religion', are echoed in many of the approaches to the sacred across the world and throughout history. As such, we can absorb many of them, if not all, to our own approach to practical spirituality and to the sacred. They stand on offer to us as tried and tested ways to achieve the best we can in living such a life. Here we can find the way to live a life that will maximise our potential and help us to evolve to the highest possible level through this lifetime.

This brings us to eight principles that we can apply to shamanism in a wider sense. The first is the principle of Mentalism. This tells us that All is Mind and matter is therefore solidified thought, which we have discovered previously. Matter and energy here become different expressions of thought, one manifest, the other not. This tells us that our intentions are all important and that our state of mind dictates our circumstances.

The second principle is that of Similarities. Mind, whether manifest or not, consists of circles within spiralling circles, showing us the mirroring effect of that which is within, also being without, or as above, so below, once again. We have also seen this applied to the movements and effect of the Sun and Moon upon us as we live. This principle can also be known as the Law of Correspondences.

The third principle is the principle of Rhythm and Vibration. This says that everything vibrates, flows and pulsates, as it is driven to do by its mere fact of existence. Thought is a central part of this vibration. This is a principle we have met directly in the teachings of the Qaballah.

The fourth principle is Polarity, the idea that everything is dual, which the Hermetic teachings also give us. The polarities are equal and opposite, and so complementary to each other. Like the yin and yang, one cannot exist without the other and each exists within the other. Ultimately, balance must be found, or the two are in perpetual conflict.

This brings the fifth principle, of Connections. This is the teaching of everything existing as energy and that this in turn exists within a greater 'energy field', each connected to the other like a spider's web. Again, this principle we have met several times before.

Shamanism's next principle is that of Cause and Effect, which includes chance as a part of its definition. This we have seen in other sacred approaches to life too, perhaps most directly in the workings of karma, from Buddhism and Yoga. Shamanism perhaps goes further in its next principle, of Frequencies, stating that every individual is a set of personal frequencies and that this is a unique vibratory pattern. As such we must accept what and who we are as a valid truth to work upon, if we find ourselves not satisfied with the present picture.

Self-Realisation, the seventh shamanic principle then follows. This tells us that we must realise that we are not our physical body, but simply live in it whilst alive on Earth. Our regard and treatment of it should therefore be as a part of sacred existence. We are told here that we are not body, mind or emotions, but we are energy, will and consciousness. This returns us to the affirmation given in the exercises for the needs of the mind, to bring the self realisation of this fundamental truth to our existence.

So we find ourselves in a living Universe that is alive of itself, as a being of energy, just as are we. It is up to each and every one of us, without exception, to find our way about this Universe and travel across the worlds if we wish. We must learn to accept and deal with the needs we have at each Elemental and Directional level; the needs of the body, heart, mind and spirit and those of the Earth upon whom we live. To do this we must look above and below, to the right and left, forward and behind and of course within. Here we find our way about ourselves and the Universe by looking directly at the seven sacred directions. This creates a sacred sphere within which each one of us has our existence and awareness, which as we have seen, is but one energy spiral existing amongst those of every living thing. Thus the web is spun.

The four Elemental directions are our main reference points in this map of existence. From the North, the needs of the Earth, we receive platonic love. Here we receive energy and learn the workings of Universal law in our lives and selves. From the East we determine that energy and find spiritual love. The needs of the mind teach us the workings of light in our lives and selves. The South gives energy and our emotions lead us to sexual love, through which we can find the power of love in our selves and lives. Lastly, the West holds the energy, and so brings physical love, teaching us the place of love itself in our selves and lives.

So we come to see the similarities between some of the major approaches to religion or the sacred life on offer to us across the globe. What becomes clear as we study these principles and approaches is that we must accept ourselves as we are and as we find us. We must then begin the 'great work' upon ourselves, determining to live in accordance with the principles we must vow to adhere to.

This work on the self is a work with no end in this life and perhaps not for many lifetimes before us. But we must accept this work and put our full being in it. This book cannot do this for you, nor can any other, for it must be done by the individual concerned. All that I can hope to do here is to offer you some ways and means to help you on your own particular (or peculiar!) path and hope that you will act on them in some way.

The principles by which you live as a means for this sacred life must be identified by you and apply to you fully and completely, in accordance with your conscience. The contents of this Chapter and indeed the whole book, may help you to discover those principles, but what the laws, virtues, principles and beliefs the religions we have looked at show us, is that you will require patience, persistence, dedication, determination and hard work in abundance in their application to every area of your life, as surely they must.

In time these will result in the correct attitude to ourself and all life. This gives the correct attitude to the world and the wider Universe, helping you to play your part fully within it, at your own particular time and place. It is thus you find your own sacredness which will ultimately lead to the only true happiness for you.

Our daily news tells us repeatedly of the violence, greed, lust and the other 'deadly sins' in our world. It is easy to understand those who have the view that if there is a hell, this is it. But many spiritual teachings tells us that the Earth is the spiritual world, where all that happens in the spiritual realms, manifests. This great dichotomy can only be answered by finding the sacred within. In the words of a wise man, 'money can't buy you love!' The hoarding of possessions or money, the path of excess, while it may lead to wisdom for a few, usually leads to poverty and depravation for the spiritual person. A real and practical application of such a spiritual way must be found that integrates with the daily life, rather than one that it takes on to it. It must infiltrate every fibre of your being and find its place at the bottom of your heart, the centre of your being, world and Universe. If you do not have this, then ultimately you have a void that remains there until you find it within yourself, where it has always existed. It is this that provides the answer to each person's misery and tears in the dead of night: the sacred within and without.

We are told by many received teachings across the world that we are approaching a new age as we enter a new millenium. This is giving us a chance to establish a new and sacred attitude and regard to and for life; all life. If we get it right, we can be entering a time of peace and prosperity the like of which we have never seen before. At present we have individuals acting for personal gain, companies doing the same and the majority of the world's wealth shared between a few, while the many starve and suffer. The concept of justice is central to many approaches to the spiritual, as is the sharing or brother (or sister) hood of all beings. With an understanding of this, coming from a sense of the sacred at the heart, we can seek to re-balance this injustice and live together.

The major and urgent work we are called to do now is to begin to help the Earth repair herself, as opposed to our current attitude that causes harm and threatens life itself. Again, this must be a regard of our heart, which can only truly come when we are inwardly aware of the existence of life within and of the Earth. Once identified and honoured as a living being, the Divine Goddess if you will, you are compelled to live your life in a sacred manner upon it. Thus the heart and Earth are closely linked, as are the words themselves.

This brings us to the highest achievement we can hope to make and one that time will judge us by, that of service. We must realise that service is our highest calling, in the sense of correct attitude to ourselves, taking first what we need to live and giving the rest freely. This means of what we have physically, emotionally, mentally and spiritually. This service brings us enlightenment in a most practical manner.

As we move through the portal in time into the new, Aquarian Age so we can identify and embrace a new spirituality that honours the sacred for the individual, in whatever form it may express itself. It is this that can become the spirituality for the new millenium and it is this that remains our brightest and best hope for imagining the best kind of world for our fellow sacred beings, our children, to inherit. What is vital is that YOU find what is sacred to you and live your life in accordance with its dictates. The choice is yours and it must be made at some point. Be blessed on your sacred road.

Bibliography

William Arkle - *The Great Gift*, Neville Spearman Ltd., 1977
Sun Bear & Wabun - *The Medicine Wheel*, Prentice Hall Press, 1980
Sun Bear, Wabun Wind & Crysalis Mulligan - *Dancing with the Wheel*, Simon & Schuster, 1991
Sun Bear, Wabun & Barry Weinstock - *The Path of Power*, Prentice Hall Press, 1987
Jenny Beekes - *Yoga of the Heart*, The White Eagle Publishing Trust, 1990
William Bloom - *Sacred Times*, Findhorn Press, 1990
John Bradshaw - *Homecoming*, Piatkus, 1990
Barbara Ann Brennan - *Hands of Light*, Bantam, 1988
Barbara Ann Brennan - *Light Emerging*, Bantam, 1993
Pauline Campanelli - *Wheel of the Year*, Llewellyn, 1989
Pauline Campanelli - *Ancient Ways*, Llewellyn, 1991
Fritjof Capra - *The Tao of Physics*, Flamingo, 1976
Philip & Stephanie Carr Gomm - *The Druid Animal Oracle*, Simon & Schuster Inc., 1994
Thorwald Dethlefsen & Rudiger Dahlke - *The Healing Power of Illness*, Element, 1990
Jennifer Dent - *Healing Homes*, Capall Bann, 1995
Pamela Eakins - *Tarot of the Spirit*, Samuel Weiser Inc., 1992
Erich Fromm - *The Art of Loving*, Unwin, 1957
Shakti Gawain - *Living in the Light*, Eden Grove Editions, 1986
M.W. & J.A. Gonzalez - *Star Spider Speaks: Teachings of the Native American Tarot*, US Games Systems, 1990
Marian Green - *A Calender of Festivals*, Element, 1991
Louise Hay - *You Can Heal Your Life*, Eden Grove Editions, 1984
Steve Hounsome - *Taming the Wolf: Full Moon Meditations*, Capall Bann 1995
Steve Hounsome - *Practical Meditation*, Capall Bann, 1996
B.K.S. Iyengar - *The Concise Light on Yoga*, Unwin, 1980
Gerald G. Jampolsky - *Love is Letting go of Fear*, Celestial Arts, 1979
Pete Jennings & Pete Sawyer - *Pathworking*, Capall Bann, 1993
Glennie Kindred - *The Sacred Tree*, Earthkind, 1995
Phyllis Krystal - *Cutting the Ties that Bind*, Element, 1989

Phyllis Kyrstal - *Cutting More Ties that Bind*, Element, 1990

C.S. Lewis - *The Problem of Pain*, Fount, 1940

Caitlin Matthews - *Singing the Soul Back Home*, Element, 1995

John Matthews - *The Celtic Shaman*, Element, 1991

Jeff Mayo - *Teach Yourself Astrology* - Hodder & Stoughton, 1964

Kenneth Meadows - *Earth Medicine*, Element, 1989

Kenneth Meadows - *The Medicine Way*, Element, 1990

Liz & Colin Murray - *The Celtic Tree Oracle*, Rider, 1988

Miyamoto Musashi - *A Book of Five Rings*, Fontana, 1984

Will Parfitt - *The Elements of Psychosynthesis*, Element, 1990

Geoffrey Parinder - *The World's Living Religions*, Pan Books Ltd., 1964

Helena Paterson - *The Handbook of Celtic Astrology*, Llewellyn, 1994

Anne Ross - *Everyday Life of the Pagan Celts*, B.T. Bateford Ltd., 1970

Jamie Sams - *Sacred Path Cards*, Harper Collins, 1990

Susan Sheppard - *The Phoenix Cards*, Destiny Books, 1990

Jose & Lena S. Stevens - *Secrets of Shamanism*, Avon Books, 1988

Lao Tsu - *Tao te Ching* - Wildwood House Ltd., 1973

Robert M. Utley - *The Lance and the Shield: The Life and Times of Sitting Bull*, Henry Holt & Company inc., 1993

Jon Manchip White - *Everyday Life of the North American Indians*, Dorset Press, 1979

Ruth White - *Working with your Chakras* - Piatkus, 1993

Stuart Wilde - *The Quickening*, White Dove International, 1988

Index

STEVE HOUNSOME - SPIRIT SEEKER MEDITATION TAPES

RELAXATION TAPE : The Fourfold Breath, Conscious Breathing, Relaxing the Body: Produced in response to an expressed need for physical and mental relaxation, this tape ncludes four exercises that have proved themselves to be of enormous value. This tape is especially suitable for sufferers of stress, tension, anxiety, insomnia etc. and is ideally suited to the maintenance of health and well being during pregnancy, study and recovery.

MEDITATION TAPE 1 - ESSENTIAL MEDITATIONS Grounding and Connecting, Tree Meditation: Side 1 is the backbone meditation of Steve's approach to the subject. This meditation brings you to the place of perfect balance, rest and peace that exists in the centre of yourself and all things. Side 2 achieves this within the setting of a tree, going on to involve all six senses in your meditation.

MEDITATION TAPE 2 - SPIRITUAL DEVELOPMENT The Sanctuary, Meeting Your Guide: Side 1 takes you to your own Sanctuary that can be used for rest, healing or contemplation. It is a wonderful place of learning, just for you. Side 1 continues from here and uses the Sanctuary for a meeting with your own guide.

MEDITATION TAPE 3 - SELF HEALING Purification Breath, The Healing Ring: Side 1 is an energy meditation that can assist in healing any aspect of dis-ease of body, mind and spirit. It is also good to do simply for a boost. Side 2 uses a breathing meditation to promote health and well being on all levels of the self.

MEDITATION TAPE 4 - PERSONAL DEVELOPMENT The Holistic Trip, The Pink Bubble: Side 1 is a guided journey that explores the house of body, mind and spirit, bringing you gifts from each. Side 2 is an energy meditation that helps you gain control of your life.

FULL MOON MEDITATION: This tape is designed to accompany the book 'Taming the Wolf: Full Moon Meditations' and contains a meditation that can be used at each Full Moon through the year.

PAST LIVES Who Were You - Past Life Awareness, Time Travelling - Past Life Journey: There are two exercises on this tape. The first is an intuitive response exercise that enables you to discover some strong past life influences affecting you now. the second is a full past life guided journey in which you can experience a past life first hand. this is not hypnosis or regression and is completely safe for anyone to perform.

PSYCHIC DEVELOPMENT Protection, Intuition, Higher Levels, Clairvoyance: This tape contains four exercises to help you acquire and develop psychic ability. The tape contains an exercise for protection so that with regular and repeated use you are able to work psychically in a safe, natural and effective manner.

TAROT MEDITATIONS: This is a series of three tapes, designed for Tarot students and those following a path of personal development. The guided visualisation journeys on them enable the cards to come alive, giving the meditator a personal experience of each one.

TAROT MEDITATION TAPE 1: Grounding and Connecting, The Temple of the Major Arcana: This tape contains a beginners meditation exercise and an introductory guided journey to The Temple of the Major Arcana. It is recommended that you begin with this tape.

TAROT MEDITATION TAPE 2: Major Arcana - The Realm of the Body, Major Arcana - The Realm of the Mind - This tape contains a guided visualisation journey that takes you through the first two realms of the Major Arcana, the Realm of the Body and the Realm of the Mind. Each journey gives you meetings with seven cards of the Major Arcana.

TAROT MEDITATION TAPE 3: Major Arcana - The Realm of Spirit, Minor Arcana Energies: This tape contains a guided journey through the last seven cards of the Major Arcana, the Realm of the Spirit, as well as an introductory meditation for the Energies of the Minor Arcana. This is based on the Elements of the four suits.

TAPE 1 - PRACTICAL SPIRITUALITY: This tape has three exercises that enable you to assess your current spiritual position. Side 1 features two 'Discrimination' and 'The World Tree'. These enable you to discover your true spiritual nature and the ability to travel between the worlds. Side Two is 'Choosing A Path', a longer guided journey that empowers you to find your own spiritual methods in life.

TAPE 2 - THE NEEDS OF THEBODY: Side 1 of this tape is an exercise that allows you to ensure the maximum efficiency of yourphysfcal energy. This can help to prevent disease occurring and ensures you are operating from the best perspective in the physical world. Side 2 contains a guided journey wherein you encounter the Element of Earth as it relates to the physical body.

TAPE 3 - THE NEEDS OF THE HEART: This tape contains exercises to help you deal with emotional aspects of your self and life. Side 1 is an exercise that takes you to an experience of the heart of love that lies at the root of all th~ngs and the Source itself. Side 2 contains a guided journey wherein you encounter the Element of Water as it relates to your emotions.

TAPE 4 - THE NEEDS OF THE MIND: This tape includes exercises to assist in the functioning of your mind. Side 1 contains breathing techniques to bring a stillness to th~ mind and lets you experience the breath as the source of life. Side 2 contains a guided journey wherein you encounter the Element of Air as it relates to the mind.

TAPE 5 - THE NEEDS OF THE SPIRIT: This tape includes exercises that empower your spirit in the everyday world. Side 1 is an exercise that brings you to a point of awareness and acceptance of who you are on a spiritual level. Side 2 contains a guided journey wherein you encounter the Element of Fire as it relate~ to your Spirit.

TAPES BY CARRIE HOUNSOME
Carrie Hounsome has produced two tapes to assist those following a more Native American path. Carrie has studied the Native American way of life closely for many years and has completed many courses of study in this respect.

POWER ANIMALS TAPE This tape includes two exercises that enable you to discover and meet a power animal to assist you in a particular project or for a period of time. Side 1 contains a guided journey to discover and meet this animal whilst Side 2 contains a journey to deepen and develop this relationship, uncovering a deeper meaning to the event.

MEDICINE WHEEL TAPE This tape contains exercises that enable the listener to orient themselves around the Sacred Directions as used by Native Americans. This provides an excellent means by which you can encounter the North East, South and West of your being and the Universe, experiencing their power in full.

Each tape is narrated by Steve Hounsome, except Power Animals and Medicine Wheel which are done by Carrie Hounsome,;they last 30 minutes per side. The meditations allow a little time at the end of the tape so you are not disturbed in any way. There is no music on any of the tapes. Each tape includes a full instruction leaflet and colour cover. All the tapes are suitable for both beginners and the experienced, having been highly acclaimed by both. The exercises are designed to be repeated again and again, and are suitable for individual or group use.

Price £7.50 incl VAT & P&P direct from Capall Bann Publishing

FREE DETAILED CATALOGUE

A detailed illustrated catalogue is available on request, SAE or International Postal Coupon appreciated. Titles are available direct from Capall Bann, post free in the UK (cheque or PO with order) or from good bookshops and specialist outlets. Titles currently available include:

Animals, Mind Body Spirit & Folklore
Angels and Goddesses - Celtic Christianity & Paganism by Michael Howard
Arthur - The Legend Unveiled by C Johnson & E Lung
Auguries and Omens - The Magical Lore of Birds by Yvonne Aburrow
Book of the Veil The by Peter Paddon
Caer Sidhe - Celtic Astrology and Astronomy by Michael Bayley
Call of the Horned Piper by Nigel Jackson
Cats' Company by Ann Walker
Celtic Lore & Druidic Ritual by Rhiannon Ryall
Compleat Vampyre - The Vampyre Shaman: Werewolves & Witchery by Nigel Jackson
Crystal Clear - A Guide to Quartz Crystal by Jennifer Dent
Earth Dance - A Year of Pagan Rituals by Jan Brodie
Earth Harmony - Places of Power, Holiness and Healing by Nigel Pennick
Earth Magic by Margaret McArthur
Enchanted Forest - The Magical Lore of Trees by Yvonne Aburrow
Familiars - Animal Powers of Britain by Anna Franklin
Healing Homes by Jennifer Dent
Herbcraft - Shamanic & Ritual Use of Herbs by Susan Lavender & Anna Franklin
In Search of Herne the Hunter by Eric Fitch
Inner Space Workbook - Developing Counselling & Magical Skills Through the Tarot
Kecks, Keddles & Kesh by Michael Bayley
Living Tarot by Ann Walker
Magical Incenses and Perfumes by Jan Brodie
Magical Lore of Cats by Marion Davies
Magical Lore of Herbs by Marion Davies
Masks of Misrule - The Horned God & His Cult in Europe by Nigel Jackson
Mysteries of the Runes by Michael Howard
Oracle of Geomancy by Nigel Pennick
Patchwork of Magic by Julia Day
Pathworking - A Practical Book of Guided Meditations by Pete Jennings
Pickingill Papers - The Origins of Gardnerian Wicca by Michael Howard
Psychic Animals by Dennis Bardens
Psychic Self Defence - Real Solutions by Jan Brodie
Runic Astrology by Nigel Pennick
Sacred Animals by Gordon MacLellan
Sacred Grove - The Mysteries of the Forest by Yvonne Aburrow
Sacred Geometry by Nigel Pennick
Sacred Lore of Horses The by Marion Davies
Sacred Ring - Pagan Origins British Folk Festivals & Customs by Michael Howard
Seasonal Magic - Diary of a Village Witch by Paddy Slade
Secret Places of the Goddess by Philip Heselton
Talking to the Earth by Gordon Maclellan
Taming the Wolf - Full Moon Meditations by Steve Hounsome
The Goddess Year by Nigel Pennick & Helen Field
West Country Wicca by Rhiannon Ryall
Witches of Oz The by Matthew & Julia Phillips

Capall Bann is owned and run by people actively involved in many of the areas in which we publish. Our list is expanding rapidly so do contact us for details on the latest releases.

Capall Bann Publishing, Freshfields, Chieveley, Berks, RG20 8TF